The
Universal Machine

BOOKS BY PAMELA MCCORDUCK

Novels:

Familiar Relations
Working to the End

Nonfiction:

Machines Who Think
The Fifth Generation
(WITH EDWARD A. FEIGENBAUM)
The Universal Machine

The
Universal Machine

Confessions of
a Technological Optimist

Pamela McCorduck

McGraw-Hill Book Company
New York St. Louis San Francisco Hamburg Mexico Toronto

Fragment of "Who Says a Painting Must Look Like Life?" from *Su Tung-p'o: Selections from a Sung Dynasty Poet,* translated by Burton Watson (Columbia University Press, 1965), reprinted by permission of Columbia University Press.

1 2 3 4 5 6 7 8 9 D O C D O C 8 7 6 5

ISBN 0-07-044882-5

LIBRARY OF CONGRESS CATALOGING IN PUBLICATION DATA

McCorduck, Pamela, 1940–
The universal machine.
1. Computers.   2. Artificial intelligence.   I. Title.
QA76.M367 1985   001.64   85-6654
ISBN 0-07-044882-5

BOOK DESIGN BY PATRICE FODERO

To Hortense Calisher
and
Herbert A. Simon

Who says a painting must look like life?
He sees only with children's eyes.
Who says a poem must stick to the theme?
Poetry is certainly lost on him.
. . . .

Who'd think one dot of red
Could call up a whole unbounded spring!

Su Tung-p'o (Sung dynasty, 1087)

Contents

Acknowledgments   xi

Prelude: Starting at the Same Time   1

Part I: TRANSITION

1. Between Two Cultures   7
2. Two Centuries   18
3. Technologies of the Intellect   30
4. Books   42
5. Texts   52
6. The Transmutations of Texts   61

Interlude: Anxiety   71

Part 2: THE MACHINE OF THE CENTURY

7. The Computer   75
8. Other Computers, Other Views   83
9. The Empire of Reason: Artificial Intelligence   94
10. The Protean Machine   105

11. The Venus of West 53rd Street 115
12. AARON 123

Interlude: The Twilight of Heroics 133

Part 3. THE VERNACULAR COMPUTER

13. The Medical Microcosm 139
14. Flatland: The Micro Universe 147
15. War 156
16. The Computer and Conciliation 168
17. Computing in Senegal 181
18. A Wider View of Third-World Computing 189
19. Computing in the Soviet Union 196
20. Work 205
21. Aiming at Computer Literacy 215
22. Computing in the Schools 225

Interlude: Fairy Tales 234

Part 4: THE NEW HUMANITIES

23. Hunter-Gatherers of the Infinite 239
24. Chaos, Chance, and Certainty 247
25. The National Football League, the Traveling
    Salesman, and Complexity 254
26. The Science of Information 262
27. The Structures of Information 269
28. The Personal Computer 277

Index 297

Acknowledgments

One point this book tries to make is that computing is very much a community effort. So is writing a book. To the following colleagues, who gave me interviews, read parts of the manuscript, or, in some cases, did both, I owe a deep gratitude: Miriam Bischoff, Harold Cohen, Lawrence Frase, Seymour Goodman, Richard Karp, Nina Macdonald, Allen Newell, Alan Perlis, Michael Rabin, Raj Reddy, Lillian Schwartz, Bernard Scott, Marshall Shulman, Charles Staples, Donald Straus, Marc Tucker, Joseph F. Traub, and Andries van Dam. I am also deeply grateful for the hospitality of William Gallagher and Deborah Wright at their computer classes in California, and for the hospitality of my hosts at the École Normale Supérieure, Dakar, Senegal, especially Mme. Fatimata Sylla, who guided me through the project and patiently answered all questions. Andrew Xu has been an invaluable assistant.

The responsibility for errors, whether of omission, commission, or interpretation, is mine alone, alas.

P.M.

Prelude: Starting at the Same Time

A few kilometers inland from Gorée Island, that melancholy piece of West African soil from which millions were transported to slavery in the New World, a schoolgirl sits in front of a computer screen. She is working slowly at a program. AV, she types, and the cursor, a small electronic dot on the screen, moves upward for *avance*, leaving a narrow electronic trail behind it. DR, she types, and the cursor moves right, *droit*. GA, she types, and the electronic dot moves left, *gauche*. She laughs with delight at the pattern she has created on the screen.

Across the Atlantic Ocean from Gorée Island, the trustees of the Museum of Modern Art in New York City examine designs for a poster that will announce the museum's reopening after a large-scale remodeling. The designs have been generated by an artist using the latest computer technology, and after some initial misgivings, the trustees are now ready to affirm, in the most public way possible, that a provocative new medium for the visual arts has arrived; that once more, art will change profoundly in the twentieth century.

Westward again, a middle-aged American lawyer is concentrating on a computer screen. Like the Senegalese schoolgirl, he

1

too is meeting the computer for the first time. Now and then he looks out the window, happy to see the sun dispelling the fog that has lingered all morning over San Francisco Bay. When his first simple program works, he feels ridiculously triumphant. Computing really isn't any more difficult than attending to the details of a contract. Why was he so worried? A good lunch and a glass of Chardonnay provided by his instructor have eased his fears more than he'd admit.

Across the Pacific, a young Japanese scientist examines code he has written for a prototype computer eventually intended to make his country the world's leading broker of information, which is the wealth of the new age. There is a bug in that code. Slowly, methodically, he will find and eliminate it. He is a child of his culture, and his culture excels at patience and perfection.

Beyond the Sea of Japan, across the great landmass of Asia, a Soviet economist has just said good-bye to an American visitor. Now he gets up to stretch, to look out the window at the gray river, to organize his thoughts. The conversation with his visitor took a strange and troubling turn. They had been discussing the economic necessity for the Soviet Union to catch up with the West in computerization, to move from a few centralized computing installations toward decentralized computing in the factories and offices, the schools, even—someday—into homes. The economist is troubled because without putting it into words he has finally understood that nothing quite like this has ever challenged the fundamental assumptions of his society: not guns, not dollars, not failed wheat crops nor failed revolutions. Power—economic, political, personal—is to be redistributed in ways that the State Planning Committee might find not altogether agreeable.

Something is happening all around the planet. In the words of Mr. Boubacai Kâne, who directs the project in Senegal that is teaching that schoolgirl how to program, "With the computer, for the first time in the history of civilization, we are all starting at the same time."

Starting what at the same time?

Many things, across the breadth and depth of the human condition. From art to medicine, from agriculture to transportation, from science to entertainment to commerce, even in war and peace, the computer is making a place for itself. Here it comes into our lives, this inevitable engine for the Age of Symbols, an age that marked its debut with the work of Sigmund Freud in one important domain, Alfred North Whitehead and Bertrand Russell in another, Ferdinand de Saussure in still a third, all taking up as central to their separate disciplines the systematic idea of representation: standing for, the object as reference to another object. Thus the symbol, and now its own machine, the computer. It enters because we want it, we need it, a human machine in a way no other ever has been.

Along with its penetration into every domain where symbols matter, the computer brings us something else. This is tentative, pregnant, barely under way; more difficult to grasp than, say, the commonsense but charming fact of a microprocessor under the Grinnell Glacier in the northern Rockies patiently calculating the pressures and movements of the glacier's interior as it happens. This something else, a novelty, is a new understanding of the very nature of symbols. As the microscope revealed the underlying structure shared by all living organisms, the cell, so the computer is revealing the underlying structures of all symbols, so varied and rich that it seems impossible to find connections among them that don't verge on superstition.

So for the first time in the history of civilization, we are all starting at the same time in a host of ways. Great themes connect such human enterprises to each other. They are simple, even familiar: symbols (hence abstraction and artifice), rationality, process, complexity, and community. But their familiarity is a gentle ruse. What we thought we knew we did not, what we dreamed of were but timid shadows of what could be.

Now at the beginning (and it is only the beginning), among our changing perceptions of ourselves, our possibilities, noble goals to strive for and catastrophes that might destroy us, we listen and hear those great themes. They are the real story—and the enduring work—of the universal machine.

PART 1

Transition

Chapter 1

Between Two Cultures

Was I drawn to science and technology or driven away from something else? I'm seventeen, a discontented English major at Berkeley, studying the poet who, they say, has pronounced the last word on the twentieth century. He is a demigod in this department and appears in every course, whether Shakespeare or Romantic Poetry, his texts an infallible measure of the distance we have come from the past. He is, of course, T. S. Eliot, and his message is not cheerful.

Passion has departed our lives, he reports: all is dreary, burnt out, hollow, straw. Yet beneath the despair lurks a kind of satisfaction, even gratitude, that passion can be dismissed as dead. (God is also declared dead just then, but the quixotic poet is trying a resurrection there.) Since it can no longer be experienced, passion has become a specimen to be examined—well, dispassionately. The poet himself provides scholarly footnotes explaining myths gone and forgotten, like the passions that once shaped them.

But. It is spring. The dogwoods bloom splendidly, Berkeley's cool air is luminous, San Francisco Bay lies fresh and inviting below us. Eliot to the contrary, passion hasn't been reduced to a squalid thing in a gloomy bed-sitter but runs through our healthy, seventeen-year-old veins like crazy. It lusts for everything: books, music, art, justice, truth, beauty, pizza, life itself. Our high spirits burden our professors, who have to try to make ends meet on a four-figure annual salary, and must publish or perish, as we undergraduates say to each other without quite understanding what that means.

More significant, memories of McCarthyism and the loyalty oath fratricides on this campus in the early 1950s are still raw. If that isn't enough, beside me in class are survivors of the Nazi horrors (me too, for that matter, except surviving the English blitz doesn't carry quite the moral cachet of surviving on the Continent). In the Telegraph Avenue coffeehouses, the Jewish question is as important for us as the Race question will be ten years later, the Woman question ten years after that. Perhaps all this permits no choice except to agree that the sour poet is right.

But I haven't been alive long enough to get weary of the world. I wonder if once I've lived as long as Eliot, as long as my professors, I'll also believe that life is one long suck on a lemon. I secretly doubt it.

Therefore, I begin to doubt my suitability as a student of literature. Further apostasy: I alone in my contemporary lit seminar argue that the standard interpretation of Tennessee Williams's play *A Streetcar Named Desire* (a brief revival running just then in New York) is wrong. That's the word I use; no patience with a polite scholar's phrases: "faulty" or "open to another interpretation." If this pretentious and morbid crackpot Blanche Du Bois is the best that high culture has to offer, then the world ought to belong to Stanley Kowalski, who, if nothing else, has vitality.

It isn't that *no* literature speaks to me. I love the jolly 1600s, with their gather-ye-rosebuds-while-ye-may poems; I love the prose of the nineteenth century, the ironic tone of its novels (which I'll reread with special pleasure all my life). But something in me seeks a voice for my own time. The past is all right, but it's only the past. I live now.

And now, a lot is happening. A few weeks into my sophomore year, in October of 1957, Sputnik—84 kilograms of earthly matter—is launched into space by the Soviets. Since Wernher von Braun has been declaring for the last five years to any reporter who will report it that *whoever controls space controls the world*, we are less enchanted by this human venture off the planet than resigned to Soviet troops goose-stepping up Channing Way. The general reaction to Sputnik is far distant from the cool ironies of the nineteenth century. Congress and everyone else, it seems, is hysterical: more engineers! More calculus! More bomb shelters! More scientists! More physics!

Thus is reset in my mind the inevitable connection among science, technology, and destruction that every child growing up in the atomic age must share. Any flirtation I had with science is suddenly ethically questionable. Well, it is not quite that tidy. I have a love affair, not a flirtation, with the earth sciences, in particular the idea of digging hominid fossils out of the dirt with the sun on my back. But imagination fails me when I'm asked what my future husband and children will do when I'm off on a field trip. If nothing else, I am cultivating myself to be a wife and mother. So I resume literature, feeling like a good girl who's had a fling with a scoundrel but come to her senses just in time.

The following spring is unusually rainy, and I lie in bed on the sleeping porch of my dormitory (the sleeping porch, a wonderful Berkeley institution that allowed you to sleep year-round with nothing but a roof and screens between you and nature; gone now, I suppose, a victim of more lawless times) listening to an air-raid siren that might have short-circuited in the rain or might finally be announcing that the Russians have come. I'm very frightened.

In my senior year, the department has a distinguished visitor, C. P. Snow. He gives a version of his "Two Cultures" talk, a new idea just then (a minor scientist and a minor novelist who has given a minor lecture, Horace Freeland Judson will say a quarter century later). The professor who leads my Virginia Woolf seminar chews over the idea that members of the literary culture should be as familiar with the second law of thermodynamics as members of the scientific culture are expected to be with Shakespeare. He sighs. "I don't even know the *first* law."

Yet he seems undisturbed. Why not? He and his colleagues have a lot of fun in the classroom at the expense of the *Untermenschen* who populate the sciences, especially the social sciences, which seem preposterous to them—a science of humans! What

next? Like most of my fellow English majors, I have uncritically
accepted and share those jokes, that preposterousness.

Despite the university's best efforts (required courses where I
learn to distinguish the three major rock types and to date the
Wisconsin glaciation to plus or minus 10,000 years), I'm so innocent of the grand issues science raises that I assume a course
in the philosophy department on the traditions of British empiricism has to do with the politics of empire. Though I can date
a glaciation, it wouldn't occur to me to date a science major—
what would we talk about?—and the idea of dating an engineer
is unthinkable. It is passion running through my veins, not
lunacy.

And yet, Snow's visit will have a profound effect on me. I lay
eyes on him only once, even though he and his wife, Pamela
Hansford Johnson, hold an open house, a tea, for students every
week and generously urge us to come and visit. I fly up the Euclid
Avenue hill, the sycamores now half bare, the light now gone, and
turn down the steps of Vine Walk to be welcome, brilliant, witty:
all in my mind. I am much too shy to take tea with Sir Charles
and Lady Pamela even once. But later I think what a single conversation with him might have done for me, how much time spent
obliquely that might have been spent directly.

Then again, perhaps not. I might have discovered for myself
his minorness—though I don't think the Two Cultures idea, however simplistic, is minor, for it addressed something important to
my time and place. In any event, Snow as dignitary in the English
Department embodies for me the idea that science, and even technology, are respectable, and respectable people can talk seriously
about them without falling from the grace of Western culture.

It will be many years before I learn to phrase something else.
Literature wants to teach me all the secrets of the human heart.
Science wants to teach me all the secrets of the universe. The
secrets of science contain the secrets of literature, but not vice
versa, and I am greedy.

By the time I understand this distinction, I've also learned that
neither literature nor science can quite deliver on their promises,
but I've also discovered that I like hanging around scientists a lot
more than I like hanging around literary types, mainly because
the scientists I know—nearly all of them engaged in the science
surrounding the computer—are not only cheerful and hopeful

about the future, but they love the present and are deeply engaged in it.

Frivolous though it may seem, this affection and admiration for who scientists are and what they do will come to shape my life in more and more decisive ways. I'm no longer seventeen, and life is beginning to toss a few lemons my way. Worse, I detect a self-earnestness that will coalesce into rigidity if I don't beware. Luckily, one of the delights of the scientific milieu where I've found myself (in every sense of that phrase) is that change, inevitable in human affairs, is regarded by these scientists as natural and welcome. With one or two vital exceptions, my literary friends see change as a monstrous imposition to be fought and resisted with all their might. I'll learn from the scientists not to resist change. Slowly, but I'll learn it.

Finally, the fact that I've found an odd perch among *computer* scientists, whose area of study is an artifact, created by human artifice, proves to be crucial. I'm used to studying and admiring artifacts, in the forms of poems and stories, melodies and paintings. The least thing computer science does for me is to open me to the beauties of technology. Machines and structures begin to reveal their aesthetics, and I am as enchanted by them as I am by any other human composition.

A decisive moment for that comes when I read an exercise by John McCarthy, one of the great pioneers in artificial intelligence. McCarthy has written it in response to—or perhaps defiance of—the times: the war in Vietnam, which has come to seem less a conflict between armies than the confrontation between technology and innocence, and, simultaneously, the newly discovered hazards of polluting water, soil, and earth, benign nature poisoned by malign man and his artifacts. All these form the background for "The Doctor's Dilemma," which begins this way:

Suspend your disbelief and imagine the following miracle to have occurred: a young doctor working in a hospital discovers that he has the power to cure anyone under the age of seventy of any sickness or injury simply by touching the patient. Any contact, however brief, between any part of the doctor's skin and the skin of the patient will cure the disease.

He has always been devoted to his work, and wants to

use this gift to benefit humanity as much as possible. However, he knows that the gift is absolutely non-transferable
(this was explained to him by the angel or flying saucerite
who gave it to him), will last for his lifetime only, and will
not persist in tissue separated from his body.

What will happen if he uses his gift?

What should he try to do and how should he go about
it?

What is the most favorable result that can be expected?

I consider myself a member of the scientific rather than
the literary culture, and my idea of the correct answers to
the above questions reflects this. However, in order to mis-
lead the reader, I shall give some pessimistic scenarios and
related literary exercises.

McCarthy then followed with a group of scenarios (some mutually exclusive), which he called "Literary Exercises in Pessimism
and Paranoia," that considered what would happen if the doctor
used his gifts, what other people might do in return, and a number
of consequences that would ensue.

The scenarios were wildly various, beginning with something
like:

The doctor uses his gift; the other doctors, jealous and
disbelieving, drive him from the hospital. He cures patients
outside; they get him for quackery and put him in jail
where he can't practice. Even in jail, he cures people, and
the prison doctor has him put in solitary confinement.
Even there he cures a guard of cancer and then the little
daughter of the warden of the prison. This arouses the
fears of the insecure, narrow-minded, brutalized, and bur-
eaucratized prison doctors to the extent that they have him
sent to a hospital for the criminally insane to be cured of
his delusion. There, they lobotomize him. Write scenes in
which doctors disbelieve the cures taking place before their
eyes, write self-justifying speeches by people who decide
to imprison him even though they know better, and write
the report justifying his commitment to the mental hospital.

Or:

He forms an organization for curing people and at first
works very hard, but gradually he grows lazy, is corrupted
by desire for money, power, fame, and women, and requires more and more flattery and obsequiousness, eventually striving single-mindedly for power, develops cruel
tastes, comes to dominate the country, and is finally as-
sassinated. Write speeches for him justifying his increased
demands at various stages. Write the self-justifying speech
of the assassin.

So the variations continued, including bureaucratic bungling,
superpower wrangling, population explosion, religious dispute,
and self-appointed guardians of the human race acting on the
race's behalf, each funnier, worse (and more depressingly plausible) than the last. McCarthy concluded:

I believe that all the above catastrophes can be avoided
and the gift made into a great benefit. Those readers who
consider themselves as members of C. P. Snow's scientific
culture should try to work out the best solution for a day
or so before turning to the next page.

On the next page McCarthy presented his own "Solution from
Morality, Common Sense and Technology." "You flunk on moral
grounds," he told his readers, "if you propose not to cure anybody.
Any attempt to cure as many people as possible gets a B. To get
an A, you must do the arithmetic and see that it is possible to cure
almost everybody for a while."

Following some simple calculations and estimates of the number of diseased people in the world under seventy years of age,
McCarthy showed that the doctor, by using a machine with a
system of conveyor belts and other pieces of extant technology,
need work only 24 minutes a day to cure all the world's illnesses
during the lifetime of his gift. Would there be problems? Perhaps,
but the miracle postulated would be decisive enough so that physicians could soon be persuaded; the mechanism for cure was
simple enough so that even bureaucrats and politicians, short-

sighted and bumbling though they often are, could manage to
produce it.

It might be necessary to protect the doctor from assassination
and the equipment from sabotage, and even then there would be
some risk of disaster, McCarthy conceded. Mental, physical, and
social side effects must also be watched for, and while the gift
would contribute to the population problem, it wouldn't be as
substantial as one might think, once the arithmetic is done—elimination of death under seventy would require stabilizing the population, a limit of 2.1 children rather than the 2.2 children that
might be allowable otherwise. "In countries with larger death rates
of young people the population effect would be larger, but ordinary medicine is already having a similar effect."

McCarthy is fascinated by technological solutions to what are
often conceived of as moral problems. He does not say that all
moral problems can be solved by technology, but he suggests that
we seek technological solutions as assiduously as we seek moral
solutions, perhaps more, since technology is usually more malleable than dogma.

Implicit in McCarthy's exercise is a message that only became
explicit for me much later, what he called "the literary problem."
Imagine, he says, that the solution he proposes to the dilemma is
correct, and that the problem is solved. But if the doctor is not a
hero of some sort, how can one make literature out of such a
situation? "The pessimistic and paranoid fantasies of the previous
section make much better literature, at least by present literary
standards," McCarthy concluded. Likewise for journalism, he might
have added.

For several years I used these scenarios as exercises for my
beginning writing students, not only because the exercises are
amusing and imaginative but also because they allow young writers
a frame to write within and an experience to write about, which
most young writers lack. As the term went on, I would ask whether
anybody had thought of a solution to the problem, but nobody
ever had. Perhaps my students were so caught up in the scenarios
of pessimism and paranoia that they couldn't think in other terms,
or perhaps they simply were not trained to think analytically and
arithmetically, so it never occurred to them to do so.

On the last day of the term, I would hand out McCarthy's
arithmetic solution. My college freshmen and sophomores

were always deeply disappointed. It was all so simple! It was a trick!

No, it was not a trick. It was a beautifully articulated lesson that would have a profound effect on me, if not on them. For me, that whimsical scenario undid once and for all the connection in my mind of science, technology, and destruction that had been caused by The Bomb and even Sputnik. Thereafter, I would look first and carefully (but not only) to what is pejoratively called "the technological fix" for problems that came along. The technological fix, it turns out, has pulled the human race out of some formidable tight spots. It is a fact of life that even when technological fixes exist—for example, to the catastrophic problems of global war fare—we cannot always apply them. But their existence gives us hope, I think, which is essential to life.

There was a more important effect on my imagination, caused in part by McCarthy's fable and in part by other matters that were beginning to capture my attention. I began to see science and technology as artifacts, as manifestations of the human imagination that were every bit as legitimate, interesting, and representative as any poem or painting. There were aesthetics, a morality, and a set of questions about the human condition that surrounded science and technology just as they surrounded art. This was startling only to somebody from an intellectual milieu that considered art the sole worthy product of the human spirit.

And that, briefly, is how I came to science and its cousin, technology. If the poets had given up on passion, the scientists had not. Thus I was drawn first to the people who did science. It took some time for me to understand what made them passionate, optimistic, excited, and happy, especially since they were supposed to be dispassionate, disinterested, and otherwise neutral. That paradox exists, and is one of their most attractive features. And as my understanding has grown, it has also suited me to be passionate about work and optimistic about the future. Differently from when I was seventeen, perhaps, but passionate and optimistic all the same.

How do I dare? Because in the last half of the calamitous twentieth century, the human race has fashioned the most civilized and human tool ever made. It is called the computer. Having fashioned it, we have in the main embraced it rapturously: it changes our lives more and more each day.

Nearly everybody understands that something called the computer revolution is upon us, but few people—including many who regularly work with a computer—would use the words civilized and human in connection with all this. Those who have shunned the computer altogether must find the claim grotesque. If they allow the idea of the thing to enter their minds at all, they dismiss it quickly as mere gadget, infernal machine, prone to spew out slapstick-style bills (not for nothing was The Little Tramp chosen to sell IBM's personal computer—and did it with stunning success). Worse, it seems an instrument designed to subvert all the ornaments of civilization that they cherish.

I stand by my claim. To put it simply, we humans have fashioned another piece of technology, a machine, to amplify the work of our minds. How this is so is the subject of this book, in detail and in general. The technologies of the intellect have always been a human concern and, I shall argue, the concern that separates us most distinctly from the other species we share the planet with. The computer is part of a continuum stretching from cave paintings through the written word, mathematics, and printing, though it breaks from the continuum in significant ways. Its dynamic properties, for example, serve to amplify our reasoning powers, whereas the previous intellectual technologies have amplified only our memories. More momentously, the computer transforms and even creates symbols instead of merely disseminating them. Finally, though its early versions might seem to contradict the idea, its present (and more so its future) versions open access to nearly infinite opportunities for individual intellectual aims.

We are all between two cultures now. Some of us race forward, others retreat. But either way, we hardly know what to make of it all. For the moment, let us acknowledge that this new technology must change us: our values, the way we think about ourselves, the expectations we hold for our own possibilities, in short, our point of view. Chatter about kilobytes and floppy disks, about whether a machine can *really* be said to think, might obscure this truth for the time being, but truth it is. We cannot stop the changes even if, in some failure of courage, we wished to. To remain ignorant or indifferent to it is to step aside from our own century's contribution to all the other magnificent intellectual adventures that have exalted the human spirit, beginning, perhaps, with the invention of language itself.

It's a commonplace that the twentieth century holds a ghastly store of tragedy for its children, who must clutch at their humanity against all despair and dread. We have seen poetry falter; we have seen the law fail us; formal religion was lost to us long ago. But in the distance, these troubled times may be remembered best for the invention—the inevitable invention—of an instrument to give us heart, for it liberates and magnifies the human property that has always served us best, our own intelligence.

Chapter 2

Two Centuries

We're inclined to feel sorry for ourselves in this paradoxical twentieth century, which, on the one hand, has prolonged its stay beyond human endurance and yet, on the other, races past us in a haste beyond our understanding. We ask aloud whether humankind has ever known such incessant plague and destruction. We fear for our own survival of such bloody-mindedness, combined as it is with confusion, treachery, dread, and the end of authority. Has the human race ever trembled on such a scale? Is anyone rash enough to harbor hope?

Well, then, if only because misery loves company, comparisons are almost irresistible. I draw them between our own century and another, the fifteenth, both of them gory, quarrelsome, and perplexing.

In both are the gravest catastrophes. Weapons of mass destruction are eagerly employed in wars that slaughter millions and despoil the land. Whole populations lie at the mercy of hoodlums, official and unofficial; disease rages; politics convulse and economies heave. Perhaps worst of all, the soul's inner ear cannot escape a certain clamor that undermines courage: it is the din of rules being broken, truths shattering. The sum of human misery, physical and spiritual, defies calculation. Examples from the twentieth century are all too familiar, but let me mention some specifics to remind us how grim the fifteenth century also was.

During the Hundred Years' War, a conflict between England and France that began in the fourteenth century but stretched well into the fifteenth, a new weapon suddenly mowed soldiers down in numbers never before seen. The outcome of the battle of Agincourt, engaged for mere moments on October 25, 1415, depended not so much on the noble courage of the English king, as Shakespeare would have it, but on the skill of his Welsh longbowmen. Inside half an hour, the French had lost 10,000 men, the English a scant 500.

Thanks, however, to oppressive new taxes (which allowed a bigger army, not to mention a more loyal one—being regularly paid has a way of promoting loyalty) and, more important, thanks to improved cannons that were able to destroy fortifications no catapult could hope to breach (the improvements borrowed from the innocent, nearly pious craft of bell-casting), the French were able to drive the English from the Continent by 1453. They could now fall to squabbling among themselves instead.

What next developed between France and Burgundy has been described by one historian as nothing less than an arms race, which culminated in a deadly mobile siege gun whose design would remain essentially unchanged for the next 400 years—and whose use would transform not only the face of European cities but also the balance of European power.

Of course, what warfare didn't accomplish the Black Death would or already had: in some parts of Europe, the population was reduced by from two-thirds to three-quarters, often literally leaving too few living to bury the dead. Nobody knew how to stop it.

One unsurprising consequence of this wholesale slaughter, natural and man-made, was massive social confusion. Economic systems, provincial or national, went berserk. In some places inflation rose 400 percent in a generation; elsewhere, horrified survivors went on a spending spree that caused a general balance of payments problem all over Europe.

Men of God seemed to have no better access to clarity of purpose: for a time during those troubled years, three rival popes reigned simultaneously. Spiritual panic drove thousands into esoteric cults, a panic compounded by official persecution of witches, most notably Joan of Arc but also many thousands of humbler folk. In 1488, responding to the growing numbers of sorcerers and witches he perceived all over Europe, Pope Innocent VIII (a name chosen with no ironic intention, we can suppose) pronounced the bull that would launch the Inquisition. Europeans prepared for the end of the world. (Surely it's arrogant to imagine that our own fears of terminal nuclear war are somehow more profound than those of fifteenth-century Europeans because we understand a reality they did not. Fear is fear.)

And Europe was not unique. Calamity prevailed nearly everywhere on the planet during that turbulent century. Constantinople fell to the Turks in a gruesome battle in 1453. The battle turned on the latest high technology, which was transferred, as we would say today, by foreign mercenaries who owed no loyalty except to profit and so cast the newest cannons for the Turks on the spot. All this ended the once mighty, but by then rotten, thousand-year Byzantine empire. The result was to cut off Europe from eastern sources of silk and spices, a deprivation that would soon spur European exploration—and exploitation—of the rest of the globe.

Meanwhile during that same century, the Indian subcontinent was wracked by wars between rival states and ruling families. In one royal family, for example, within the space of three decades, the king (who had already come to power under dubious circumstances) was murdered by his son, who in turn was murdered by a brother, whose throne was then usurped by a general, who himself would be replaced by a regent, who promptly seized power from the general's sons he nominally represented.

At the same time in China, a testy emperor (compensating, perhaps, for his own shady rise to power) caused, on one occasion alone, the slaughter of 5,000 of his overseas compatriots in Sumatra when they failed to pay suitable tribute to his grandness. He launched similarly ruthless but instructive invasions all over Asia to consolidate his dynasty's power. Those invasions would prove untenable in the long run, serving only to wreck the imperial treasury and mire the central administration in intrigues and disputes that distracted it from the really serious problems of administration.

Asia too had suffered dreadfully from the plague, probably

spread by marauding Mongols who brought not only pestilence but also a rule so repressive in the Middle East that, by the mid-1400s, countless small but once prosperous peasant economies had systematically been ruined. The only place on the planet that could be called even relatively serene during the fifteenth century was the Americas, but, as we know, their time was at hand. *Aztec conquests*

All this and more in those extraordinary years between 1400 and 1500. No one who has spent much time in the twentieth century will need help in drawing the obvious parallels between then and now—arms races, economic ruin, disasters natural and man-made, crises of authority. Still, my point is not to demonstrate that the human race has always suffered a state of chaos and pain and that therefore we should desist from self-pity at once. It is rather to say that in the middle of that tumult—and made feasible by some of the same circumstances that caused the tumult—there appeared in Europe an instrument as powerful as any weapon, as devastating as any epidemic, more influential in its effects than any usurper of thrones or general of armies. It was the printing press.

A comparison between the computer and the printing press verges on the hackneyed, but there are good reasons for it nonetheless. Both instruments are processors of information. Both appeared when nothing quite like them had existed before, and both began to make their effects felt immediately (a situation that isn't invariable with new technology). Both devices were less the result of a singular breakthrough than of an evolving set of technologies. Like the computer, the printing press had no one certain inventor; it was a technology whose time had come. Advances in metallurgy, ink, the falling price of paper (a complicated result of several technological and eonomic changes), and the demand of the growing middle class for reading matter, all drove artisans to experiment with an automated means of writing until somebody—perhaps a German named Johann Gutenberg, perhaps not—managed to do it.

Once the techniques were fused into a single device, printing spread rapidly from Germany to Italy, Switzerland, and Bohemia, to the Netherlands, France, Spain, England, and Hungary (on the site of the first Hungarian printshop, whose production began in 1473, modern tourists can have a drink in a cozy bar that commemorates the publication of the first Hungarian book). The new instrument not only revolutionized the production of books, it also introduced new methods of working, new jobs, and new ways of thinking about things.

The press did not change an illiterate society into a literate one, as we usually assume. Its effect is more subtly described as changing a scribal culture into a print culture, a transformation that everyone agrees was momentous, but whose profoundest effects are still not entirely understood. The most thorough study, Elizabeth L. Eisenstein's *The Printing Press as an Agent of Change*, not only corrects our misunderstanding of pre-print and post-print Europe, and answers many questions we might not think to ask, but is at pains to remind us how many questions remain. So much the more for the computer, come as it has only a half century ago, changing its role as we watch from giant luxury to miniature disposable, from calculator to universal symbol processor.

There's another parallel between the two centuries and their emblematic machines. It's larger, vaguer, harder to grasp. In the fifteenth century, a new class rose to prominence, its rise aided by an instrument that both embodied new intellectual preoccupations (in the case of the press, standardization, interchangeability, and systematization) and helped achieve them. This new class is casually called the bourgeoisie, but a more precise term is the lay intelligentsia. They thought for themselves, and would lead revolutions to come: social, political, scientific, industrial.

In the twentieth century another new class rises to prominence. We have no term for it just yet, since its members appear in so many places, whether science, finance, public service, industry, medicine, or the arts. In earlier times they might have been called (somewhat contemptuously) reductionists, for they deal in symbolic codes that stand for much larger phenomena. Or they might have been called rationalists, for they rely heavily on reasoning, cause and effect, and logic, however imperfect the knowledge they have. Some have called them knowledge workers, but this seems to me too broad: the real power elite are a species of poet, both inventing and deciphering the codes their tasks require; they will moreover understand when processes are parallel, weakly or strongly linked, which level of a hierarchical system (appearing ubiquitously in nature and society) deserves proper attention, and when to shift between levels to achieve the most leverage.

As the scribes were already literate and preceded the print

[handwritten margin note: Not the same at all, but maybe the lay intelligentsia was important.]

revolution, precursors of the new class are already among us, concerned with processing information on a scale that only a machine can manage. The members of our new class have machines to help them think, and they are already leading revolutions.

In both cases, the very invention of the machine was impelled by long-standing desires and then rapidly, almost rapturously, adopted by groups that became virtual cultures unto themselves. In both cases, a new kind of power accrues and is consolidated with the help of the instrument. At first it is personal: independence from local teachers, independence from ancient authority, new creativity from mental energies set free by the machine. The new power then becomes communal: a reexamination of theological and political power; the beginning of sound quantitative analyses of nature—for to open the Book of Nature required a preliminary encoding of data into ever more sophisticated equations, diagrams, models, and charts, writes Elizabeth Eisenstein. In short, the communications shift of the fifteenth century produced fundamental alterations in prevailing patterns of continuity and change in every area of human interest.

Perhaps amusingly, surely inevitably, both devices were stoutly resisted by the established, centralized powers, who soon found themselves overtaken. Those established powers were forced to adopt the new technology and tried, too late, to control it.

Thus in 1501, when it seemed clear that the printing press would not simply go away and that it was not a mere fad of the inconsequential (until then) middle classes, Pope Alexander VI, sounding like ever so many who have taken it upon themselves to protect us all, declared:

> The art of printing is very useful insofar as it furthers the circulation of useful and tested books; but it can be very harmful if it is permitted to widen the audience of pernicious works. It will therefore be necessary to maintain full control over the printers so that they may be prevented from bringing into print writings which are antagonistic to the Catholic faith or which are likely to cause trouble to believers.

From his point of view he was right to be alarmed but deluded about maintaining full control. In the fifty or so years since the printing press had emerged, the number of European volumes had soared from an estimated scores of thousands of handwritten volumes to between 6 and 9 million printed volumes (one authority says 20 million, but this seems incredible to me). The 9 million figure works out to roughly a doubling rate every seven years, not quite as fast as computing power has doubled in our time but not so bad, either. Printed books were cheap; even an artisan could afford one or two. As the pope finally realized, the press would change everything.

For example, and most germane to the Church, the press was to be directly responsible for transforming a little parochial quarrel in Germany into the Reformation and surely was to be equally responsible for the scientific revolution of the seventeenth century—not to mention its effect on national languages, literature, and individual consciousness.

The printing press, I repeat, emerged as the Renaissance was already under way and transformed its character from Italianate to Germanic. (Delicious boosterism: the press was immediately touted by the Germans as proof that they were just as accomplished as the Italians.) It can even be argued that the press sustained what would have been just one more resurgence of antiquarian values, similar to many that had come before, into a distinct movement with lasting effect called "the Renaissance." That the individual was beginning to matter in a way individuals had not mattered before is as evident in the painting of the fifteenth century as it is in the earnest efforts of the bourgeoisie to improve themselves by purchasing self-help books. Art became humanized, specifically individualized, and newly intellectualized: with printed books suddenly available everywhere to narrate stories, paintings were released to do other things.

In a similar way, the computer has emerged as the move toward quantification, precision, models of rule-based behavior, and individual control in a whole variety of human activities is already well under way, but it offers opportunities to understand and do such things better. In addition, it will surely reform our intellectual and perhaps our spiritual life in ways we can hardly anticipate.

It is self-evident that the demands on the intellect made by reading are different from those made by listening or watching. Beyond that, it seems we have little firm information. A modest amount of research has been done with tribes that have no written language, and other research is under way with illiterate adults who live in a generally literate society. Although such adults may know the meaning of a simple word like "hot" or "cold," they cannot grasp the metaphorical equivalent of "hot stuff." They also lack the ability to connect cause and effect, to predict, to tell much difference between the past, the present, and the future. They cannot move easily from the personal to the impersonal; they cannot grasp a multiplicity of points of view; their ability to generalize is nearly nil.

Only recently—and I mean within the last few years—has any serious attention been paid to the general effects of literacy upon human cognition, which might seem odd, but there it is. As late as 1979, Eisenstein could complain bitterly about it: the effects of literacy were assumed to be obvious and well known, she said, but are not. Others agreed, and joined her in blaming the anti-science and anti-technology biases of those most concerned with literature: preposterous to think of literature as a *technology!* goes the common wisdom of the litterateurs.

On the contrary, says a new view (one I share, as the next chapter will show), it can be enlightening to examine literature as a species of technology. Fresh research, led not by professors of literature, of course, but by cognitive psychologists, sociologists, and anthropologists, suggests common patterns of thought among college students in remedial writing courses, tribes with little or no contact with written language, and children who watch a lot of TV, the patterns being those cited above. The cognitive participation required by literature exercises the brain in wondrous ways. (This, as opposed to the passivity possible before other media— or, I should guess, the wired-in nature of our visual and audial perception acquired over millennia of evolution, which other media call upon. In other words, it is "natural" to see and hear; it is not natural to read.) These are preliminary findings, exciting much dispute.

However, they allow me to speculate that a computationally illiterate citizen of the future will lack other skills: the ability to deal with many variables, or a group of simultaneous, related causes and effects known as a process (the language, a linear thing, does not bend gracefully to the concept). Perhaps such citizens will be unable to deal effectively with hierarchical systems, will misunderstand or miss altogether significant connections between apparently unrelated events, or be unable to distinguish among what can be known, might be known, and never can be known.

Perhaps they will never discover their own possibilities for action, that they can play an important role in shaping their destiny instead of waiting passively for it to happen.

But what must be stressed is that literacy—textual or computational—has implications far beyond its immediate uses. Well before the introduction of the printing press, even the modest amount of literacy that then existed in Europe had already affected art and architecture: an elite class of court and church artisans had come under the sway, whether they knew it or not, of the literate. In gothic architecture, for example, the great cathedrals are an integration of structure and appearance that demands a literate mind to receive its symbolic message. "Written culture effectively imposed divisions of space and time onto experience, dividing land into precise boundaries and books into chapters. Gothic architecture merely applied the same notions of didacticism and reckoning to another area and on a grander scale," medievalist Brian Stock observes.

He goes on to point out that literacy also affected economics: Europeans could now think of the abstraction called money (which arose in the twelfth and thirteenth centuries, replacing barter, gifts, and other forms of goods distribution) as an objectification of their economic concerns; thus supply and demand entered the pricing structure, and the economy could be thought of as a process over time (itself a notion undergoing revision and objectification).

Literacy in pre-print Europe also affected work, law, custom, and the way individuals communicated with one another. The notion of modern times as distinct from olden times—historical consciousness—emerged once more, having enjoyed currency with the Greeks when they become literate but having later been lost in oral cultures. At the same time, if we can judge from the few oral cultures that have survived to the present, the arts of human memory and listening declined dramatically. There was no particular merit in heroic feats of memory or well-disciplined attention when cheap books existed to do the job painlessly.

So thanks to literacy, power shifted from the supernatural to humans themselves, who were ambivalent about exercising it. They worried; they spoke of alienation from what had once been and, unsurprisingly, looked wistfully backward to the intimacies of an oral culture. But as much as they longed for the simplicities of the past, European intellectuals (what an apt term) could not give up the power that literate abstraction gave them over their lives. Gradually, they came to terms with all these formalizations and abstractions called law, philosophy, and theology—the text—by supposing that this new technical instrument called writing would restore to them a lost spiritual unity with God.

A century or so later, the printing press springs upon a Europe so eagerly aroused that printing spreads at the astonishing rates cited earlier. The mechanization of writing will bring about changes that are related to, but different from, the changes already made as a consequence of literacy among that earlier small but influential elite.

The heart of those changes will be community, but community that transcends the local neighborhood and, paradoxically, intensifies individualism. Book publishing and its concomitant literacy are to be directly responsible for the transformation of intellectual work from an isolated and solitary human activity into something cooperative and collective, speeding up the collection and validation of knowledge drastically. (The natural sciences are the most conspicuous example, but that will come later than the fifteenth century.) At the same time, in Eisenstein's words, based on carefully assembled evidence, printing stimulated "a heightened sense of individuality and personality—a sense which continues to distinguish Western civilization from other civilizations even now."

We return again to numbers. Between 1450 and 1501 Europe could boast a book for every five persons, and the ratio was even higher in Germany and the Low Countries where printing had first taken hold. Who was reading? Not the peasants, who would remain illiterate for centuries, nor the aristocracy, which, when it felt the need for learning (which was rather seldom), could rely on scribes. It was the rising middle class, the lay intelligentsia, with business to conduct and books to keep, in the narrowest sense of the term. They would soon be joined by scientists and political theorists, engineers and generals.

This was secular literacy, which swelled university enrollments and turned a handsome profit for the printers. The printers, by the way, from the outset had been interested as much in profit as in good works. If their products ran first to religious books, grammars, dictionaries, encyclopedias, and textbooks, it was because those were what the new literate class wanted; soon it also wanted almanacs, that is, records and forecasts of astronomical events, and even self-help science and medical books. One printer, fired up, we can suppose, by doing what was proper and not necessarily what was profitable, decided to publish books in Greek alongside the Latin and vernacular books of most publishers' lists. He was soon forced to offer his stock at cost and then at a loss; Greek books didn't provide the immediate edification that book buyers craved. When I'm discouraged by the banality of the most widely used software today, I remind myself of printing's callow youth.

There were graver effects. Printing turned a series of local religious scuffles into a systematized, continent-wide madness. Witch-hunts began to increase significantly in the fifteenth century and reached a frenzy in the sixteenth, organized and carried out by literate Dominicans who relied on a widely disseminated printed code for the proper detection of witches. Tens of thousands of people would fall victim to such nice scrupulosity. Literal fundamentalism and the official censorship of words, deeds, and thought were as much a by-product of printing as the coming Enlightenment.

Just as there are obvious differences between the fifteenth and twentieth centuries, so too there are obvious and significant differences between their two characteristic devices. The printing press is an instrument that mechanizes human writing, itself a technology that mechanized human *memory*. Computers, roughly speaking, mechanize and amplify not only memory but also another aspect of the human mind, which is *reasoning*.

The importance in both cases lies in the qualitative change brought about by quantitative increases. With the computer, we are on the threshold, in the words of John McCarthy, of putting a hundred years' thought into every decision. But that is only the simplest way of expressing it.

We understand that technologies of the intellect have profound and unexpected results. In the past, they have simultaneously reflected and reformed the human intellect and, with it, human culture and values. As the rapid proliferation of mechanized printing helped to change nearly everything, so we can anticipate that the computer will also mark some startling changes in human fortunes. Those changes will be perceived as both good and bad. But such evaluations are tricky. Pope Alexander's objections were really to the diminution of his earthly powers. Was that a change for good or bad?

Another example: could the rising European nation-states, each built on a national language, which had been codified by

printing, be considered improvements over the crumbling eccle-
siastical empire they replaced, or just different? Was the shift that
we can begin to detect in the fifteenth century in the relationships
among humans from one of status and hierarchy—class, aristocracy, clergy—to one of contract, however imperfect, good for
humans or bad for them? In any case, both changes began to take
place about this time, not caused but certainly enlarged by the
printing press, and they implied that a closed order was an obsolete way of looking at the world. The news was that the world
had open bounds. Christopher Columbus set out to prove that
literally in 1492.

The trends toward nationalism, secularism, individualism, and
the breaking of bounds were under way before the advent of the
printing press. But the printing press accelerated those trends
mightily because it was a technology so apt for the projects humans
were eager to accomplish, including, eventually, the overthrow of
the divine right of kings and the establishment of representative
governments, a distinct improvement, in my view, in the human
condition. Eisenstein argues that printing increased creativity by
making "food for thought much more abundant" and allowing
"mental energies to be much more efficiently used." All this because the press had moved us from an age of script to an age of
print? Yes. And more, much more.

Here now is our new technology, and I write of it for several
purposes. One purpose is to look at specific examples of the impact
of computing on various human enterprises, such as medicine,
art, and labor. Another is to look at the major ideas that the
practice of computing itself is introducing, including new ways of
thinking, new structures of knowledge, and new approaches to
what, up to now, have been intractable problems for us.

Somewhat like the Europeans of the fifteenth century, we are
in transit between cultures. The new one shows signs of looking
different from what we are used to; power is shifting and feels
strange. We denounce the changes, blaming the machine that
began as symptom and has become cause. History suggests we
won't like everything that's going to happen.

And yet, as the printing press was, on the whole, an instrument
to give heart and hope to the sorely beset citizens of the fifteenth
century (though perhaps few of them perceived it as that), I believe the computer is an instrument to give us heart and hope
too—and even more abundant food for thought.

Chapter 3

Technologies of the Intellect

We think of tools as something for the shed or as implements hauled in by an artisan to fix leaky pipes, bad wiring. But by now it must be clear that workers in the realm of the mind have tools too, whole technologies, if you will, that serve the same purpose as any artisan's: they make work more effective, exciting, pleasant, and precise. They are the winches and pulleys, the miter boxes and wheels that amplify our powers in every direction.

For the moment I dwell on two of the best-known artifacts in the intellectual's tool kit, the alphabet and printed books. Some tools. Not only did they help us craft better ways of thinking and sharing thought, but they each caused a panorama of transformations in dozens of different fields that eventually changed civilization—mainly for the better, but not unmixed. Equally important, those changes were shaped not only according to the inherent powers of the technology itself but also according to the values of the culture that had produced each tool.

Their histories also illustrate two different ways that the technologies of the intellect (and indeed, most technologies) work. In the first, the true alphabet, a small but significant change to an evolving technology made a decisive and finally overwhelming difference. In the second, printed books, a substantial increase in quantity made a great change in quality.

The question, of course, is why? What is it about literacy that gives us this intellectual leverage, that confers not only the ability to decode but also the unexpected skills of generalization, reasoning about cause and effect, and all the other things I mentioned? At present, nobody knows for sure. I offer a modest proposal, drawn from information-processing psychology.

We have good scientific evidence that the human memory is organized hierarchically in lists and in lists of lists, an organization that usually exhibits itself in an associative fashion. Thus experts are such because their knowledge is, first, extensive and, second, well-organized. They have good lists. Herbert Simon compares the organization of long-term memory to a library:

> The information stored by topics (nodes), liberally cross-referenced (associational links), and with an elaborate index (recognition capability) that gives direct access through multiple entries to the topics. Long-term memory operates like a second environment, parallel to the environment sensed through eyes and ears, through which the problem solver can search and to whose contents he can respond.

Experts—whether chess players or physicians—are those who have encountered so many examples in their fields of expertise that they can "chunk" (form into meaningful units of information) each example of their experience and store those chunks in linked list structures of memory, instead of allowing the experience to straggle here and there in their brains like a displaced person. (As it happens, it takes about a decade of training for most people to reach their peak professional proficiency, which psychologists believe corresponds to the acquisition of about 50,000 chunks. As Simon points out, when a profession demands more than a decade of preparation, specialization occurs, and professionals make more and more use of outside aids such as books.)

Now then, the amount of information to be gained about the world at large through one's own senses is limited, mainly by what any one human can experience and think about in a lifetime. Writing—and then printing—dramatically increased the level of information a person was exposed to, providing a kind of prefabricated and often abstract, but wide-ranging, experience that is a precondition to any expertise. (In some cases, the memory structures are prefabricated as well.) Thus it seems to me that the literate become "experts" about the world in ways the illiterate cannot, with memory lists that hold not only their own chunks, or units of meaningful information, but the community's as well. Why this should affect not only the information but also the cognitive processes is to rephrase Yeats's famous question: how shall we know the dancer from the dance? One subtly becomes the other.

None of this, so far as I know, has been proved about literacy, but it seems to me plausible.

In any event, our newest intellectual tool, the computer, has begun to exhibit all the usual effects of technologies of the intellect: small but significant changes to an evolving technology that make decisive and finally overwhelming differences; a substantial increase in quantity that makes a great change in quality; and as we shall later see, a shape that comes not only according to the inherent powers of the technology itself but also according to the values of the culture where it finds itself.

Although we understand that we are only at the beginning, we can nevertheless see that the computer is already helping us achieve what no other intellecltual tool (nor human head, for that matter) has ever done. As always, the results in the long run are frankly unpredictable.

We press ahead anyway, noticing small changes and wondering if they will lead to big ones. Mathematicians, those first practitioners of abstract expressionism, even have a phrase for it: is a problem ill-conditioned or well-conditioned? they ask. This has nothing to do with muscle tone. They are asking whether small changes in certain beginning conditions will make only small changes in the end results (a well-conditioned problem) or whether small changes can make disproportionately large, even catastrophic, changes in the end (an ill-conditioned problem).

We can ask the same questions of life but are seldom confident in our answers. Does the end of the snail darter mean only the end of an exotic zoological species or does its extinction have implications far beyond that? Will a rise of just 2 degrees centigrade in the average temperature of the earth's surface really turn New York City into Daytona Beach? The military, contributing still another colorful metaphor to our everyday language, asks the question this way: will a small technological edge in, say, a weapon—a shade of gray—convert the battlefield into black and white, winner-take-all?

And, of course, we raise the same sorts of questions about the technologies and tools surrounding the human intellect. Why the glory that was Greece? I once asked an innocent dinner partner, a professor of classics. He bit his lip. At last he answered: "If I had to give one reason alone, I suppose I'd say written language." Just that? Written language? Is culture an ill-conditioned problem? One small shade of gray and winner-take-all? So it seems. For later I was to come across Eric Havelock's *The Literate Revolution in Greece and Its Cultural Consequences* and discover that the Yale scholar makes the same argument, but in persuasive detail, and provides us, as it happens, with a perfect illustration of the power of a shade of gray in an intellectual contest.

Written language alone wasn't the issue. There were many languages in the Mediterranean basin around 700 B.C., and a fair number of them were beginning to be written down in some awkward form or other. These scripts were partial answers to a problem that was growing more and more urgent as life forced its complications on the young human race. The problem, of course, was how to represent what people said to each other in a form that would be economical, would endure beyond fallible human memory (in fact, could travel through time and space), would contain a minimum of ambiguity, and yet would capture all the nuances of human speech.

The Phoenicians, those no-nonsense traders, had supplied part of the answer. So had the Semites. But both scripts, based on syllables, failed to solve the problem altogether. In this evolving technology called writing, then, the Greeks made one small but crucial change. Instead of using syllables as the atomic units of writing, the Greeks introduced the abstraction we now call letters. They dissolved the syllable into its acoustic components, which meant that an alphabet of only twenty-three signs, "a piece of explosive technology," in Havelock's words, could represent spoken language conveniently, exhaustively, and unambiguously.

From this apparently small but highly significant advantage there flowed an astonishing set of results, including new ways of thinking, new ways of looking at the world, and new ways of describing it all, not only in language but soon in the plastic arts as well. Not Greek genes but Greek orthography supplied the shade of gray that made the situation black and white, that made Western culture the intellectual child of Greek thought. Winner-take-all. (I cannot resist pointing out that the alphabet also displayed one of the greatest of intellectual meta-tools, the power of abstraction.)

A similar (but not identical) transformation is owed to the printing press. Like written language, mechanical printing acted as an artificial memory, but now the memory, a communal treasure, was greatly enlarged. Such growth illustrates what scientists like to call "the order of magnitude effect," the idea that if something is increased by tens, by hundreds, by thousands, and by millions, there will come about not only a quantitative change but a qualitative change as well.

I have already mentioned the religious and scientific revolutions the printing press supported and its lasting effects on national languages, literature, and consciousness. The geopolitical revolutions were profound as well: when Europeans went out into the rest of the planet with their new ways of organizing and their rapid dissemination of technology (thanks to printing, which had now become a tool to spread tools), the melancholy result for nonliterate civilizations, and even for literate ones that didn't share the European cultural values of trade and national aggrandizement, was all but black and white. Winner-take-all would be known more politely later as the European hegemony.

By now nearly everybody understands that the computer is no mere calculating device but a tool that can manipulate symbols of all kinds. (I suppose we owe this, if nothing else, to the great but short-lived video game mania of the early eighties. For years computer specialists were telling us about the symbolic possibilities of the device, but we just didn't get it; then one morning the world woke up and shrugged yes, of course. Pac-Man doesn't crunch numbers.)

It bears repeating that this new piece of intellectual technology stands in relation to our reasoning powers as written language stands to our memories. It has amplified the faculty of reason and will soon automate the process. It is dynamic, not static. Like the changes brought about by the proliferation of printed books, the new tool in our kit introduces a qualitative change in our intellectual life.

Does that qualitative change imply that life is, because of the computer, once more an ill-conditioned problem? To be sure, the computer is physically small. Miniaturization is its destiny. A computer now sits on my desk at home that any multinational conglomerate would have been proud to own twenty years ago. I am not a multinational group but a writer, and I bought it out of my dinky royalties. If I laid out the same money today, two years later, I could get an even more powerful machine—or pay 40 percent less for what I have. Soon, I suppose, we can expect computers the size of head lice, and eventually we may hide them in our tresses for occasions of quick, on-the-spot processing.

Small can be beautiful, small can be powerful, and the history of technologies of the intellect tells us that there, particularly, small improvements can turn shades of gray dramatically into black and white; or more patiently, that incremental changes in quantities can eventually change the quality of culture and human life in general. Of course it will be so with computing, a prediction so obvious and safe it hardly seems worth mentioning. The hard trick is to predict what shape the changes will take.

Nobody knows. Prophets must humbly remind themselves that a nonhuman mechanism with the capacity to reason is a singularity in human history. Since it is a singularity, we can say nothing for certain.

But we are free to guess. No matter how wonderful reasoning machines will be, there are some things they will never be able to do. For example, they will not be able to guarantee the constancy of your lover; they will not instill filial piety into your children; they will not categorically eliminate wickedness from the planet, nor even cure your flatfeet, though they have a better chance of doing that than solving the other problems I've just mentioned. They will not give you deeper self-knowledge, I think, if you already resist self-knowledge.

In other words, many important aspects of human life (the stuff of drama, the stuff of passion) will remain more or less the same. If we put aside those parts of the human experience for now, it isn't because they aren't important. It is because the computer has little to say or do for them. But some things *are* going to change, in fact will never be the same again. For one thing, the stuff of community drama or global passion. For another, matters of the intellect.

I write these words on a third-generation computer (inte-

5th generation promises

grated circuits), but my attention lately has been on the fifth generation, promised to us by the Japanese for the 1990s. These are to be intelligent machines, intelligent by any definition we can reasonably propose. (Whether these machines can *really* think or are only faking it is a topic that leaves me—and the Japanese—cold, though I am quite aware that many in the Western world consider it so hot they can hardly be civil about it. *De gustibus.*)

The fifth-generation machines will be able to understand us as we speak to them, or write to them, or show them pictures. We can state a task in terms of a goal: suggest a plausible diagnosis for this disease and the best way to treat it. How can my firm increase its productivity? Tell me why humans are known to eat raw fish but not raw meat.

And we will not have to instruct them where to look for the answers; they are to be supplied with automatic reasoning processes and enormous knowledge bases that include not only the knowledge found in textbooks, which is useful enough, but also the knowledge that humans acquire as they become experts in a given field, the judgmental, rule-of-thumb knowledge that can be learned only in the clinic, the courtroom, at the workbench, in the field. The advice offered by our automated reasoning machine will come to us in the form we want it, spoken, written, or pictorial; but more significant, in the intellectual form we can use best: goodbye information glut and hello useful knowledge. Since they will be equipped with the means to explain themselves, we can ask them why they gave us such advice and to justify their line of reasoning so that we can judge its soundness.

The development of the fifth generation represents a brilliant intellectual strategy on the part of the Japanese. (It also represents a brilliant economic strategy, with profound shades-of-gray, winner-take-all economic implications.) If the Japanese are first and alone in this development, there are surely profound cultural implications, for, as I have said, changes come not only according to the inherent powers of a given technology of the intellect but also according to the values of the culture that produced it. Europeans had printing and took its powers into the world. The Chinese also had printing and used it to fix themselves immutably in time and space.

The main question in the minds of most informed people is not whether such machines can be produced but when. Concerted research and development has been under way in Tokyo since 1982 for what is planned as a ten-year national project. It is based on prototypes developed in the United States but will carry research and development far beyond what now exists. Whether the research goals will be reached within the ten-year period is an open question, but the Japanese believe their project is so important to the long-term health of their nation that, if necessary, they are prepared to take half again or even twice as long to achieve their aims.

Those American prototypes upon which an important part of the Japanese project is based are known generically as "expert systems." These are computer programs whose performance equals and often exceeds human performance in certain narrow but important fields of intellectual endeavor, such as specialized medical diagnosis, computer configuration, mineral prospecting, or signal analysis (to name only a few areas where such systems have been developed).

Expert systems have already begun to provide their users with that shade of gray that resolves itself into a black-and-white advantage, winner-take-all. Those who object to this must remember that the winners are not only rich oil and computer companies but also such people as cancer patients whose chemotherapy is complicated beyond human wit and are thus alive because there are smart machines to manage the complexities. But other problems of distribution will surely arise, which I will address in a moment.

In our terms, expert systems are the rudimentary equivalent of the written word. The fifth generation of computers, however, will be the equivalent of the printing press, in that it aims to bring the power of expert systems technology not only to fortunate and wealthy experts who might want intelligent assistance but to anybody and everybody who might want that same expertise.

Several factors make me hopeful about this general distribution. The first is the Western tradition (cheerfully adopted by the Japanese) of turning a profit. As printshops were the new profit centers of the fifteenth- and sixteenth-century information revolution, knowledge sources may very well play the same role in the next century. Moreover, I am hopeful, though not certain, that market competition and economies of scale will keep prices low. The entrepreneur's trick is always to make the product cheap enough to discourage do-it-yourself projects but costly enough to maintain the business. Even so, some knowledge is inappropriate for the private sector to monopolize or, on the contrary, is essential but unprofitable, and community consensus will have to be mobilized to regulate and perhaps subsidize in such cases.

Then there's the peculiar nature of information processing, whether through a printing press or a computer, which makes it a highly dispersed or decentralized activity. Given a certain level of literacy, it goes on wherever human heads congregate. Putting a lid on things only works temporarily, if at all, as post-print European governments discovered (a censored author would cross a border and continue writing and publishing, or somebody else would come along and take up the cause) and as both the United States and the Soviet Union are discovering today, in their separate ways (though many developing countries seem not to believe it and are doomed to find out the hard way). Dozens of problems arise that we could not have anticipated, having to do with intellectual property rights, say, or transborder data flow, and we must feel our way along unsteadily, using mutual interests and the rather irrelevant precedents of real property to help us.

In any event, whether it comes from the Japanese or elsewhere—and signs are that both Americans and Europeans are stirred enough to mount competition to the Japanese challenge—we shall have a new technology of the intellect that will change processes of every kind, from manufacturing to management, from design to growing wheat in the heartland, from scholarship to (perhaps) citizenship.

How? Research in expert systems has already shown us. We begin with a task for the machine to do. The task is specified very precisely, drawing on all the expertise a team of human experts can muster. But the moment the program and the knowledge are laid out in detail before those experts, they can see at once how to make improvements. Add the machine's tirelessness, capacious memory, and enormous processing power, its inability to grow bored or forgetful, and you can see how the program surpasses human performance.

Thus even if no *new* knowledge is brought to bear on a process, be it design, management, or harvesting, the very act of bringing to it a mechanism that embodies the expertise of the best human experts (one or, for that matter, many geographically scattered experts) will change the quality of the process significantly for the better.

Better processes allow better productivity, superior products, leverage: and while this is true of the marketplace it is equally true of the life of the mind. The alphabet didn't just release the Greeks from having to memorize tiresome syllabaries; it freed them to think about things that nobody without a powerful system of writing could have thought about.

And then, if this new technology of the intellect begins to give us new knowledge—knowledge that human beings wouldn't have stumbled on because they don't have the time or energy to do the kinds of searches that might uncover it or because the clever combining of pieces of old knowledge is beyond our flesh-and-blood brains—the changes will be much more startling.

Users—and vendors—of such devices will find themselves holding a shade-of-gray advantage that could transform an intellectual challenge into black and white. And the implacable secret of it all is something we have always known: knowledge is power.

The Japanese are optimistic about all this, and so am I. But optimistic does not mean insensitive to the risks, at least the ones we can predict, which are probably the easiest to deal with. Such uncertainties—the most important being that we do not know how to imbue humans with the critical intelligence necessary to evaluate the knowledge they are exposed to—are enough to make some people cry hold, enough! I am not among them. Risks considered, I say knowledge is still preferable to ignorance—not exactly a stance of stunning bravado in a community of the intellect. And knowledge is what's coming. These machines will automatically pare and shape (abstract, of course, that powerful meta-tool in the thinker's tool kit) large quantities of information into knowledge we want, when we want it, so that with our limited human brains we can comprehend and make use of it.

Implicitly, we have been talking all this time about something we can now make explicit. It is the continuing democratization of knowledge that began with written language and was drastically increased with the invention of the printing press.

More knowledge brings not only more power but also more responsibility, both individual and collective, and that we shall have to shoulder without excessive or unseemly grumbling. It won't be easy, but it will surely be exhilarating.

Do we understand our various human cultures well enough to anticipate what any one of them will let loose in the world if it has intellectual power that exceeds that of its neighbors, the shade of gray that transforms the game to black and white? Probably not. It's easy to say that we want to shape the world justly, peacefully, and respectfully for our species in its glorious diversity, but the task of moving all that beyond platitude is a heavy and mysterious responsibility.

One small piece of insurance against cultural hegemony is the existence of multitudes of tool designers, designing multitudes of tools, each appropriate to the culture it is designed for. In a sense, this situation exists, for as I have said, the Europeans (especially the British and the French) and the Americans are beginning to believe that the Japanese mean it and are moving toward their own workbenches to see what they can come up with. It doesn't take such sophisticated technology to begin to make a difference. A project at Bar Ilan University in Israel to store all the historical precedents of Jewish law in a form that will allow questions and answers to be easily consulted and compared is already changing the practice of law there; moreover, it is having a subtle sociological effect as previously neglected commentaries from the Sephardic tradition appear right beside the dominant Ashkenazic traditions and thus must be taken into account.

Another small piece of insurance is in the nature of the technology itself, which, unlike other machines, does not demand interchangeable parts for its efficient use but, on the contrary, permits nearly endless amounts of individualization. As the printing press had the paradoxical effect of both enhancing community identity *and* sharpening individual worth, the computer could do the same, only more so.

But insurance is not the same as a guarantee against catastrophe, and we are obliged to be alert. The new technology will bring along its own versions of Grand Inquisitors: let us say, for an early example, poorly maintained criminal data bases, believed too gullibly and applied indiscriminately, or an arrogant confidence that the computer can tell us whether we should risk destroying the planet in the name of self-defense. The new technology will force us to part, perhaps painfully, from some ideas we are reverent about and replace them with revisions, even as the printing press evicted Galen and Aristotle from the halls of science and placed them, instead, in the museum of charming historical curiosities. We cannot say now which ideas they will be; we can only be assured that it will happen.

Yet I remain optimistic, and history is the source of my optimism. Here we are with a new tool in our intellectual tool kit, primitive compared to what it will be and yet already powerful, waiting to be used as we see fit. It has the potential to help us through that ill-conditioned problem called real life, enlarging the kinds of subjects we feel confident to address, and, of course, changing the way we think about them. It can transform shades of gray into black and white, where the human race is the winner that takes all.

In my most extravagantly optimistic moments, I believe we stand on the threshold of another golden age, another renaissance, big—and in my view, good—changes ahead. Those changes will trouble the Establishment (because they will inevitably disestablish the Establishment) but excite the adventuresome and enrich us all. That is what technologies of the intellect have always promised—and always delivered.

Chapter 4

Books

Can it be possible, then, that what I call the inevitable machine of the twentieth century will eventually usurp that of the fifteenth century? Many fear it. But with certain qualifications, and depending upon how we define "eventually," I doubt it.

When I was a child, my family immigrated to the United States. Like many families who made post–World War II immigrations, we knew some hard times at the beginning. My refuge was the children's room of the public library in Rutherford, New Jersey, directed by Miss Ralph, a no-nonsense but loving keeper of the books, who guided a troubled seven-year-old through the shelves, encouraging my fantasies and soothing my soul.

At least to a degree. I wanted to bound ahead, read everything I could get my hands on. I had started high and mighty—the first book I read on my own was an unbowdlerized copy of Grimm's, given to my mother when she was a child. The rich variety of human experience in the unexpurgated Grimm's mocked the prissy stuff the experts said was good for children my age. The mockery came for reasons the experts might not have suspected: Grimm was real life, full of struggles between good and evil, poor and rich, young and old; full of strangers making their way in strange lands, up against strange ways, where only a quick wit saved you from destruction.

Books approved for children my age, on the other hand, were astonishing make-believe. Children in them were clean and well fed, had rooms of their own, endlessly patient parents with infinity to explain matters, loving grandparents, affectionate pets, jolly policemen and greengrocers, lawns in the summer and sleds in the winter. They suffered spats, not life and death struggles. Such poor as there were in these books weren't to admire or even to identify with but were vaguely pitiful outsiders who evoked your condescension even as they claimed your tolerance.

A part of me knew it was pap and was bored. But another part of me saw it as a fortunate introduction to the new society: child anthropologist, I would study its ways and learn. In still another, more calculating part of my mind, I dreamed that if I read every silly book Miss Ralph gave me, and did it as quickly and as diligently as possible, she'd finally allow me to read the good stuff. None of this passed between Miss Ralph and me in so many words: I was not only troubled, but shy, and excessively polite, and afraid of hurting the librarian's feelings. But oh how I longed for better things.

Years later my feelings toward books were just as strong but different. I stopped once and tried to analyze the rush of excitement that came over me when I stood at the threshold of a great library. It was just how I felt when I faced a party full of strangers: an anticipatory tingle saying, here are unimaginable stories assembled for your delight; dive in.

To this day, I roam the stacks of the great libraries where I am lucky enough to have access and simply breathe in the piquant aroma of old bound paper and ink. I smell decay, I suppose, since the acid-based paper most books have been printed on for the past fifty years is slowly destroying itself. A cynic might smile and read some larger sign of the folly of a lifetime's devotion to books, to what is soon to be irrevocably lost. A worse cynic would note the whistle I have to wear around my neck to keep the molesters at bay, the library stacks housing much more of the real world than they used to. True, I do not like having to look over my shoulder each time I hear footsteps to see who goes.

As I earned some money from books, both teaching out of them and writing them, I spent it extravagantly on—what else?—

more books. I still do depend on books, and I still read and write them. I close my day peacefully, reading or writing before I put out the light. But of course, something has happened.

A year or so ago, writing out a check for a book I very much needed, I only noticed the warning to allow six weeks for delivery after I'd signed my name. The product I was ordering was already manufactured and sitting on a warehouse shelf. There was no need for customized slipcovers, color choices, or other variations from the norm. Presumably, my order would arrive, a clerk would pull the item off the shelf, pack it indifferently (no need to worry about fragility), and put it in the mail to me.

Was it coming from Ulan Bator? No, it was coming from Princeton, New Jersey, an hour and a half's drive away. Was the company expecting such a tidal wave of orders that no known clerical system could cope without six weeks' grace? Probably not: the product was a $45 book on certain aspects of medieval literacy, fascinating to me, but not to tidal waves of others.

I needed information that might be in that book for a talk I'd be giving within the month. Such information would be interesting later on but not as useful. I posted off the order with the forlorn hope that somehow the book would come soon.

I might have gone to the great university library two blocks away—after all, that would allow me to see if the information I needed was really in that book instead of wagering a hopeful $45 that it was—but my library, though better than most, takes time to process a book before it gets on the shelf and this book was newly published.

I might have tried my local bookstore, but of the nearly 50,000 book titles published each year, that shop can order only a fraction of them. Special orders take six weeks, and there's a surcharge of $3 (last time I looked). The surcharge costs about the same as a long-distance call, so these days I call publishers directly to see if they'll take my credit card. A voice in Princeton seemed flustered by that; evidently the idea hangs heavy that no scholar needs information in a hurry. (Though I offer as counterevidence another scholarly press, the M.I.T. Press, feet firmly in the twentieth century, that not only will take my credit card but will express a book to me if I'm willing to pay the freight. I usually am.)

Both the book industry and my beloved libraries would seem to be among the first and most conspicuous casualties of the computer revolution.

In my more peevish moments, I complain: send silent letters to the editor, all editors, declaring pompously that as a member of a family that spends thousands of dollars a year on books I am surely entitled, et cetera, et cetera. Yet the truth is that readers' needs are changing, and the book business is, in the main, having a hard time responding. It is once again a matter of being between two cultures.

There is something else. It may or may not be significant that our family outlay on books in 1982 was eclipsed for the first time by outlay on electronics. We bought a personal computer. While we weren't the last on our block, we weren't the first, either, simply because we had professional access to computers. Like a lot of people, we discovered that conveniences we had at the office (and in our case at home in the form of a terminal) were too good not to introduce elsewhere in our lives.

At the moment, information across computer networks is costly—though $45 for a book that has a lot of information I don't really want, and only might have some information I do want, will take six weeks to arrive, and then must be housed, compares less than splendidly with commercial data-base subscriptions and search costs. However, information in such commercial data bases is at present fragmented, highly specialized, and sloppily verified. When I tried to find out who originally had said "God is in the details" through such a source, I received twenty citations of journalists making various attributions (including "as somebody said"), all permissively leaving me to decide who, if any of them, was right. Such specialization, fragmentation, and sloppy scholarship were also characteristic of the early printed book, so things will surely improve on-line in the future.

And yet pushed, I cannot believe that sitting down at my electronic terminal I will ever feel the thrills I feel in a library or when I hold in my hands a splendid example of the bookbinder's art. There's no deeper truth in that; it is only my own history. "Books are the way we first came to knowledge," says my mentor and friend, and I think yes, books were my generation's apples— the serpent beguiled us and we did eat. And loved it. But the next generation's Apples are something else. I can believe—in fact, I wish and hope it for them—that a younger generation will sit down at their terminals with that same thrill of anticipation that my generation, and generations before me, felt in the presence of books.

For the times move on. The most visionary librarians and publishers understand that their fates are converging with electronics. The tough problem is what to do just now. When he was head of the Project on Information and Technology in Washington, D.C., Marc Tucker likened it to viewing the Promised Land across the Red Sea. Everybody knows that's where they want to be eventually, but how is the Red Sea to be parted and who will pay the costs?

Publishers think individual users should and are moving quickly toward a fee-for-use: every time you pull something up on your screen or off your facsimile transmitter, you'll be charged, which effectively limits browsing to the well-off. This shift of cost from the community to the individual user is contrary to the centuries-old tradition of libraries and gives the control of access to publishers in the profit sector. As I argued earlier, we can hope that competition will keep prices low, but there is no certainty. Most scholars are unaware of, or indifferent to, this impending change in scholarship. Instead, they resist change in its superficial forms (using automated search, for example) while a change of substance is being thrust upon them.

The situation is further confused for scholarship—meaning any inquiry, scientific or humanistic—since there are at present no international standards, little linkage among data bases (which in any case are often unknown to the very people who could most use them), and copyright problems. All these puzzles must be worked out in painstaking detail, but with attention to the long-range effects, which is easy to say and far harder to do.

For a while, some colleges made news (but the novelty soon wore thin) by requiring incoming freshmen to purchase personal microcomputers, regardless of their major field of study or intentions in the world. The impulse is partly sound: the automatic manipulation of data is a fact of many people's lives, and when students arrive at college, they have a right to expect computing to be at least as good as they had it at home (imagine attending a college whose library wasn't as good as the one Mom and Dad have). But except for the most mundane applications, microcomputers are not yet the gateway to the knowledge we hope for and will not be until a host of other problems are solved.

At the same time, it's an ill-kept secret that those in universities who allocate computing live in fear of the day that students of the humanities and arts discover what students of science, business, and law, say, have already discovered—that the computer, even in its present impeded form, is indispensable to effective scholarship—if only as a wonderful drudge called a word processor—and demand their share of the computational resources.

Patricia Battin, vice president and university librarian of Columbia University, who has been president of the pioneering Research Libraries Group (an organization of twenty-six university research libraries, which aims to reshape information services for scholars), envisions a merger of university libraries and computer centers that will provide an "information infrastructure to stimulate the continuing autonomous use of information sources." It's a process, not an entity, evolving in response to client needs and technology imperatives. Still, she calls it a Scholarly Information Center, and its duties and purposes are manifold. It must establish new policies for centrally subsidized services, with a series of optional, incremental fee-based services available in addition on request. The goal, of course, is to permit the electronic scholar of the 1990s "to rummage around in the bibliographic wealth of recorded knowledge, organized in meaningful fashion with logically controlled searches." This means access to data bases, files, and all works published on optical disks; high-resolution graphics capability; capacity to order off-line prints of machine-readable text; links to printed works through on-line indexes of books, tables of contents, and so on, and acccess to current scholarly work through topic indexes, in addition to on-line training and consultation services supplied by the Scholarly Information Center.

Battin continues:

> According to the traditional cliché, the library is the heart of the university. I think it is time for a new metaphor—and that metaphor is more appropriately the DNA. The new process will be a helix—we provide a basic set of services and technical capacities, users interact and experiment with the new technical dimensions and develop new requirements which then influence the evolution of a new shape for the infrastructure. As the genetic code of the university, the character and quality of the Scholarly Information Center will determine the character and quality of the institution.

Is this, then, the end of the book? Not now, not for a long time, surely. As I've argued elsewhere, whatever aims to replace books would have to match their portability, the high resolution of ink on paper, the ease of access. I say nothing about economics, which are knottier problems yet.

And yet for those of us poised between two technologies, the frustrations are great. Rising expectations have hit for gathering information. I resent having to move my body physically from my pleasant study; I resent having to put a whistle around my neck as I enter the dark library stacks; I resent the frustrations of books that are checked out to somebody else, missing, otherwise inaccessible—a fact I can discover only by going to see for myself.

When I first used a university library, human pages stood between me and the pages of books. Those human pages behaved like the most simpleminded of, well, machines: if the book I asked for was out, it wasn't their business to look on either side of the empty space and fetch a substitute. That had to wait until I was a graduate student and was considered responsible enough to be let loose in the stacks to browse by myself. (At just about the same time, however, labor costs became so prohibitive that libraries could no longer afford human pages, so the stacks became free-for-alls, with what effects on the book stock I cannot tell; my unscientific recollection is that doing it yourself, molesters not-withstanding, is still preferable to the interference of human pages.)

Three observations. The first is that we keep comparing the computer to the printing press, although many other inventions have had an impact on the human condition before and since. The second is that those who worry most (or loudest, at any rate) about the computer are lovers of books. (Moviemakers seem pleased about the introduction of the computer into their technology; musicians protest, but more because of the computer's effect on employment than because of its musical impact; dancers are using computers for dance notation and physical conditioning; paint-ers—well, I shall treat painters presently.) Why do we keep re-turning to that comparison with the printing press, and why do booklovers seem to feel threatened the most?

"Reading," William Gass has written, "is reasoning, figuring things out through thoughts, making arrangements out of ar-rangements until we've understood a text so fully it is nothing but feeling and pure response, until its conceptual turns are like the reversals of mood in a marriage—petty, sad, ecstatic, common-place, foreseeable, amazing."

Reading, in other words, is a part of that fundamental human intellectual endeavor called the processing of symbols. It is supple enough in its powers of abstraction to go everywhere, from nursery rhymes to high energy physics (though it sometimes requires special languages, mathematics, say, to illuminate a topic fully). By mechanizing the production of text, reading has intellectually enfranchised the millions with both the ideas it conveys and the processes it demands.

Yet Gass might just as well be describing computing. The reader with his book, the user with her computer are responding to information in sibling ways. One difference—and it is a significant one—is that many functions now performed by humans reading and writing text will come more and more to be performed *for* humans *by* the computer. I mean, for example, the recasting of information into summaries and abstractions, the drawing of inferences, and the venturing of generalizations that offer understanding, mastery, and, eventually, intellectual leverage. In short, computing offers the immense power of codes, symbols, standing-for, which I have already argued is the lingua franca of the new rising class. Up to now, such power as we've had along these lines has belonged to literate human heads alone.

At some level, readers recognize this. Perhaps that is why so many of them fear the computer. Though they speak of the tactile pleasures of the book, perhaps they are really voicing their uneasiness at the idea of turning over to a mechanism such subtle business as reasoning, figuring things out through thoughts, making arrangements out of arrangements, and finally understanding. Though they complain, with justification, about the difficulties of electronic scholarly search, perhaps they are really complaining about the difficulty of being curator of the former revolution, while the new revolution is being carried out by others, in this case, the engineers and computer scientists. Perhaps, finally, they fear what the popular press says bluntly: such an automated process of reasoning, figuring things out through thoughts, and so on, if it can be done, must be resisted or else we shall be transformed into a race of intellectual sloths.

We've had such warnings before. E. M. Forster's short story "The Machine Stops," written at the turn of the century (less, perhaps, to prophesy than to prick the irritating optimism of his enemy, H. G. Wells), envisioned a future human race bereft of any physical skills except the ability to push buttons. The human race, ever contrary, has become unexpectedly obsessed with physical fitness. But the subtext of Forster's story, human dependence upon artifacts, is troubling. We rely more intimately upon our artifacts every day. This is because grown-up life consists of trade-offs, and most of us trade some personal independence for advantages we think lie in, say, our vulnerable cities or our fragile telecommunications networks or even in our books (artifacts too, after all).

It remains an astringent fact that the real risks of the new are not what we expected and often cannot be perceived until after the trade is made. We are never "ready" for such changes (we are not biologically "ready" for the agricultural revolution, but too late now). So we gamble, hoping that checks and balances provided by other human artifacts (law, moral philosophy, community sentiment) will help us if we go too far. The odds are in our favor, but not a sure thing.

When the reasoning computer is widely available—not if—I think it will be good for us, on the whole. Computing demands a subtlety of intellectual powers to take advantage of it, which will have to be acquired the usual way (though I hope we can improve on that process thanks to the computer's contributions to cognitive psychology). I will not think it intellectual sloth to subcontract to the machine those tasks the machine can do better if that frees me to go and do other things, to climb perhaps to a higher level of understanding, which gives me still further leverage. Instead of fearing, readers are the very people most entitled to take proprietary interest.

Maybe it would help if we didn't call it a computer, which has all those overtones of counting and reckoning. The French call the universal machine *l'ordinateur,* which I find much more satisfying, since its roots are in the Old French word for ordering and arranging, more illustrative of the machine's functions than mere counting. (In a final bit of poetic closure, that Old French word comes from the Latin technical term for the order of threads in the woof: weaving, as we shall see, being the mother of text.) But computer is what we call it in English, reflecting its historical uses.

So although computing is reasoning, making arrangements out of arrangements, and still more, the book—bound and bounded though it is—is not soon to be replaced. I cannot imagine computer literacy without ordinary literacy as its precondition; more banal but equally a problem, the cost of sophisticated electronic scholarship is very high, and that outlay will not happen soon, whether by scholars, by entrepreneurs, or by society at large. So the printed text will not soon be replaced but instead slowly be supplemented by electronic text.

The third observation, a central one, may be the most troubling to booklovers, and remains to be examined. When the project to computerize the commentary on Jewish law got under way at Bar Ilan University in Israel, the programmers faced a puzzle. Jewish law prohibits the name of God once written from being erased or the paper upon which it is written from being destroyed. Could the name of God be erased from the video screen, the disks, the tape? The rabbis pondered the programmers' question and finally ruled that these media were not considered writing; they could be erased. In other words, electronic text is impermanent, flimsy, malleable, contingent. Where is Truth in impermanence, flimsiness, malleability, and contingency?

Right there.

Chapter 5

Texts

Text. The word is meant to be so rich in associations: it's an early metaphor and signifies weaving—of words, of thoughts, of beliefs—in the most extended sense. In medieval scholarly communities, texts formed and reformed social organizations, pushed the uses of the word into new forms, and meantime caused some nasty theological quarrels. (I suppose they still do.) Texts can be pleasurable, sensational; Barthes' erotic language is apt. We are ever in the thrall of texts: one chronicler of Chinese history reports with amusement about a group of scholars who tried to destroy bandits by chanting the Confucian classics at them. Martyrs to the word, predictably.

But if written text (by hand or mechanized) was considered woven thought, what shall we call electronic text? People who write or read on electronic screens already see something much more complicated than warp and woof, bobbin and shuttle at work, and understand that it is just the beginning.

The words flow faster. At the terminal in my Manhattan apartment I draft a letter to the editor, responding to a nearly libelous book review. I transmit its text to my co-author, who happens to be at home in Palo Alto (although he needn't be—he could be anywhere in the country where he has access to the network we use, visiting another university or research laboratory, for example). He thinks I'm far too restrained and serious. "Let's slice this meatball up," he writes to me. "Okay," I say, "give me some time to think about it."

Another text, very different in tone and attitude. He likes this, makes his own changes, and an amended draft comes back to me. I laugh at his turns of phrase (as he, I hope, has laughed at mine) and without complications I make a hard, or paper-and-ink, copy of the letter that will go by conventional post (known among computer types as snail-mail) to its recipient. The whole exchange between us has taken place in a matter of hours, oblivious of time-zone differences, of whether we two are in our offices, at home, or out of town. Both of us have slept, eaten, carried on our normal lives and, moreover, have each controlled the rate at which we corresponded with each other. In technical terms, our communication is asynchronous.

Sometimes I check my electronic mail just before I go to bed, sometimes I check it as dinner is cooking. My co-author, on the other hand, spends a lot more time at his terminal than I do at mine, so gets a brief signal—a beep—as he is working to let him know that mail has arrived for him, and he can read it if he likes. Sometimes he likes; sometimes he keeps on working, knowing that the message will keep, which is one of electronic mail's great virtues over telephone interruptions.

Now, multiply the actors in that little drama by scores, and you can see some of the implications of electronic text. Such weavings are taking place every day. Sometimes the topic is as innocuous as selling a pair of skis (electronic bulletin boards are both local and nationwide) or as harmful as disclosing code for penetrating private networks; sometimes the subject is erotica (an "adult" group greets one another on a number of networks) and sometimes the subject is professional. Computer networks have been used to lay out specifications for the design of computer chips, with widely dispersed groups easily and conveniently contributing to the highly difficult and complicated design, and sometimes networks have been used to debate issues of interest to the community, such as when undergraduates and faculty discussed the proposition that Carnegie-Mellon University should be fully wired for electronic exchange. (Nobody knows exactly why, but studies at IBM and similar industrial installations have shown that electronic communication has had virtually no effect on basic scientific research, which is still done face to face, whereas in engineering, electronic communication is very important, and in management, even more so.)

I pen a letter and am appalled at my handwriting. The keyboard, through which thousands of my words pour each day, is obliterating this sign—this signature—of myself.

Of course, I leave an electronic signature in a way I didn't with my typewriter. One of our national spy agencies is constructing an electronic envelope around its premises to keep the errant electronic texts from flying hither and yon. I cannot afford such a thing, so conceivably, somebody could stand outside my house and spy: posted like a lovesick fool, he catches my every keystroke in his electronic butterfly net, the thousands of preliminaries as well as the good stuff. What devotion!

My journal, where I still handwrite entries daily, lets me check the state of my motor skills. All right. But technology giveth and technology taketh away. Nobody reads my handwritten journal, not even me (very often). However, safe behind the confessional-box grille of printed text, I expose myself publicly. After a fashion. "Are you imagining, as you read me, that I am portraying myself?" Colette teased. "Have patience: this is merely my model."

A word-processing system (when we inevitably get rid of that awkward phrase, some variant on text might take its place, texting, say) increases my productivity three or four times. Since I am a pieceworker, and paid accordingly, this is good for me. Unfortunately, I can't go back. The first summer after I started using such a system, I arrived at my summer home as usual, where I usually do my most productive (least interrupted) work. There I realized that no amount of writing obligations would drive me back to my faithful old electric typewriter. Jean-Paul Sartre once estimated that 90 percent of his work was rewriting, and I am not as smart as he was. So the text editor I use is a dream come true. The only drawback is that now I am greedy for more—more power, more speed, more memory, more functions—which is endemic in the computing world.

I write on a stand-alone device, which is to say a personal computer that is not connected to any other computer (except by the telephone, which is another story). In a room near my study is the terminal that connects to a large academic computer network around the world (which is how I communicated with my co-author), but for all other writing I use my own computer, mainly for flexibility.

There are many implications in all this, but for the moment I wish only to address matters of text itself. Electronic texts increase productivity, but that raises questions. If authors, for example, begin in great numbers to submit their writing on disks for automatic composition and publication, which dispenses with an editor and compositor, should they get the money they save the publisher?

A committee began in 1983 to study these questions and develop industry standards. Co-sponsored by the Association of American Publishers and the Council on Library Resources, the committee involves a number of interested parties such as the Authors Guild, the Library of Congress, the National Library of Medicine, and other groups. Perhaps we shall no longer need to allow six weeks for delivery, and authors will see their work published, in its old-fashioned sense of "made public," much sooner than the months and sometimes years they now must wait.

Productivity is a matter of not only quantity but quality. Are we windy writers to be allowed to foist anything we want on the world without intervention? A writer who has felt the heavy hand of a clumsy editor would celebrate such a turn, but the truth is that writers are sometimes so close to their work that the help of a sensitive and gifted editor is vital.

It happens that a portion of editing can be done automatically. Some people might find that upsetting—what could be more intimate and human than the process of writing and the even more delicate process of editing that text to make it say what it means in the most effective way? Does the specter of a robot Harold Ross or Maxwell Perkins lurk in the electronic shadows? Not quite.

Bell Laboratories faced this problem a few years ago in a slightly different form. The numbers of documents were growing at fission rates, which raised two important questions. How could they be managed, and how could they be made more understandable? Computer programs were being produced that could help people do all sorts of useful things, but, unfortunately, the descriptions of what those programs did and how they accomplished it, known as documentation, were in shambles. People who design computer programs and systems (not unlike experimental scientists, say) are notoriously more interested in producing lovely systems than in telling the world how to use their designs. When they shift themselves to such disclosure, they aren't very good at it.

A small group of linguists, psychologists, and computer specialists wondered whether the problems might be ameliorated, if not altogether solved, by automation. ("We got tired of being asked, 'Is this clear?'" Lawrence Frase, a psychologist in the Bell group, laughs now.) The answer was yes, the editing process could be automated to a large degree, and thus was born the Writer's Workbench, a set of programs that can scan your prose for diverse characteristics, depending on your aims, and coach and coax you toward good writing.

"It was pretty arrogant at first," Frase says, and another member of the Workbench team, linguist Nina Macdonald, recalls that people were a bit put off by its prescriptiveness. All this has been modified: now the Writer's Workbench suggests, without rapping your knuckles. In text analysis and editorial feedback it aims to be "rational, diverse, evaluative, modifiable, specific, and informative."

Principles of good writing in English are fairly widely agreed upon, at least for expository prose, and the team members consulted a large number of books that attempt to explicate those principles. On their desks and bookshelves I saw Strunk and White, Fowler, *The Chicago Manual of Style,* and many other handbooks familiar to any professional writer.

In addition, the Workbenchers used what psychologists and linguists are discovering about those rules. For instance, nearly every stylebook exhorts writers to use the active rather than the passive voice: Use "Mary smacked John" instead of "John was smacked by Mary." The rule books talk about the active voice as more vigorous and aesthetically satisfying, but psychological research has shown that people remember active versions of a sentence better than passive versions and verify its facts faster, important points in transmitting information of any kind but especially in scientific documentation. Thus a Workbench client can learn why certain rules are laid down.

The rules of good writing are agreed upon but not absolute. Obviously, a writer should spell correctly and write grammatically;

the writing level should be appropriate for the reader; the sentences should vary in length to hold the reader's interest, examples should be concrete, and so on. The various programs of the Writer's Workbench examine prose for all these factors. An elementary program even checks the organization of ideas, but it makes no judgment about their soundness. Lacking intelligence of any kind, something the designers hope to remedy in the future, the Writer's Workbench cannot make sophisticated judgments about content or form or even more subtle judgments about suitability to the occasion.

For example, one user was told that his prose was verbose, that it contained many more long words than readers wanted. He stuck by his writing. As a member of a minority group, he argued, he was always having to prove himself to the majority. The proof the majority demanded, in his view, was pomposity. He knew better, but the majority didn't. Nina Macdonald, who told me this story, shrugged. "I think he saw things as they are. I sure couldn't argue with him."

Within its limitations, the Writer's Workbench has proved to be extremely useful. But as Macdonald points out, its most useful functions are its least interesting: spelling and punctuation checks, noting consecutive occurrences of the same word, wordiness, split infinitives, and the like. Unfortunately, as any instructor of elementary composition knows, most writing errors are dismally repetitive. If there is pleasure in watching a student struggle to transform ideas from clichés to authentic expression, from the slovenly ungrammatical to the powerfully grammatical; if there is pleasure in watching a human being discover the treasure of his native tongue (and there are such pleasures and they are profound), the tedium of correcting compositions poisons those pleasures fatally. That is why teaching composition in college is the gruntwork of the English department, left mainly to graduate students and disdained by senior professors.

So it is that the Writer's Workbench has been adopted at a small number of colleges and universities, with some success. The students seem to like having their prose examined by a machine, whose opinion they don't care about, before it is put before a human, whose opinion matters. The Writer's Workbench, at first a corrective, becomes a pedagogical tool: novice writers begin to anticipate the program's diagnoses and fix faults ahead of time.

For fun, I gave the Writer's Workbench two pieces of my own prose. The first piece is the raw stuff of my journal, censored but not edited. In addition, I gave it some paragraphs from a book I published a few years ago. On their own, the researchers chose a chapter from a book I had recently co-authored (but, to my amazement, picked a technical chapter that I had written, not a chapter by my scientist co-author).

Here is the material from my journal as the program received it:

August 3, 1983

Just as I was writing the entry above, the phone rang and it was Mark Harris, who'd been in Berkeley visiting Serendipity Books (which is handling his literary papers, which are for sale) and also visiting his old teacher, Henry Nash Smith. We were delighted to have him here for an impromptu dinner. I thought he looked exceptionally well. The most memorable thing he said, among many memorable things, was that scholars of English are always astonished to discover that the passions writers write about aren't synthetic but real, and writers have them. In some ways it was as if we'd hardly interrupted a conversation we'd begun many years ago, but there was also the sense that time was pressing and much important must be left out. Heard his version of the great Arizona State University lawsuit that sounded more sensible than any others I'd heard.

Mom, San and I to lunch and had such a delightful time we simply moved on to San's to continue. There we got a call from John, happy to share with us that our offer on the Santa Rosa property has been accepted. Now the loan must be approved, but we're 90% there. We were very happy!

A curiosity: since I got to California, driving the freeways has made me extremely nervous. I wondered if I had a full-blown phobia lurking nearby. Yesterday, with the news of the *Times* review, I drove down to Palo Alto with my California-driver-since-sixteen confidence. Better yet, it hadn't gone away today, though of course the thrill was somewhat attenuated.

Monday a visit from R., a nice man, I suppose, but like all men, a talker, not a listener. I found my patience wearing thin after two and a half hours.

An earlier talk with a man who runs . . . , an entrepreneur with no vision, no particular skills, no insight; simply a guy turning a buck. No blame for that, but no great honor, either.

Monday night a rock group played at the Keystone. Their name: Artificial Intelligence.

August 21, 1983

To Peter and Dorothy Denning's in Portola Valley on Friday night for dinner, Peter serving his altogether astonishing French Bordeaux, one a 1950, the other 1968, and me limp with admiration pour les deux, but especially the 1968.

The Workbench informed me that while my journal entries could be read by eighth and ninth graders, my published prose was accessible only to high school seniors and college freshmen. The program also went on to tell me about sentence length, sentence types (simple and compound), my uses of the verb "to be," my use of passives, nominalizations (nouns created from verbs—impediments to remembering), and expletives (words or phrases that add no information).

I was pleased to see that the expletives and nominalizations were low in all samples, chastened that word lengths were long. I was surprised that an eighth grader might read my journal (I'd have thought the ideas were more complicated) and pleased that my published prose was accessible to high school seniors and college freshmen (I'd worked hard to simplify technical ideas). I expected a scolding for my sexist remark about all men, but the Workbench, which does monitor such things, must concur. Unlike my high school English teachers, the program had no objections to sentence fragments or the pronoun "I."

Regular users have reported that they like the immediate, objective criticism of the Writer's Workbench, and the specific advice about their prose, which, though sometimes confusing, is still preferable to the vague advice and subjective opinions of human reviewers. Users like the time it saves, its privacy, and the way it alerts them to principles of good writing. But they've found it difficult to apply some of the advice, and they objected to the length of some of the program commentary.

Other firms have also felt the need. IBM has an experimental system, EPISTLE, under way, which evaluates text for grammar and style. The text is displayed on a screen with grammatical errors, for example, highlighted in color. When the user wishes to focus on a particular error, he points at it with a lightpen. A box, known as a window, then appears on the screen near the error, with an explanation of the error and possible remedies. The user can choose one of those; alternatively, he can ask for more help (an expanded description of the error, the system's strategies for selecting the recommended corrections, and a strategy for the user to apply in making up his own remedy) or decide to ignore the system's advice altogether. The program also signals style errors on several different levels, whether poor words, phrases, or paragraphs.

But the possibilities of text in the computer are hardly exhausted by gentle correctives, as we shall see next.

Chapter 6

The Transmutations
of Texts

When the Lord looked down and saw that the children of man were building a tower to reach heaven, he said to himself, "Now nothing will be restrained from them, which they have imagined to do," and then exercised the first recorded use of divide-and-conquer, scattering them abroad and confounding the language of all the earth. Translation has been a trial ever since.

In the mid-1940s it seemed an inspired thing to put computers to work on automatic translation. For many reasons, the early projects were not a great success (though not as ridiculous as they have sometimes been described), and in 1966 a panel of experts from the National Science Foundation declared the project hopeless for the foreseeable future and recommended against any future government funding, which effectively killed automatic translation research in the United States. I think the project seemed hopeless to the scientists who comprised the panel not because automatic translation was impossible but because it was difficult to do perfectly. Tellingly, work continued in Europe and Japan.

In the early 1970s a rumor moved uncertainly around the artificial intelligence community that somebody—no one was sure just who—was ignoring the advice of the august panel. The in-

surgents were said to be doing automatic translations from English
into Vietnamese for the U.S. Army. Nothing fancy: maintenance
manuals, instruction booklets, that sort of thing, but by machine,
with some message at the end. Not long after the need for English-
to-Vietnamese manuals came to an end, the rumors began again
that the same group was now engaged in English-to-Farsi translations, again for the military.

The rumors proved to be true, and while the sages were struggling with what might be the true nature of complete and thorough language understanding, the Logos Corporation was
producing translations by machine—not perfectly, but usefully,
and with ever-improving accuracy.

The Vietnamese project led to work in French, Russian, Farsi,
Spanish, and German, each project teaching the systems designers
something new. At last what has emerged is a universal, which is
to say, language-independent, automatic translator, which when
I visited Logos happened to be producing German-to-English
translations for a large manufacturing company in Germany. (Development was under way in Japanese, English, German, French,
and a number of target languages.)

The translator is highly flexible. It allows topic-specific semantics—for example, the German word "panzer" in military terminology means armorplate, in particular, a kind of tank; in zoology,
it means shell; and in computing it means metallic skin—and the
system can take such context into account. The system also permits
company-specific semantics (a word in one firm might have a
slightly different meaning in another firm even though both firms
are in the same business). It can, without help from a human
translator, select the correct nuance of the verb "to run," for
example, from among dozens of nuances stored in the semantic
memory. Because the size of this memory is virtually limitless, and
because the machine never tires and never forgets, its translations
are becoming increasingly useful.

Americans can hardly appreciate the desperate need the rest
of the world has for automatic translation. High-tech products in
particular have a short market life, and no company can wait
around to market its products internationally while a human translator takes on the job of translating all customer documents, repair
manuals, or patents. Translations must be finished by the time
the product is ready to be shipped or may as well not be done at

all. The European Economic Community, an early patron of machine translation, and recently a Logos client, is committed to publishing all its documents in all languages of all ten member nations. The task is impossible without a machine solution, and so the EEC has budgeted $25 million to produce a universal translator called EUROTRA, an ambitious project that many feel is still some years off.

But the first commercial product of Logos is on the market, a German-to-English, English-to-German translator, which is licensed for a relatively modest fee plus pennies per word of translation. Since the automatic translator runs on ordinary Wang word processors, they can be used for clerical work during the day at a firm and turned over to translating at night, or the translations can be run as "background" jobs on the fancier Wang configurations. Logos has worked at making the system as easy to use as possible—human translators need a two-week training period to learn the system (which for most of them also includes using a word processor for the first time) and then can be left alone, able to update or specify new meanings for their dictionaries as needed. Help is always available by telephone.

Like humans, the automatic translator deals well but not perfectly with linguistic complexity and ambiguity. It has seven levels of abstraction, which reduce the complexity of natural language and at the same time preserve semantic content. The translator also relies on massive dictionaries, which can be easily updated with floppy disks. The present general dictionary of German-to-English contains 100,000 entries, but there can be any number of sub-dictionaries for specific companies and subjects and for private use.

The system serves human translators and works best for relatively straightforward text—poesy will not soon be translated automatically. Typically, the human selects the text to be translated from the electronic library and pushes the button to get the automatic translation going. The system can translate approximately 20,000 words in 24 hours; and so, depending on the length of the document, a completed translation is subsequently returned to the screen for post-editing by the human translator. Thus the Logos translation can be considered the first draft or something to scan for information. "While Logos is broadly capable, and never forgets a transfer," its creators write, "it is not a skilled,

professional human translator. Before a translated document is
ready for publication and distribution, a competent translator must
review it, and edit it. . . . The human translator is essentially the
manager of this process—not a limiting variable." Again, usually
from 10 to 20 percent of the text requires post-editing. Translators
working with the Logos system have been able to turn out as many
as forty pages of technical translation a day, though on a sustained
basis twenty to thirty pages a day is more typical. Without machine
aid, the usual product is about eight pages a day.

Logos Corporation's founder and president, Bernard Scott,
and its chief operating officer, Charles Staples, willingly mused
for me about dreams for the future: automatic abstracting and
translating, individual translations by scanner for individual scholars, as unthinkable a luxury now as a personal chamber music
ensemble was before the automatic reproduction of sound.

I'm amused that the automatic translation goals of the Japanese fifth-generation machines (goals that cannot possibly be reached
I am still assured solemnly by cocktail party experts) are in the
1990s to achieve what Logos has already produced, although the
Japanese machine translation project is planned to be part of an
integrated system and, having faster machines to run on, will
doubtless produce the documents faster. But Logos is building a
faster version of its system too.

On that pleasant autumn afternoon, surrounded by the signs
of both the nineteenth century—the railroad, church bells ringing
in the village—and the twentieth, I asked Scott what he believed
accounted for Logos's success. Touching on one of the great themes
of computing, he said: "No question, it all hinges on the cooperative atmosphere we've had here. You can't get very far on a
computer without cooperation, as you know. And you can't fake
it. The work must be honest, the cooperation real. Fifteen key
people here have hung together through thick and thin, giving
me just that, honest work. Cooperation. And a certain humility;
without it there can't be any real cooperation. Imagine this. If
man's pride led to the breakup of language into many separate
tongues, will it be his pride that separates or his humility that
unites that leads man on the path to discerning the language
behind languages?"

But of course cooperation is fundamental to text, to language
itself. You and I must agree, at least to an extent, on the meanings

of words before we can speak to each other. (We don't agree completely, of course, or else we'd revoke the franchises of lawyers, diplomats, and philosophers, but we normally enter into a discourse that suffices for getting along.) In computing that cooperation takes a slightly different form: we agree on goals; but our goals are so ambitious that neither of us is capable of reaching them alone or even together; it must be several of us, many of us, working in coordination. This is one salient fact of computing, and as I intend to argue later, one of the most important worldwide effects of computing might be its introduction of a new ethos of cooperation. Nothing can be hurt by automatic access to each other's languages.

But there are other ways that text becomes a way of knitting the human community together. Consider hypertext, a term invented, so far as I know, by Ted Nelson, a systems designer and self-described rogue intellectual. In his brilliant little essay *Literary Machines,* he argues for nonsequential writing, a simple and flexible form of reading and writing on the personal computer screen.

Literature, Nelson maintains, is a system of interconnected writings. The sheet of paper, the book, that we see alone and discrete is really invisibly connected—by ideas—to other sheets of paper, some written by other writers, some by the same writer. The links take the form of referrals and quotations, but they can also take the form of disagreement and reevaluation. Nelson envisions storing text in segments of individual changes and fragments, assimilating each change as it arrives, but keeping former changes, integrating them all by means of an indexing method that allows you to reconstruct any previous instant.

"This is the true structure of text, because text is best viewed as an evolving, Protean structure," he says, and no writer would disagree. And of course this needn't be the text of only one writer, but the text of many writers, as a Brown University experiment with hypertext in the mid-1970s showed.

In an introductory poetry course, Brown instructors employed the ideas of hypertext to ease beginning students into the mysteries of a poem. "The individual facing the poem is required (often with little apparent guidance from the text) not merely to read the text itself, but also to place it within a context," writes James V. Catano, who was a teaching assistant in the course. That context includes not only the poem's own literary reflections but also the responses of the readers, both professional and novice. Thus students were presented with the text and its background in such a way that they could manipulate the material any way it suited them.

Professor Andries van Dam of Brown's computer sciences program had been looking for courses in the humanities that might make use of his text-editing system called FRESS to produce hypertext, and the notion seemed made to order for teaching poetry, producing a computer-based collection of background to poems but also permitting the students themselves to participate, recording and sharing their reactions as they changed over time. The screen work wouldn't replace classroom discussion but complement it. The project was a middle ground between normal classroom procedures and conventional computer-aided instruction.

Thus ten major poems were supplied with biographical material, other poems by the poet, related poems by other poets, and several critical articles. These could be linked together anywhere within the text, and students could refer to the separate materials through a simple command that would cause the material to be displayed on a split screen so that texts could be compared. Catano says, "This capacity of the screen would reinforce the idea of the poem as the center of a web of interconnected materials. After placing the poem in one window, each student could use the strands of the web to 'pull' other selected materials into the three remaining windows. The poem would cease to exist in a vacuum; rather it would be the central point of a progressively revealed body of documents and ideas."

Moreover, students would add their own responses, be able to browse through responses by other students and also comments by the course's three instructors.

To everybody's surprise, the students produced a large quantity of commentary, typically more than twice as much as the most productive members of a control group in a normal section of the course. The quality of those comments, while harder to judge, seemed significantly better not only to experienced instructors but also to outside evaluators. The preestablished hypertext links (prepared by the instructors) were enthusiastically followed, although students themselves were less likely to trailblaze.

Professor of English Robert Scholes, who was in charge of the experimental course, says, "We discovered, as we were using the system, that what we had here was a communications instrument of extraordinary richness and subtlety, something that changed the whole dynamic of the course. It wasn't simply something that altered students' study habits. We had expected that and I think that did happen. We got more work from students than one normally gets in a course organized in a normal way. We also got a kind of rapport with the students, a kind of interaction that we hadn't expected." The instructors were so pleased with the results that they hoped to spread the technique to upper level seminars in English and philosophy. But it would be nearly ten years before significant funding came to resume the experiment.

Translations and hypertext are texts connected organically to other texts, but texts can be transmuted into other things, pictures, for example. In 1984, Brown and M.I.T. were awarded a total of $3 million between them by the Annenberg/Corporation for Public Broadcasting Project for an electronic seminar to help scholars synthesize ideas, no longer hypertext but hypermedia. (M.I.T. planned a novel interactive adventure game as a means of teaching foreign languages.) Hypermedia suggests that not text alone but graphics, and even sound, have their place in scholarly research and teaching.

The idea of combining media for a clearer understanding of ideas has an honorable history in computing. In the early 1970s a group under the direction of Alan Kay at Xerox Palo Alto Research Center produced a new programming language called Smalltalk. Kay had set himself a task: how simple could a formal language be and still work? Unlike most other programming languages, Smalltalk tied commands to graphics as well as text. Complicated ideas could be presented so naturally and obviously that beginners with no idea of how a computer works could sit down and get going at once. (Users of the Macintosh will find many of the early Smalltalk features incorporated into their machine, such as icons, the mouse, and menus, although not the feature that Kay believes is fundamental, easy communication between machines.)

Kay's own special interest was the Dynabook, a concept he envisaged as a hand-held, high-performance computer with a high-resolution display, input and output devices supporting visual and audio communications paths, and network connections to shared information resources. It was to be highly portable: "In my original image, you had to be able to carry a couple of sacks of groceries as well, or you'd find some excuse to leave the thing behind."

As a product, Smalltalk's implementation on a Xerox computer was turned down in favor of a word-processing system that made more sense to Xerox executives who saw themselves in the office machine sales business. Eventually Kay left Xerox to become chief scientist at Atari, where he got involved, among other things, with a project to implement the *Encyclopaedia Britannica* in a Smalltalk-like environment. But the video-game income supporting his research suddenly dried up, and the encyclopedia project languished. Kay moved on to Apple, where he is the first Apple Fellow, free to do what moves him.

I hope it's the encyclopedia, myself. Kay had envisioned the new encyclopedia as a dynamic body of knowledge with guides: "I don't like the 'oracle' image of the computer; I prefer the 'librarian' image, which is, you don't expect the librarian to have the answer, but to know where the answer is." Thus the dynamic encyclopedia could not only guide you to the answer but also coach you, select for you, and, perhaps most important of all, change your point of view.

I've imagined such a thing and wish it would soon arrive. For me it's the ultimate transmutation of text: knowledge how, where, and when I want it. It could work like this: I pose a question, why do humans eat raw fish and not raw meat? And a helping hand, an automatic librarian, begins suggesting information for me to look at (better yet—and it is not out of the question—begins abstracting and presenting me with germane hints). Perhaps the first information I get is about human digestive systems and how they can easily digest raw fish but not raw meat. (I receive not only textual descriptions but graphical demonstrations that make such concepts clearer.) But that isn't quite what I had in mind, so I ask for more, and learn about the relative difference in muscles between those animals that live on dry land, and have one relation to gravity, and those that live in water, and have a different relation to gravity, and (now we're getting warmer) the natural limits imposed on a people who live on a small, largely unfarmable island that is nevertheless surrounded by seas full of protein-rich fish, an island that has few forests for cooking fuel—raw fish suddenly becomes a cultural imperative instead of a culinary oddity.

I don't need an oracle; it needn't read my mind. It need only help, sifting and connecting and presenting points of view to me, which ultimately gives me more than knowledge: it gives me intellectual leverage. The raw fish example is not accidental. The first nation to announce that it was systematically working toward such a general purpose intellectual amplifier was Japan, sending a minor shock through the computing world. Other national groups have since announced such plans of their own.

And yet when I reflect upon these transmutations of text that the computer has so far brought about, I am struck how relatively unrevolutionary they are. That is, all this error-correcting and, yes, even translating and summarizing is different only in quantity. It is what we humans have been doing all along, only faster. (The order-of-magnitude effect suggests that a speedup of tens of times will change not only the quantity but the quality of a phenomenon, and so it shall with texts, but I'm driving at something else.) To see how the computer is changing medicine, say, or manufacturing, is to see genuinely novel changes introduced. Not so (so far) in texts.

One reason for this apparent lack of change might be that many of the brightest people who care about texts have been repelled by computers, but that will pass.

A more plausible reason for the relatively superficial impact of the computer on texts might be that the symbolic system called written language has been pushed about as far as it can go, computer or no. This is not true, as we know, of graphic representations: the graphics people are eagerly pressing computer technology in richer directions, whether into the interior of a cell or out into deep space. "Reading is, after all, a terrible waste of our human perceptual bandwidth, even if it is enjoyable," says one graphics specialist, misunderstanding, I think, the extraordinary achievement in symbolism, abstraction, and thus intellectual economy that is the written word. Ancient Chinese proverbs to the contrary, writing is considered a large step up from pictographs. But he is correct that reading does not take advantage of the full human perceptual bandwidth. We read by seeing (or with Braille, touching) and perhaps simultaneously listening to unrelated music, smelling unrelated odors. (But not with equal attention. I listen to music as I read and usually as I write, but a favorite movement suddenly claims my attention, and I get up and turn up the volume, slow or stop my business with text for the duration.)

In any event, for the time being we shall still perceive what the computer presents to us in the way of transmuted text at pretty much the same rate we now perceive text.

That leaves us to speculate that text is the end of a great, honorable, powerful, but perhaps fully evolved technology of the intellect. If that is so, then the computer will continue to make no more than its orders-of-magnitude changes on text without the revolutionary transformations we can already see in other fields.

Then again, something else, perhaps an astonishing tapestry of text and graphics, changing under our hands as we turn it in the light, now this way, now that, will come to replace text or, rather, exalt the weaving of thoughts and ideas to a simultaneous richness, subtlety, and accessibility that was unimaginable before the computer's processes. It will be even more supple and universal than text (which fails at certain critical moments, alas), and we shall be off again to capture, explain, and shape the world to our minds' content.

Interlude: Anxiety

In the space of a few weeks a lot of new electronic equipment arrives together by coincidence. In addition to the his and hers computers we already have, we are blessed with new video and sound equipment, a third very different kind of computer, even new telephones. Warranty cards are neglected; there are too many to remember.

Though I love to get information through text, manuals dishearten me as a rule, and these are the most disheartening I have ever seen. Yet I have no choice: my intuitions and all past experience fail me. I must sit down and read, take myself slowly through the steps. With intuition and experience no use, I am suddenly childlike but without a child's joy. That is because I am not a child but an adult; I can see how much better the device might have been designed, how much better the manual could have been written, and that the difficulties are not my intellectual challenge but somebody else's intellectual slovenliness.

Slovenliness: the top-of-the-line laser readout compact disk player, which allows me play forward, backward, by track, by phrase, at random and so forth, nevertheless cannot do the simple task of stopping automatically at the end of a disk. For this, I must jump up and stop it manually, or else it starts at the beginning all over again. I call the shop. "A design flaw," I say. "It's not a flaw," the salesman explains, "the manufacturer intended it that way." "But if it's stupid, and I can't override it, then that's called a design flaw," I say. "It's not a flaw," he repeats impatiently, "the manufacture *intended* it."

So it takes me the better part of the morning just to master the television, and hours of concentration for the videocassette recorder. Because I think I ought to be able to do it all easily, I'm shaken by how hard it is for me, which magnifies those anxieties one inevitably feels when faced with the novel and, of course, compounds my difficulties.

The machines are not only complicated but have bugs. Repair shops are called, appointments made, days fragmented while I await the experts. Since I work at home, it ought to follow that waiting for these deliverymen, installers, and repairers should have no great impact on my work, but they shatter my concentration, which is vital to me.

After a few months I learn to operate everything minimally. I'm nagged by the fact that I cannot find time to master each device, that as miraculous as what I have is, the astounding miracles remain latent. For my life goes on at full pace: writing, lecturing, traveling, doing research, exercising, seeing friends, going to the theater, the cleaners, the bank (which is in a fury with me: having signed up for the home electronic banking, I refuse to activate it and cannot explain that I am simply overloaded and can't take on one more electronic routine, no matter how simple and easy).

This will pass. Each machine will yield itself by turn. Meanwhile, even minimal operations are rewarding. But I will never forget the helplessness under assault I felt, as humbling an experience as a technophile can have. It must be how technophobes feel all the time. For a little while I have dwelled in their world and it is a fearsome, humiliating place.

PART 2

The Machine of the Century

Chapter 7

The Computer

It may be helpful to stop and ask just what a computer is. I don't mean its physical parts, especially since the technology changes almost daily, or so it seems—vacuum tubes are replaced by transistors; transistors by integrated circuits; microprocessors and very large scale integrated circuits appear, known awkwardly as VLSIs. The science journals are full of things to come: biological memories, gallium arsenide, Josephson junctions (largely abandoned for now, but perhaps to make a comeback), computers that dissipate next to no energy, and scientists say they still don't know all there is to know about ordinary silicon.

Rather, let us raise the question to a higher level of abstraction, even beyond the organizational elements that characterize all computers; to wit, processor(s), memory, and input and output devices. For it happens that the functional simplicity of these elements has revealed a new view of what computers, human minds, and symbols may be.

I have already mentioned that somehow the idea of computer as symbol processor, not mere number cruncher, penetrated the general intellectual consciousness with unexpected spontaneity a few years ago, this after many years of earnest efforts by computer scientists to make us understand that notion. I attributed our sudden grasp of it to the widespread popularity of video games; I suppose I could just as well have attributed it to word processing or spreadsheet programs that illustrated themselves with bar graphs and pie charts. Regardless, having been told for years that the machine processed symbols of all kinds, an idea that seemed enduringly bizarre, we not only have made our peace with that idea but have assimilated it in our everyday thoughts.

The computer is a processor of symbols, but it is even more. *It is itself a physical system.* In this subtle, surprising, and novel idea lies the computer's profound powers of abstraction, its ability to simulate other systems, its powers of symbolic computation, its intelligence.

That the computer is a physical symbol system was eloquently and explicitly explained for the first time—at least in terms outsiders could understand—in an address composed by Allen Newell and Herbert Simon, both of Carnegie-Mellon University, when, in 1975, they shared the Turing Award, computing's equivalent of the Nobel prize. I expect they chose that occasion to explicate (not invent) a working hypothesis that they and most other researchers in artificial intelligence had used for two decades because they understood that they were addressing not only outsiders but a whole raft of computing insiders who also failed to grasp the startling idea.

It is this: the computer has permitted an explanation, at a rather basic and scientific level, of what symbols are. The explanation goes beyond metaphor to theory, which is to say, it makes a scientific proposition about nature, empirically derived (and susceptible to empirical testing), that accounts for phenomena that would otherwise by inexplicable. It is furthermore the result of a long and gradual development.

"All sciences characterize the essential nature of the systems they study. Such characterizations are inevitably qualitative in nature," Newell and Simon suggested, "because here are set the terms within which more detailed (often meaning quantitative) knowledge can be developed: the cell doctrine in biology, which states that the basic building block of all living organisms is the cell; plate tectonics in geology; the germ theory of disease; the doctrine of atomism in chemistry. *In computing, the qualitative description that defines and forms the science is the idea of a physical symbol system.*" (My emphasis.)

Physical denotes that such systems clearly obey the laws of physics—they are realizable by engineered systems made of engineered components. A *symbol system* is a collection of patterns and processes, the processes capable of producing, destroying, and modifying the symbols. The most important property of patterns is that they can designate objects, processes, or other patterns. When patterns designate processes, they can be interpreted. Interpretation means carrying out the designated processes.

And then the zinger: "The two most significant classes of symbol systems with which we are acquainted are human beings and computers."

Symbols, Newell and Simon argue, lie at the root of intelligent action, which is, of course, the primary topic of artificial intelligence and, for that matter, a primary question for all of computer science.

> For all information is processed by computers in the service of ends, and we measure the intelligence of a system by its ability to achieve stated ends in the face of variations, difficulties, and complexities posed by the task environment. This general investment of computer science in attaining intelligence is obscured when the tasks being accomplished are limited in scope, for then the full variations in the environment can be accurately foreseen. It becomes more obvious as we extend computers to more global, complex, and knowledge-intensive tasks—as we attempt to make them our agents, capable of handling on their own the full contingencies of the natural world.

It strikes me that this hypothesis is deep in the *Zeitgeist* of the twentieth century, our self-conscious age, which has devoted so much of its intellectual energy to examining signs and symbols *as* signs and symbols. From Sigmund Freud in one important domain to the work of Whitehead and Russell in another; from the work of Ferdinand de Saussure (who posited the existence of a general science of signs, or semiology, in 1916) to Roland Barthes and his recent influential inquiries into linguistics and other cultural symbols to the painter Frank Stella, who makes a good case that abstraction is the twentieth century's major contribution to visual art, we are a century giddy with codes. The computer then becomes the inevitable machine of the Age of Symbols.

Seventy-five years later, Newell and Simon have taken up the dilemma of Henry Adams at the Gallery of Machines at the Great Exposition of 1900 in Paris. They do not say that, but I think they have. Adams describes himself, with macabre jocularity, lying on the floor before the dynamo, "historical neck broken by the sudden irruption of forces totally new." He has wrestled with the doctrine he senses is wrong but cannot reply to, that all the steam in the world could not, like the Virgin, build Chartres. Wrong, he cries, as down he goes, but he has no way to explain why it is wrong, why the energy and forces—a word he especially likes—that built Chartres are kin, perhaps even identical, to what powers the dynamo. This quintessentially American (or Franco-American) dilemma is taken up and answered, provisionally at least, in the physical symbol system hypothesis.

Newell and Simon compare the physical symbol system theory to the cell theory of biology. Fair enough. I put myself in the company of one of my distinguished ancestors, the Thirteenth Earl of Shrewsbury, let's say. We ride in a carriage between field and forest, the vast demesne of the Talbots, and I mention that the trees on the right, the corn on the left, the birds, the matched bays that draw the carriage, even his lordship and I, share a common structure called the cell that underlies all living things, regardless of their glorious diversity. He thinks this over, concludes I'm a religious quack, luckily a harmless thing in a woman. Eventually an instrument—the microscope, of course—presents the evidence for this universal and frankly surprising structure. I say surprising, for it takes nearly two hundred years after the instrument's invention for the cell theory to be articulated, and cell biology is still a field with many fascinating unanswered questions.

Thus the physical symbol system hypothesis. There is a structure, says this hypothesis, that underlies all symbols, whether personal ornament or poem, tirade or traffic light. We are as befuddled by that assertion as our ancestors would have been to hear that every living thing also shares a common structure. We examine it tentatively, skeptically.

Yet once sensitive to this way of looking at the world, we're bound to discover that we humans aren't the only creators of symbol systems. Perhaps the most elaborate language among the animals is not spoken by the other primates (where we expected) but by the carnivores that hunt in packs—wild dogs, for example—whose instructions to each other ("take up the left side," "grab it at the back," "you, forward, quick!") are gradually being decoded by animal behaviorists. If we include chemical messages, which we are now able to decode in much greater detail than before, thanks to devices such as gas chromatographs that can interpret chemicals at much finer levels, we discover that the content of those messages is considerably more elaborate than we dreamed. "I was here," "this is my territory," "I am in heat," turn out to be very crude approximations of messages that are more like "I, Ozymandias, King of the Lions, was here on May 14, having had a good meal three days earlier, and consorted with La Belle Leonie that day 72 times, which may be a record. Correction; which *is* a record, but only to be expected from such a magnificent beast as I."

It was in this twentieth-century spirit of examining symbol systems as entities in themselves that Newell and Simon explicated their own hypotheses. They traced the mathematical and logical antecedents of physical symbol systems, laying particular stress on the development of list processing—a programming technique first developed by them and their colleague, J. C. Shaw (and lifted to a further level of machine-independent abstraction by John McCarthy in his language LISP), which allowed lists to hold addresses of other lists.

In other words, lists are symbolic of, and can thus refer to, other lists. Simple as this structure is, it creates a genuine dynamic memory structure in the machine—a machine that until then had been perceived as having a fixed structure. Here at last was the designating symbol and means of manipulating it in complex ways. And the essence of the matter would be this: *such a structure of physical symbol systems is capable of intelligent behavior.* Hence artificial intelligence, which has provoked, exasperated, and inspired computer science since the formation of the discipline. Hence the power of the computer to model human symbolic behavior, a new tool in the psychology of thought. List processing was the first of the dynamic structures computer scientists discovered (or invented, if you prefer, although Newell and Simon have said elsewhere that list processing was inspired by what psychologists knew about human associative memory at mid-century). There would be other such structures.

And here for me is the difference between those other physical symbol systems I mentioned, such as animal communication (for whether they are auditory, behavioral, or chemical, such communications are physical embodiments of information, which is to say, symbols), on the one hand, and humans and computers, on the other. The difference lies in the degree of dynamic structure the human and the computer systems are capable of. (It may also lie in memory size, but of that I am less certain: big memories aren't necessarily smart memories.) The dynamic structure may be conceptually simple (we don't know that for sure about the cognition of human beings yet), but it is capable of great power, elaboration, and a certain degree of autonomy.

So that is a computer: a physical symbol system. It can augment and give insight into the physical symbol systems called human minds, although everybody agrees that we understand both systems, whether human or computer, very imperfectly. We know how to build some kinds of computers, but computer science is empirical: once built, the computers must be tested to discover their capacities, and they are full of surprises. For example, constructing computers with more than a handful of parallel processors, say, is a subject of enormous debate just now and intense experimental investigation around the world.

I believe the physical symbol system hypothesis is one of the great ideas of the twentieth century, its profundity masked, perhaps, by its simplicity. Like the cell theory of biology, it is a framework within which to study highly complex behavior (a qualitative characterization of intelligent behavior, in Newell and Simon's words) but not an answer to all questions about that behavior. That it arose in computer science, specifically artificial intelligence research, is not accidental. Those functionally simple elements of the machine, the processor, memory, and input and output devices, laid bare principles that are otherwise elusive in the other significant class of symbol systems called human beings.

However, it's only a hypothesis and may be wrong. Empirical investigations will show us one way or the other, and those are well under way. Meanwhile, the hypothesis has some interesting philosophical consequences.

What is mind? What is body? What is consciousness? What is knowing? Those questions have been asked since classical Greece at least.

The physical symbol system hypothesis obviates such questions. Mind can be realized only in a physical system, so mind without body is impossible, a contradiction in terms. Consciousness is the ability of a system to contain a model (or several models) of itself and its behavior. Bodies follow physical laws. Knowing is—ah, knowing is not yet altogether known, for this is science-in-progress, the answer to emerge next week, next year, ten years hence. And maybe somewhere else. But workers in the field suspect that knowing has a great deal to do with how knowledge is represented in the system: some knowledge representations work better than others, and the ability to represent knowledge effectively, to make it quickly accessible when appropriate, lies in the representation. In mind, it seems, function follows form.

"The brevity and simplicity of these answers reveals again the magician's trick—it was all over before it started. That is, once the information-processing view is adopted, these answers (more or less) follow," Newell once wrote. Put another way, if you believe disease is caused by germs and not by human sin, you turn your attention to the germs, and a patient's moral behavior—insofar as curing is concerned—is beside the point. (At least in principle; we still have some leftover problems with that in practice.)

Some people are deeply offended that a mechanism (and, by extension, a mechanistic hypothesis) has intruded itself into studies of mind. Some are particularly offended that the mechanism is a device we have created by ourselves (although we make human minds that way, known as babies, and train those minds with all sorts of human-fashioned devices, beginning with language). Some are troubled by technology in general and/or jealous of the supremacy of the human race, and believe that the computer as an instrument to understand and exhibit intelligence is both ridiculous and threatening. This latter is a group I often find in delicious contradiction with itself: as they vaunt humanity with one hand, they pummel it with the other for cheekily exhibiting its most human characteristics. Alas for all such troubled souls, both the human race and the computer are more complicated business than sentimentality, mysticism, or polemics allow.

A physical symbol system, whether human or computer, still contains countless mysteries. It may comfort the worriers that those mysteries are unlikely to be revealed in my lifetime, at least. But I'm sorry to have to say so, for I would love to know.

I began by asking what a computer is, beyond the accident of its temporary technology. The answer is that a computer is many things (or more precisely, many phenomena exhibit computational behavior, and the computer is thus becoming a fruitful model to explain matters in a number of scientific fields, including physics, chemistry, biology, astronomy). A computer is a physical symbol system and has the capacity for intelligent behavior. This hypothesis is in the process of being proved by computer programs that demonstrate what would be called intelligence in humans. I say "in the process" most carefully. Artificial intelligence is severely limited at the moment to dozens of special cases, and as potent as those special cases are, we do not yet understand enough about intelligence, human or otherwise, to create a generally intelligent agent (as we presume humans are, although we may be wrong in that presumption).

The computer is more. Broadly speaking, computational devices fall into two categories, the symbolic, which we know generally as "computers," and another class of computational devices known as the self-referential. A look at other computers and other views might enlighten us.

Chapter 8

Other Computers, Other Views

Some ten years after the Turing address, responding to the award of an honorary degree from Columbia University, Herbert Simon gave a talk called "Cohabiting the Planet with Computers." It was the end of a two-day symposium, and many of the speakers had described an astonishing and wondrous new future to come. Simon has always found contrariness irresistible, and this occasion was no exception.

"As I listen to public discussion about computers," he said, "and particularly discussion about computers as intelligent systems, systems that think, I hear many expressions of uneasiness about living in this kind of world. There seems to be special uneasiness about cohabiting a world with computers when some of them might turn out to be smarter than we humans are."

But he wanted us to be at our ease. "In the case of computers, perhaps we would feel better and more relaxed in living in the world with them—in the kind of world that all the speakers in the past two days have described—if we recognized that in most ways it is not at all a new world." We are already thoroughly familiar with computers and have been for a long time, he suggested. The novelty electronics brings is largely a novelty of understanding what mind is, not a novelty that requires us to understand and live in a new kind of world.

By examining some longtime nonelectronic computer companions, Simon hoped we might not only be at ease with the electronic variety but be able to think about them in a new way, especially the linkages between those computers throughout the whole office, the whole company, or, for that matter, the whole world.

"I shall propose four examples of networked computers. Unless you are a pantheist, you will find it hard to think of the first two of them as minds, but they certainly are computers. The third and fourth examples are computers that also are definitely minds."

His first example was the solar system, a very large distributed system, with computations going on simultaneously in all of its components, each responding to the presence and location of others. It is a physical system, which is to say, it is self-referential; it doesn't make computations about other systems but about itself. Thus it is not a symbolic computer, as some of the others he would mention. (Symbolic computers, in contrast, denote something other than themselves; they are able not only to talk to themselves and about themselves but to talk about other things as well. This is not a case of an analogy masquerading as an equivalence; it rests on the physical symbol system hypothesis about computers.) However, the solar system is interesting in the present world of computers because its computations are highly distributed. It's an example of a parallel computer, each planetary body (really each molecule or atom in the planetary bodies) a component.

Its lessons for us are, first, that order can emerge from highly decentralized but interrelated forces: "We can have design without a Designer." Next, the very terms of our own existence, the human condition, are defined by the computations performed by this system, our own organic molecules. Finally, while we must obey its laws, they give us wide latitude for deciding and choosing. It occurs to me that this could be Robert Venturi describing successful architecture, which admits control *and* spontaneity, correctness *and* ease, improvisations within the whole. In fact, it refers to early work that Simon and an associate did to understand the nature of hierarchies, but about that, more later.

His second example of a physical computer system was the atmosphere, the weather. "In a certain sense, it is an even more decentralized physical computer than the solar system, decentralized right down to the level of the individual gaseous molecules. It has so many degrees of freedom that building a meteorological orrery or model of any kind stretches the capacities of even our largest computers."

Its lesson for us as a computer is that even a determinate machine can behave in ways so nearly chaotic that it almost forecloses the possibilities of prediction: we can glimpse only statistical order in it. "And as with the solar system, the atmospheric system has the gravest consequences for our own lives. We deal with those consequences mainly not by fighting the system, but by adapting to it. We've made only minor and I think dubiously successful attempts to intervene in an active way in the computation by such measures as cloud seeding of hurricanes, or cloud seedings to end droughts in Iowa."

And then he said provocatively:

> We respect and we fear, sometimes, both of these physical computing systems—the solar system and the atmospheric system—because in a very real sense, they are smarter than we are. They can do all sorts of things that we can't comprehend. We recognize the control they exercise over our lives and our very nature, but we don't perceive them as denying our humanity. Rather, they define it. We also don't perceive them as impinging on our freedom, for we don't define our freedom in such a way that obedience of natural law is an infringement of that freedom.

Not long after this talk, I asked Simon for a definition of computer. "It's just as Al and I said in our Turing lecture," he replied, and though Simon and I were communicating between New York and Pittsburgh by electronic mail, I could almost see a Simonian smile coming on. "A computer is a physical symbol system. Ah, you will say, neither the planets nor the atmosphere are physical symbol systems. Oh, I reply, the planetary system is just the Lord's metaphor for a computation of the equations of motion—thinking we would not understand the computation in abstract form, He provided us with a physical embodiment of it."
"The weather that kept Dorothea [his wife] in the house last week was just an analog computation of the aerodynamic equations of

the atmosphere. Realizing that should make you more comfortable the next time it is freezing in New York." Perhaps it will.

Simon and computing were made for each other. He is perfectly at home with the simultaneous abstraction and the attention to real-world limits that the computer imposes. He is an empirical scientist, moving out in the real world to observe afresh how those other symbol processors, human beings, really do it, and taking it back to the computer to see how the machine can be made to do it too.

When I was that discontented English major in the 1950s I had a part-time job in the school of business at Berkeley, paying my college expenses by typing course outlines and exams. It was hard not to notice that in nearly every course, from municipal management to theory of the firm, from administrative behavior to computer applications in business (an exotic and little-patronized course in those days), there was inevitably a required book by somebody named Herbert A. Simon. English-major snob, I figured business for a thin field if one man wrote all its textbooks. But of course he was their Eliot, with at least as much to say about the twentieth century as the poet, and most of it far more to the point. When, some fifteen years later, I finally met Simon face to face, I was nearly speechless with awe, so deep a hold had he taken on my imagination by then.

Of Simon's four familiar computers, his next two were explicitly symbolic: "They get their work done, they operate, by creating, modifying, and exchanging symbols." They were the political and economic systems. The most obvious ways the political system computes is by electing and legislating. As it happens, the political system contributed a very important idea in the early days of electronic computing, when hardware reliability was a much worse problem than it is now. The idea was conceived, by John von Neumann among others, of making every computation an odd number of times, and in case of disagreement among the outcomes, accepting the majority vote. "So the idea in computing of using majority logic was taken over quite directly from the computing system that we call a democratic political system."

Simon went on to draw further comparisons, including the disappointment we often feel because the computational power of our political system does not seem to match the difficulty of the problems we pose to it. Moreover, there are often spectacular computational failures, the stuff of history books. Yet despite its inscrutability and the enormous influence it has on our lives, our political system still maintains, most of the time, a tolerable level of order and tranquility and sometimes even some measure of justice in a large society; moreover, it can permit an enormous amount of human freedom and self-determination, including the freedom to alter and loosen the constraints themselves, "to modify the connections, you might say, of the hardware and the program by which it operates."

His final example of a familiar computer was the economy, also a distributed computer that organizes a complex system with explicit recognition of individual differences in values and preferences. Sufficiently idealized, it even lends itself to mathematical abstractions. But we don't understand this computer very well either, except to suffer from its instability (a property that arises especially because each component computer in the economic system can try to outguess the future behaviors of the other components, communicate, and thereby synchronize their mutual attempts to outguess each other). "With all these defects," Simon observed, "the economic system operates tolerably a large part of the time."

What can we say in general about computers in our lives, then, the systems that do symbolic computation? Simon asked, and summarized his view that a distributed computing system with intelligence at each of its nodes can organize, more or less well, the affairs of society, while at the same time it allows enormous autonomy to its components, accommodating diversity and even conflict of values.

The introduction of electronic components into these existing distributive computers, the solar system, the weather, the political system, the economy (and, I would add, many other systems besides, including art and language), will not change the basic characteristics of those systems; the consequences of introducing more intelligence into them hinge on the quality of the intelligence that is supplied.

Simon believes that society is not a zero-sum game: if we introduce electronic intelligent agents to the system, it will increase the overall intelligence of all aspects of the system, not remove intelligence from one part (the humans) to give to another (the computers).

He concluded with some skepticism about revolutions, particularly those that aim, as the Russian and the Chinese revolutions have, to produce a New Man. They have not. A technological revolution is likely to have no more luck.

But—we shall know more. We shall have more intelligence, artificial to be sure, to augment our natural intelligence. We may use it well or badly, but we shall have it. Simon returned to his four familiar computers:

> Let's ask of these familiar computational systems the question that is now so frequently asked of electronic computers. Do these systems control us? Yes, in certain important senses they do, for they set vital limits to our behavior and its consequences. But usually we don't think of them as controlling us; usually we view them as defining the space within which we do our own computations.
>
> Nor is our computational space a fixed space; human intelligence has continually enlarged it over the past history of our species. When human intelligence is generously augmented with machine intelligence, we will have means again for enlarging the space of our thoughts, and our hopes, and our actions. . . . But we retain our hope and belief that, on balance, our new intelligence will bring some measure of improvement in the human condition. As in the past, we will prefer knowledge to ignorance.

In any event, we shall push ahead. Alan Perlis, who for many years was one of Simon's colleagues at Carnegie and who is now a professor of computer science at Yale, also spoke to me one afternoon about the idea of the computer in general. I had asked him whether the computer might transcend human intelligence. His answer was yes; that was inevitable and we would make it so. As he gave me his reasons for believing that, it all seemed to me an engaging complement to Simon's views of humans and their familiar computers, natural and artificial.

"Evolution has put humans in an N-dimensional hypercube," Perlis said, using one of his favorite images. "We exist in time over a period of roughly a hundred years. Air pressure, 14.7 pounds per square inch, give or take something. Temperature, a span of 150 degrees, something like that. Composition of the atmosphere: oxygen, nitrogen, and so forth. And our brains, if you will, have been engaged in a kind of feverish search, ever since man first began to think, for ways of stretching this hypercube along one or more dimensions. Everything we do is aimed at that. Writing is aimed so that we can, in a sense, transfer information from one hypercube to another. The space program, all of science, is aimed at developing for us a view of the universe in which we can escape this damn hypercube. In our minds, we can make models of extended hypercubes that we cannot participate in ourselves. The computer, it seems to me, is (so far at least) the ultimate hypercube-stretcher for us. Not only can we think about these things now, but we can essentially propagate surrogates of ourselves into environments that we will never be able to exist in."

Why are we humans cursed with wanting to escape our natural hypercube, or as Simon would put it, extend our computational space?

"It's not a curse," Perlis protested. "It's part of the grand evolutionary plan. It's just the way the world is. And to me it makes sense. It explains why we do the things we do. And it doesn't rationalize them in the sense of giving a higher ethic to them, it just explains why we do it. We do it because we must. It's more than just advantage," he said, using a term he'd defined earlier as the urge we have to get ahead of our fellow humans. "I think that, of course, is the side of the human being that makes him such a cherished thing: we do many things just because we have to do them, as a means of self-fulfillment rather than just to get an advantage.

"So the computer really is an extraordinary instrument. I think in many ways it's more important than theoretical physics, for example, even though theoretical physics has within it the possibility of finding other ways to rupture the hypercube for us, and extend it. We don't know what things lie there. But certainly from the standpoint of making and manipulating models of the world we live in, would like to live in, could live in, can't live in, the computer is the paramount tool that we have."

Then the computer is inevitable?

"Oh, yes. Look at its history." Each step, as he sees it, was driven by human realizations of the computer's generality, of its potential capacity if only it were extended here, expanded there.

"At each stage, the limitations of the computer drove us to call upon our bank accounts in physics to withdraw material, techniques, to expand the machine. And we kept on expanding it. No sooner do we have networks than we begin to realize that these networks are now something very different just because of the dispersion of the problem-solving sources, the anonymity of it."

Perlis prefers the term computability to intelligence, but he means approximately the same thing by computability that Simon means by intelligence, the process of manipulating symbols systematically toward goals. Indeed, it is Perlis's view that process is more important than goals and that this insight has come to us from computing.

"Process is more important than goals are to the continuing development of society. Obviously goals are extraordinarily important to the human being and his social organization—there has to be a reason *for*. But processes transcend particular goals, particular times, and particular societies. They are transferable from generation to generation almost without being dragged down by semantic details. In a very real sense they are the purest objects we can pass on to our descendants, because they aren't clouded by our own search for advantage. Our descendants need not have the same search, and will probably not, because of the different circumstances under which they live. But the processes they can use and improve upon, and the computer is, of course, nothing but a device upon which one executes process. One can't think of anything *except* in terms of process. As a result, anybody who works around a computer, no matter from where he starts, or what problem he's trying to solve, ultimately comes to realize that his major intellectual effort is associated with the invention, description, and organization of processes. His ability to propagate those processes to other people for other purposes is in a real sense the measure of his success with the computer."

It is also, I believe, a good measure of success in any intellectual endeavor that reaches out to other human beings. And while we are usually interested in the explicit content of symbols, we are often interested in abstracting the systematic way they relate to each other, which is what begins to transform a collection of observations into science, a collection of expressions into art.

And so around the computer a science is emerging, an empirical science, as I've said, with both experimental and theoretical components, which not only will reveal aspects of the nature of computation, or symbol processing, but will also permit us to look at familiar phenomena in new and perhaps even useful ways. Eventually Simon will be able to describe the computational elements of such disparate events as the solar system, the weather, politics, and economics. He might have mentioned biological systems as well, the computational model there so widely held that it seems unbelievable it only emerged in the late 1960s. Once again, the computer's functional simplicity lays bare processes that might go unnoticed in the noisy complexity of other systems.

I understand that scientists do not demand of science that it be useful: for them it is enough that it be valid. But the rest of us, ill-equipped to appreciate science for its own sake alone, are curious to know what it all has to do with our lives.

Simply put, the computer and the science surrounding it have everything to do with our lives, from new forms of art to new forms of medicine, from new ways of work to new ways of communicating. We're entitled to hope that our new knowledge about the nature of symbols and symbolic systems will grow, permitting us to design better systems, more effective, more just, perhaps more beautiful. Certainly more intelligent.

Simon argues that whatever the changes, they won't produce the New Man, that we shall still read Euripides with understanding (though even Simon would concede that as a woman of the late twentieth century I receive *Medea* rather differently from its first audiences. As a man of the late twentieth century, so does he). Perlis argues that the machine is inevitable, and as I stand back and see the twentieth century's preoccupation, its obsession even, with symbols, I must agree.

So, is this the Computer Revolution? Will it produce the New, uh, Human? Imagine a citizen of the twenty-first century, living in a world where information does not provoke an endless struggle to cope but confers orderly personal power at the same time it discloses process and connections. Will such a citizen behave more rationally, in the best sense of that word? Or will the hapless soul fall into a paralysis of indecision, so many events put in train when even a sparrow falls? I hope for an embrace of the rational and assume that part of our future citizen's intellectual endowment is a firm grasp of the difference between loosely coupled and tightly coupled systems: our citizen should know that the fall of one sparrow has limited (but never entirely predictable) effects.

Then again, farther down the road and despite everybody's

best efforts, it could happen that our artifacts move so far beyond our human capabilities that they really cannot explain to us what they're about in any sense we can comprehend. Would this mean the return of mystery and magic to our society? Would we stand before our intelligent artifacts the way our ancestors once stood before the cereal crop: in awe, in pleasure, in reverence, and a certain amount of fear? If so, I imagine we should then begin great cycles of myths and tales about intelligence. It would not be the Golden Age of Reason, and it would not be entirely new.

Or, less fancifully, suppose the idea that mind can arise only from matter, and no other place, takes widespread hold. Surely this will pose some pretty problems for metaphysicians and theologians. Does a world like that have room for a deity? What is transcendence? What is the Good? Will such an idea, once in place, then make us more careful about matter, not just the stuff of human heads (which we are not memorably careful about at the moment) but *all* matter? Surely we shall abandon the easy opposition of materialism vs. spiritualism, and a new definition of the spiritual, passing beyond those simplicities, will come to guide our efforts toward wise and ethical action.

I like to imagine it a more serene world, human intelligence set free to address all sorts of issues that, up to now, have been beyond us; but it will still be full of surprises and challenges and, yes, heartbreak. Anyone with a more precise measure of the sparrow's fall also has an unsparing measure of his own importance in the grander systems. It might be humbling and, for some, demoralizing. The other side of that, of course, is a new sense of community, of being an essential and unique part of things in a way that was imperceptible before. As with the printing press, it is likely that both effects will be felt by the human spirit simultaneously.

In an important sense, Simon is correct: comes the revolution, it will be the Same Old Us, the reptile brain buried deep under the neocortex to make trouble unless it is fed, sheltered, warmed, gratified. At the same time, human history can plausibly be viewed as a series of symbolic constructions called law, custom, culture, religion, and war, changing in time and distinct from place to place, their purpose to transform the energy of that short-range self-absorption into something longer range and transcendent. The neocortex produces those symbolic structures effusively, not in conflict with the other parts of its systems, inner and outer, but in concert. The symbolic structures in their turn make their changes upon us, amending our terms of the acceptable, the possible, the permissible. Not new, but not the same, either.

All this is what drives us to press against the confines of our hypercubes with such enormous longing.

Chapter 9

The Empire of Reason:
Artificial Intelligence

Without question, it is a New World. And it is sometimes confusing, for as Henry Steele Commager said of America, it was invented before it was discovered. The invention of America, Commager noted, "embraced the Blessed Isles, the Fortunate Isles, Avalon, El Dorado and Atlantis; even the sensible Edmund Spenser thought that his countrymen might find Faery Land in the new world."

Just so: in science fiction, artificial intelligences—in the form of malevolent robots (or benevolent ones, for that matter), in the form of self-aggrandizing computer networks and anything else the human mind can imagine—have been presented to us in all-talking, full-color, lurid detail.

The reality, then, is disappointing. There are programs that understand a few thousand words of continuously spoken language, about the level of a three-year-old human being; programs that can prospect for minerals like wizards—but how many of us need to prospect for minerals, or interpret mass spectrograms, or play masters' level chess, or recapitulate the discovery processes of the physical sciences, to name a few of the outstanding programs in the artificial intelligence grab bag? I sometimes wonder if the petulance exhibited by outsiders is less their outrage at the grand dreams than their disappointment that reality is, just now, so far from those dreams.

Petulance there is. William Bradford first thought Cape Cod "a hideous and desolate wilderness, full of wild beasts and wild men" but later changed his mind. He, at least, lived there. The most vicious (and amusing) attacks on the New World came from Europeans who hadn't been there but knew how awful it was and did their very best to expose it for the noxious and backward place it really was. At the same time, the New World's most extravagant promoters were also strangers to its shores. Enthralled by the ideas of El Dorado, fountains of youth, and heaven knows what other fabulous illusions, they stirred Europeans into unreal expectations ("a new Olympus, a new Arcady, a new Athens, a new Greece," said one rapturous Frenchman; "this people is the hope of the human race. It may become the model," said another—but then he had met the stupendous Benjamin Franklin and could be forgiven for being dazzled). Such extreme hopes were bound to lead to disappointment. Thus too with the New World of artificial intelligence.

There are other parallels. I could summarize the history of artificial intelligence as an adventure story, with heroes, great deeds, high hopes, suspense, enormous obstacles to success, and all the other elements such a story ought to have. It doesn't exactly have villains, but it does have cowards who carp and criticize and vilify our heroes as they're embarking on their great adventure.

To my story, then: they are young men, our heroes, full of high spirits, as young men often are. One day, thanks to unusual, perhaps unique, historical circumstances, they are presented with a splendid, an overwhelmingly tempting opportunity. It is the chance—and only a chance, no guarantee—to turn a grand human dream into reality. There are risks, there are dangers, there is, frankly, little real hope of complete success in their own lifetimes. There is a grave possibility that they will have risked their lives, their fortunes, and their sacred honor for nothing at all in the end. But, being heroes, of course they have no choice but to give it a try.

Thus they bid farewell to the safe and the familiar and remove themselves from the ordinary lives of human beings. They move to a New World, which is full equally of promise and peril. They do what they can to extract the reality from the dream.

Not in a vacuum, naturally. The cowards who won't follow them have nevertheless transshipped their criticism, scorn, mockery. It's a bracing thing to examine the archives and read those words—they drip with sarcasm, they slander with vituperation, they puff with outrage. They even lie. How dare the heroes presume to try such an experiment? How idiotic can they be to attempt what everybody knows is impossible? How dare our heroes make such promises which they can never ever keep? And unspoken is the great dread that if our heroes succeed even a little bit, then things will never be the same in the world again.

As time goes on, the words of the critics are so harsh—and the way of our heroes so hard—that it begins to seem that all we can hear are those words. Our heroes look less heroic than presumptuous, foolhardy, perhaps even deliberately deceitful. At best they look hopelessly utopian, idealistic. And every time they fail (and they fail very often, because they have set themselves such a difficult task) the critics gloat with delight. Didn't we tell you so? Aren't you sorry now you embarked on this stupid, ill-conceived, ridiculous adventure, an offense to all decent and right-thinking people.

Is this the story of the Founding Fathers of the American republic, or the founding fathers of artificial intelligence? Both. And in both cases, the story is far from over yet. As all adventure stories do, it must have crises. Heroes are human and stumble; heroes fall out and quarrel among themselves; heroes are betrayed by those who are less than heroic. But the beauty and strength and nobility of the dream transcend all that and keep the adventure alive, despite our human frailties. And even when everything isn't perfect, it's still pretty good.

There are other important parallels between these two great intellectual adventure stories besides the fact that the adventures themselves were undertaken by young men who should have known better but luckily did not. Both adventures have been among the most momentous undertakings of their time. Both have challenged the established order to its foundations. Perhaps the most significant similarity of all is that both adventures share a great faith, and place a great trust, in reason.

Commager called the young United States "the Empire of Reason." "The Old World imagined, invented, and formulated the Enlightenment; the New World—certainly the Anglo-American part of it—realized and fulfilled it." In its political institutions, its heritage, its assumptions both stated and not, the United States is the child of the Age of Reason. And a fortunate child in that, I'd say. So would countless millions who have come here, also putting their trust in reason.

Artificial intelligence is devoted to the development of reasoning machines, that is, computers capable of imitating the human thinking process. The idea of a reasoning machine is not wholly original with Americans. In fact, I have traced its roots to ancient Greece and have recently discovered similar ideas floating around during the Chou dynasty, which is roughly parallel in time with classical Greece. But those who, at least until recently, have taken on the task, engaged in the adventure, of making the dream a reality are Americans.

Readers of my earlier *Machines Who Think* will see that thinking machines were certainly dreamed about, often with great intelligence and ingenuity, in the Old World, particularly in England. But the machines lurched into reality in the United States. I believe it is no accident that the Empire of Reason is the place where reasoning machines were first invented and nurtured. For at the same time we have been the Empire of Reason, we have also been, in Daniel Boorstin's words, "a land of Otherwise. Nothing is more distinctive, nor has made us more un-European, than our disbelief in the ancient and well-documented impossibilities. Every day we receive invitations to try something new. And we still give the traditional, exuberant American answer: 'Why not?' "

Well, reasoning machines. Thinking machines. Intelligent systems. *Why not?* They are not impossible, as some people once thought. They are not silly, or fraudulent, or even wicked. They are very difficult to bring about, perhaps more difficult than anybody first expected, but not impossible.

"The first AI researchers were tremendously naive," says a smug critic with the benefit of a quarter century's hindsight. So they were. So are we all when we commence: a good thing, I'd say, or nothing significant would ever get done. Sailors who were recruited to ship out for the New World often were not told the destination, for fear the difficulties would incite mutinies.

It has required large parts of Yankee ingenuity—unfettered, it must be said, by ideology—to bring about the level of accomplishment that now exists in artificial intelligence. (You could write a plausible history of the field that argues progress was made *only* when ideology was abandoned, when scientists plunged into experiments with try-anything-now flair. It is very American, that mistrust of ideology.)

So: equal parts of Yankee ingenuity, Yankee pragmatism, Yankee bravado, and, last but not least, the Yankee dollar have made reasoning machines, intelligent systems, artificial intelligence, as American a project as apple pie. It might have been done elsewhere in the beginning, but it was not. It was first done here, and for a long time, only here. It is done elsewhere now; the Japanese (using exactly the same formula of ingenuity, pragmatism, bravado, and cash, not to mention hard work) may provide the next capital of the Empire. But the origins of the technology that made it possible, and the belief that it not only could be done but was worth doing, are deep in the American grain, which is to say that place called the Empire of Reason and the Republic of Technology.

Another thing about this New World of artificial intelligence. Suppose we really are face to face with an unanticipated novelty. Lacking better words, we call what the machines do *thinking, reasoning*, the functions we are familiar with in humans. But maybe we are repeating the experience of Christopher Columbus, who was so monomaniacal about the Orient that he insisted, against all the evidence, on calling his discovery "the Indies." (Thanks to him, the Empire of Reason has a Bureau of Indian Affairs to this day.) But it wasn't the news of the Indies that he took back to Europe, it was something no one was expecting. The New World would eventually be named after its mappers, especially Amerigo Vespucci. So, supposing this artificial intelligence is new business altogether: instead of thinking, reasoning, why not Newelling, Simoning, McCarthying, Minskying, Feigenbauming—I find the idea enchanting.

"I'm certainly glad to see you're writing about something in computing besides artificial intelligence," a friend said as I began this book. "Some people think you've really been captured by those people in AI." Some people would be right; though captivated is the word I'd use. If the Brothers Grimm opened me to the literary imagination, the brotherhood of AI (for in those days it was a fraternity, though happily, no longer) opened me to the scientific imagination.

The founding fathers of artificial intelligence are cartographers of the symbolic realm, just as the Founding Fathers of the original Empire of Reason were. And what a smart bunch! Commager says the original Empire was lucky enough to have such brilliant founders because politics afforded the only opportunity for a bright, ambitious young man in the New World to make a difference. Artificial intelligence attracted its polymath founding fathers for much the same reasons: where else could you address yourself to anything whatsoever that mattered, from music to mathematics, from the laws of nature to rules of thumb?

Artificial intelligence continues to be invented before it is discovered. Ponderous debates are held about its propriety long before we really understand what shapes it may take. Its reality continues to exasperate; its promise makes us reach out beyond ourselves and what we already know.

I have written elsewhere about the general uneasiness caused by artificial intelligence, namely, the threat to egos, the evocation of the monstrous, the sacrilegious overtones, and so on, but one more source of discomfort occurs to me. That is, we feel responsible for the artificial in ways we do not for natural events. So we should. Therefore, when things go wrong in the world of human affairs, we sternly judge each other (and occasionally ourselves) for shortsightedness, self-interest, even sinfulness. Our responsibility in the realm of the artificial is appropriate, but it also puts us under a drastic strain. For the fact is that in systems of any complexity, natural or artificial, it now exceeds anybody's wit to predict precisely what will occur when changes are introduced.

Nathaniel Hawthorne understood Americans perfectly well in this regard when he invented Hester Prynne, walking abroad with the fantastically embroidered letter A that she had stitched herself, threads of scarlet and gold (I picture the needle going in and out, off and on, positive-negative, its simple little elements slowly composing an elaborate whole: dear Hester, a few centuries later, you might have been programming in assembly language).

The letter A stood for adultery, but as Hawthorne implied, it also stood for artifice, and in the end, unsanctified art. The scorners of artifice, especially artificial intelligence, still employ the moralistic tone of the Reverend Mr. Dimmesdale, but I suppose we shall not discover unsuspected connections, nor ultimately inter their bones together with the corpse of what they condemn, as readers of *The Scarlet Letter* are satisfied to see it all turn out. Like the Puritans, however, the scorners are hardest on what is most human about us: in this case, not our urge to connect passionately, which we share with almost every other living creature, but our enchantment with symbols, with artifice, which is ours alone in the animal kingdom. It is our nature.

Let me state it more strongly: to the degree that humans do it, creating, transforming, and reasoning with symbols is the most human thing we do. Some object to that assertion and would substitute compassion or altruism or love or, for that matter, rage, cruelty, or jealousy, as much more human. But I think it can be shown that other animals exhibit compassion, altruism, perhaps even love: on the African savanna, I have seen a warthog parent successfully stand its ground against a cheetah who was menacing its shoats. It hesitated before making its stand; in fact, at first it ran away. It understood the danger. It seemed to make one choice, and then the opposite. Compassion? Altruism in the form of parental love? Instinct? The terms are meaningless here. Likewise, animals rage and do gratuitously cruel things to each other. There are even animals who seem, in a primitive way, to employ some symbolic reasoning.

But only we humans construct a symbolic universe of such elaborate proportions that it can transform the planet. It astonishes me to meditate on the fact that there is no such thing as a no-frills human culture, where clothing is only to cover, food only to eat, shelter only to protect. From the most basic of our gestures to the most abstract, we invest every instance with symbolic significance, usually layers deep and sometimes contradictory, presenting them all for our fellow humans to take note of, as they will. Ideas begin in our heads and find embodiment in our bridges, our temples, our mathematical systems and our poems, our trash heaps and our bedroom slippers. Our urge to make symbols is as basic as our urge to eat, and much more our own. As we do it, it's unique.

A nascent science of all this, the realm of the artificial, is underway, sometimes quantitative, sometimes not. It introduces new models of what a science might be, but they still conform to the larger requirements of science, that it be empirically verifiable, that it offer explanations for a host of phenomena, that it offer reliable predictions. Since the singular attribute of artificial systems is their symbolic processing, the computer is central to this endeavor, both as scientific model and as tool. As a science, AI aims for the same things all science aims for: an underlying theory or set of theories that can serve as a basis for predicting, to some useful degree, alternative future developments.

In artificial intelligence we have a kind of ultimate symbol system or extension of our symbolic functions, an artifact that excells at reasoning (but performs dismally at seeing, sensing, and moving about in the real world, our legacy of millions of years of evolution). It complements the reasoning of human heads and may eventually do it better.

Meanwhile, since creating, transforming, and reasoning about symbols is our nature, our responsibility lies in doing it as well as we can.

How well can that be? Hester Prynne thought she knew, but Hawthorne had put her in a more complicated world than first met the eye: rules were contradictory and complex; keeping one rule meant breaking another. With the best of intentions, with abject self-denial, she still sinned. In the end, as she cries out to a fellow sinner, she can speak for us all: "Thou shalt forgive me! Let God punish! Thou shalt forgive!"

So yes, since we created them, we're responsible for them. In principle we can alter, perhaps improve, human artifacts small and large, including aspects of our society, our beliefs, and the lot of our fellow humans. That is what we mean by moral choice, requiring moral intelligence, moral responsibility. But it is staggeringly complicated and cannot be accomplished by good intentions alone. Mistakes are inevitable.

We've made many such choices, alterations, and among them we have some things to be proud of: medicine, the green revolution, the idea of political self-determination (if not always its reality), mass education (though it could be improved in quantity and quality). Yet each of these has had its unexpected drawbacks.

For example, relying heavily on the advice of sociologists, the United States Supreme Court decided that there could be no equality in education without racial balance and so ordered the forced integration of primary public schools. The results of this well-meant introduction of rationality (and human decency) have been more mixed than we could have dreamed. Should we therefore not have tried? That seems to me a greater indecency.

Ultimately, the human condition—an omnibus term for the

large, complex, artificial systems that we've surrounded ourselves
with—can be successfully changed only to the extent that we understand what we're doing. Understanding the human condition
is limited by the concepts and tools we bring to that study, just as
studying the natural sciences has been. In biology, where we build
upon more than a hundred years of solid scientific research, errors
still occur. In the symbolic domains—let us say politics, for example, or intelligence, the life of the mind—we have no such solid
knowledge, and so changes are made mainly on intuition and
hope. (The American Founding Fathers had extravagant amounts
of both, but they also had open eyes: power would be distributed
and intricately checked and balanced to save society from itself.)

A fundamental premise of artificial intelligence research is that
general laws exist governing the behavior of intelligent systems,
whether humans or computers, in the aggregate or individually—
or inevitably, flesh together with artifact. These general laws, parallel to but different from the laws of the natural sciences, can
eventually be teased out of the detailed phenomena of intelligent
systems.

It is a controversial premise, aiming at a controversial goal.
The American Founding Fathers would have been quite at ease
with it, just as the founding fathers of artificial intelligence are,
but the rest of the world, as usual, views premise and goal dimly.
We do not know if science will eventually give us such a powerful
and predictive set of laws about our artificial systems, but I hope
so. The computer will be central to all this, beginning with, but
not limited to, artificial intelligence—again, because its relative
simplicity allows it to model and thereby illuminate intelligent or
symbolic processes of all kinds.

But it is the beginning. Artificial intelligence research has been
under way about thirty years and has far to go. We are entitled
to impatience but not surprise when our goals are sometimes
beyond our best intentions and are furthermore confounded by
the complex, contradictory circumstances of real life.

Objections are raised to the intrusion of the mechanistic, or
the rational, into an area that is presumed to be sublimely irrational. Even worse, it seems we may already have an excess of
rationality at the microlevel of human existence that has thrown
the macrolevel, the larger society, out of kilter and, paradoxically,
into extreme irrationality. The last argument is well taken: we

need only look at the arms race, where it could be cataclysmic. But it appears in more innocent sectors of human endeavor too, such as science, government, and commerce. Could the computer, and particularly its form called artificial intelligence, be one of those excessive pieces of rationality at the microlevel that will cause gross perturbations at the macrolevel?

Nobody knows if this is so. We are only now getting the first shreds of evidence one way or the other, since for many years artificial intelligence was so innocent of obvious utility that for most people it was a joke and a rather bad one at that. In the last ten years, however, AI, in the form of something called expert systems, has gone out into the world. (Expert systems are described in Chapter 3, "Technologies of the Intellect.") Expert systems represent a new stage in the mechanization of human reason, lushly orchestrated by large amounts of human knowledge. They make their way through tasks noble and banal, from offering lifesaving medical advice to estimating the cost of steam boilers. Probably the most widely used expert system is called ACE, for Automated Cable Expertise, which helps diagnose failures in telephone lines for a million customers in the southwestern United States. ACE is eminently useful but lacks the dramatic flair to chill the fearful or even thrill the hopeful. This is the present humdrum reality of artificial intelligence in the real world.

Since the United States Defense Department has been one of the great patrons of artificial intelligence, it is hardly surprising that expert systems are being developed for battlefield tactics, the integration of sonar signals, and other martial uses. This has some unexpected and, it can be argued, relatively good consequences. I will take that up in Chapter 15, on the computer and war. On the other hand, an equally enthusiastic patron of artificial intelligence has been the National Institutes of Health, and so, many more expert systems exist in medicine than in the military. Wealthy multinational corporations can afford to develop expert systems to help them in whatever their commercial purposes are: less wealthy firms and ordinary individuals have to make do with pre-fabricated programs, though the price of these is dropping sharply.

Is this natural? If not natural, certainly predictable. Is it good? That's a moral issue, and less clear. However, thanks to the pioneering efforts of the affluent, the Japanese plan to bring artificial intelligence to Everyman. They could not have launched such an attempt without the original patronage of those who can afford to take chances.

In the end, I think, our salvation as a species lies in self-help: by introducing knowledge and its rational uses not only at the microlevel but also at the macrolevel and learning to see the connections. This cannot be done by unaided, or natural, human reason alone, and it certainly cannot be done by human passion alone, either. Only now are we beginning to grasp the notion of dynamic hierarchies, macrolevels, and microlevels, and we have even murkier notions about distributed systems, but computer science research has made us see their importance and continues to suggest ways to understand them.

To come to peace with the artificial, and what we can make of it in our own best interests, is a good step in the evolution of human consciousness. The computer can help us achieve that tranquility and help us identify and pursue those best interests in more effective ways (as well as tell us when we are attempting the equivalent of squaring the circle or inventing a perpetual-motion machine).

Here at last is the best news of all about the artificial: there *are* alternatives, there *is* human choice. This more than anything is the grand premise of both Empires of Reason. James Madison studied all the confederations of states that had gone before and failed, identified their difficulties, decided that it need not be done that way, and so found a new set of principles and translated them into new institutions. Thomas Jefferson wanted the Constitution rewritten every nineteen years as "a salutary restraint on living generations from unjust and unnecessary burdens on their successors."

In the newest Empire of Reason, he gets his wish. The constitution is under perpetual amendment and much is novel and odd, changing even as we watch. The new principles and new institutions (in a scientific sense) are just now being discovered. Meanwhile, we grope toward understanding what our alternatives and choices are in this domain of the artificial, this Empire of Reason, surely comical in our bumblings. We laugh—and well we might. But let us be forgiving of our confusions at the same time. As Hester Prynne knew, judgment comes inexorably enough.

Chapter 10

The Protean Machine

The machine moves into the world and, like all artifacts, enters into a delicate reciprocal relationship, imposing shape and receiving form back. It is villain and savior, not just in the eye of the beholder but in fact.

Not long ago I attended a planning meeting for a conference on the computer. Since it was sponsored by a scientific academy, and its main audience would be scientists, I was surprised by some of the criticisms of the preliminary draft of the program.

"It glorifies the computer!" one scientist sputtered.

"Where's the balance? Where are the critics?" another demanded.

For a scientific conference, these questions seemed bizarre. Creationists aren't brought on to "balance" programs devoted to biology, nor are disciples of Velikovsky sought to even the score on programs in astrophysics. When a chemistry conference is about chemistry, nobody thinks it excessive glorification. What else should it be about?

Computing as a science certainly has its controversies. Is the von Neumann design obsolete? Can anybody get more than six processors to work simultaneously? Is structured programming really superior? These are some of the big questions just now, and a crashing bore to anybody outside the field, of course. No lay debates on alternative designs of operating systems take place, nor impassioned rhetoric about relational data bases, though both areas could perhaps capture the amateur's attention if he worked a bit at understanding them.

I said all this to no effect. The balance and the redress of glorification sought by the offended members of the planning committee were extra-scientific.

So official "critics" were subsequently invited to the conference, congratulated themselves for saying once more that the computer would never *really* think but would only be faking it and in any case wouldn't have the consciousness of knowing it was thinking, couldn't *intend* to think, and, most telling of all, would never replace humans. That is true in one important sense but untrue in another, as Seymour Papert pointed out after one of the critics had had some fun: "You laugh," he told the hilarious audience, "because really, you're scared. Because for a long time a computer only seemed like a threat to blue-collar workers, and not to you. And now you know it's going to be capable of taking your job too." The laughter stopped at once.

I think it stopped not so much because jobs were at issue but because the audience was reminded of something anyone who encounters computers knows: the computer raises big questions. It asks—and is suggesting answers to—what life is, intelligence, mind. The computer, as Sherry Turkle puts it in her study *The Second Self*, is an evocative machine: it incites self-reflection and permits a multitude of answers, some of them contradictory.

Computer scientists may well look over enviously at their colleagues in other scientific fields for the undisturbed peace they seem to enjoy to pursue matters as they will, but it's too late. We're all in on the game. An eminent historian, a specialist in the nineteenth century, tells a computer scientist that he sees this twentieth-century machine as Napoleonic, pushing its imperialism—and luck—to the limit. "Don't claim everything," he warns (or pleads), "it just isn't right." It isn't even possible.

Still, I understand the irritation computer scientists sometimes feel. To be a computer scientist is often to be an unwilling audience for personal revelations, fears, prejudices, and nostalgia for what never was. One must not only be still and listen, one must be still for blame.

For computers, it's said, are depersonalizing everything. True, these days we can sit at our terminals connected to various networks, making new friends; and since *noms d'ordinateur* are commonplace, we're often in the dark about the gender, age, status, pigmentation, level of personal hygiene, and so on of our computer correspondents.

In an ideal world, we'd deal sensibly, democratically, and justly with all these human characteristics. The fair-minded among us already try. But meanwhile, in this imperfect world, the computer can help a friendship stay happily uncluttered as it begins to take shape. (When I mentioned this feature of computer networks briefly in another book, a reviewer professed shock at such behavior, not being resident on the same planet as I, I must assume. He was one of two people who mentioned the passage. The other was the anchor of a news program aimed mainly at the New York City black community. She herself was black and laughed ruefully: "Oh, sister, the sooner the better.") Face to face with each other, we judge and are judged on specious grounds. We try to guard against it, having learned that clothes really don't make the man and that birds of a feather don't always flock together. But those rules of thumb are helpful often enough to beguile us despite our best efforts. The computer as a communications medium simply prevents that from happening quite so easily.

Related to this, technology in general and the computer specifically are accused of oversimplifying human relations. Abbe Mowshowitz laments "the rich kinship structures of the past . . . drastically weakened or completely destroyed. In some parts of the world even the nuclear family is virtually destroyed." Mowshowitz was writing in 1974 and couldn't anticipate the uproar caused some years later by the prospect of the electronic cottage. By the early 1980s, the complaint was against the "fortress family" (in the words of still another critic), faulted for speaking to no one but themselves.

But what about that famous exchange among a group of Stanford students who worried that all the time they were spending in front of terminals was warping their social lives? Reprinted in *Psychology Today,* with suitably grave cluckings from a psychologist, the discourse captured the imagination of many, though it seemed to me no different from the anxieties most undergraduates endure on any number of personal topics, a painful constant of the human condition.

But surely there are people who'd rather hack than do anything? Yes, and the computer lets them do it. Institutions, such as universities and computer manufacturers, have taken advantage of that and attract hackers to produce systems and machines. Whether that particular obsession is more harmful than intense involvement with books or a musical instrument is not at all clear to me. Turkle's study of hackers reveals a rich and complex world, with a refined social and epistemological structure, including some antagonisms toward ordinary computer scientists who simply want to get things done and don't share the hackers' reverent aesthetics of the machine and their dedication to ever better computing. The hacker culture—an extreme one, everybody admits—seems to lack complicated and intimate human relationships. It backs off from sensuality. It is a priesthood, but without the blessings or the heavenly rewards promised by the Church.*

Perhaps I ought to disapprove, but I don't. I've tasted the joys of obsession myself, and my sympathies are, on the whole, with the obsessed. An obsession can be an exalting experience. Moreover, it might help to calm fears if we recall that withdrawing from one's fellows by choice is an old pattern in human behavior and seemed neither startling nor reprehensible when it was done for religious reasons, or because a man earned his livelihood setting traps in the wilderness or a family had the opportunity to homestead new and remote territory. Did we once have more respect for freedom of choice? That seems unlikely, but if so, the computer restores that choice to people who find other people intolerable.

Personally, I'd leave the hackers (and the marathoners and the Trappists, for that matter) alone. If they want to stop, ways can be found. We run big risks by obliging human beings to conform to behavior we think is good for them. That kind of busybodying too soon degenerates into sanctimoniousness. Perhaps hackers are missing something by not attending to the sensual side of life, by evading intimate human relationships, but

*Turkle's study is limited to American hackers, almost all at MIT. I think it can be argued that the lack of complicated and intimate human relationships are as typical of the dominant American culture as they are hackeresque: certainly American culture is anti-sensuous, if not anti-sensual. Since, as she asserts, we make the machine and its surroundings what we want, how interesting it would be to see hackers in, say, Martinique, with its astonishing French-African amalgam, or Singapore.

those of us who fritter away our time in a variety of experiences are missing something too. Everybody cannot have everything.

The dangers in all this? Obsessions for their own sake can run away with us, fail to make connections with greater purposes. It seems the hackers in our weapons laboratories keep making bigger, better, and ultimately more catastrophic weapons when we already have plenty to blow us all to smithereens. But the men who display the most egregious hacker behavior when it comes to weapons systems are politicians, apple-pie normal by every other standard. The extravagant Star Wars initiative was a civilian idea, and the provocative anti-satellite weapons my government insists on testing are considered neither sensible nor necessary by scientists and industrialists. Hacking, it would seem, is normal American male behavior, only more so. Its truly dangerous excesses don't take place in computer laboratories but in houses of state.

In any event, the stereotypes about the computer, which is to say the facile evocations, persist. Praising a new building for computer science at Columbia University, *Interior Design* used phrases like "unexpected and delightful" and "fancifully lyrical." The reviewer concluded:

> On the whole, this is a tough interior, not a soft one, but it is a tough interior set to music. One may question the appropriateness of this manner of detailing to the icily futuristic world of computer science, but—for the present, at least—the computers are still operated by humans, and Kliment/Halsband's design efforts are admirably, pleasurably humane.

Yet at Skidmore, Owings, and Merrill's One Chase Plaza, a much-praised building of 1960, everything down to the last ashtray was dictated by the architects and their interior designers, standards that could not be deviated from, since the brutes who actually worked in the building were considered far too ignorant to be trusted with the surroundings they spent most of their waking hours in. One very senior executive had thumbed his nose at all that, and his suite was a startling contrast to the rest of the 1960s Boxe Internationale, having wood-paneled walls and Remington paintings, but no one else had been permitted such personal expression. Architects should be the last to throw stones about the icily futuristic, for the same tale can be told about Le

Corbusier's postwar worker housing in Marseilles. By now I suppose Chase employees have risen up and turned their workplace into something more idiosyncratic and human; the French workers certainly have.

Idiosyncratic and human. This is the main message from Sherry Turkle's study: the computer is a setting for diversity. Whether challenger or helper, the computer is, in large part, what we ourselves bring to it. The hackers confess their sense of being different long before they discover the computer (and other hackers).

So the computer accommodates the dreamers as well as the no-nonsense pragmatists. This is prettily illustrated in Turkle's distinction between the "hards" and the "softs" in styles of computer mastery among children. The categories are roughly equivalent to the analytics and the romantics, the Apollonians and the Dionysians. The "hards" impose their will upon the machine, have their say, have their way, plan, engineer, make it turn out right. They see the world that way too, a place to have your own way, lead, shape. The "softs" are more interactive, more contemplative, try something, see how it goes, and then try something else. The "softs" see the world as something they fit themselves to, beyond their direct control. The computer, protean machine, not only accommodates both styles: it allows them to thrive.

But the computer goes beyond the expression of personality.

> It is a constructive as well as a projective medium. For example, it allows "softs" such as Kevin to operate in a domain of machines and formal systems that has been thought to be the exclusive cultural preserve of the "hards." For the first time Kevin could march into a mathematical world with hysterical colors flying full mast.

And women, who traditionally tend toward the soft rather than the hard and who are traditionally ill at ease in "objective science" (the quotes signal the dubiousness of that phrase) with its abstractions and rigid boundaries between subject and object, find a way of being "soft" and yet intellectually effective with machines and formal systems. In dealing with a medium that can be negotiated with, responded to, and psychologized, women too have access to a world formerly denied.

If Turkle has made the fullest documentation of this, she codifies computer folklore from way back. Melvin Conway once observed that people build computer structures like their own organizations. Thus IBM's computer structures tend to be hierarchical, while Digital's structures tend to be democratic, not to say anarchic. Gordon Bell elaborates:

> The early MIT computers were both configured and programmed to act like members of the university community. Computers developed in other settings were similarly structured like their organizations. IBM computers were "business machines" with cashier-like windows for depositing piles of cards for processing, and the memory units called storage.

And structures refer, of course, not only to physical machines. A program control structure called "the blackboard," which allows many sources of expertise to contribute and compare their ideas simultaneously during the execution of a program so that the program can decide what to do next, and which has had notable success in artificial intelligence applications, grew out of the consensual—not democratic—milieu of Carnegie-Mellon's computer science department in the 1970s. Pascal, a language designed by the Swiss scientist Niklaus Wirth, has been attacked by Yale's Alan Perlis as a "language of manners," so inflexibly Swiss it's rigid. (In fairness, Wirth confesses himself astonished at Pascal's longevity. "I did the best with the resources I had, but that isn't how I'd do it now.")

Perlis has strong feelings about programming languages, and even makes his beginning computer science majors at Yale memorize programs in APL (A Programming Language) the way English instructors once made their students memorize poetry. COBOL, the language of business data applications, Perlis says, is like the language of a business letter—windy, inelegant, and full of stock phrases, but by the time you've written a week's worth of code, you think you've accomplished something. BASIC is even worse, for though it can be learned in four hours, it takes a hundred hours to write anything worth writing.

Perlis observes that most programming languages have been developed in the United States (he went to China in 1972, hoping that the Chinese, in their isolation, had invented different kinds of programming languages but was disappointed to find they'd only adopted dialects of ALGOL and FORTRAN). He offers two reasons why Americans dominate in languages: "We're a very process-oriented people. We're interested in how you say things to get things done. Second, we are a very undisciplined people, and certainly this was true in the fifties and sixties when computing was really taking root. Everybody said hell, I can develop a language as good as his. And in the late fifties, early sixties, hardly a week went by when there wasn't a new language on the horizon. They've all died more or less, but the inventiveness, the urge to invent, is always there."

Perlis doesn't even think it's accidental that the computer has been most successfully developed in the United States. "The computer field requires a tremendous combination of disparate talents, inventiveness, independence, entrepreneurship, business, just name it. And now with the Japanese, the interesting thing is they have fastened on one part of the computer field which is the complex structured organization of integrated circuitry that fits with their view of art and sculpture, literature, you name it. The microcircuit world is a new world of flower arrangement for the Japanese. *It is.* But inventing languages, that's different. To invent language means that you push your authority down somebody else's throat, or attempt to. And the Japanese don't do that. So the microcircuitry is an extraordinary but limited part of computing. Which leads me to wonder whether the Japanese will really be able to make as much out of computers as we think they're going to."

The computer is an extension, a reflection of what we think is important, what oppresses us. Thus an office worker compelled to sit, earplugged and screenbound, without the pleasures of human involvement that make otherwise tedious work bearable, sees the computer very differently from a hacker who can't wait to sit down at the screen. While they may spend the same number of hours at the machine (the hacker probably spends more), the office worker does it to earn a living, and usually in an environment that she has had no say in designing and perhaps toward goals that she has no stake in, whereas the hacker does it for fun, for mastery, for whatever his personal purposes, and harms nobody save himself, if harm it is. The difference is large, and not at all subtle. (I use the personal pronouns deliberately; they reflect a general state of affairs.)

We make the computer's meaning what we will. If life seems

What does the hacker's sister do and why? Male and female children?

impersonal, overly complicated, unyielding, full of vague dread, as well blame the computer as any other phenomenon. Its sinister nature is immediately apparent: it's just like all the other bad machines, only worse, because it can go beyond brute force and outfox—and humiliate—you. Or, alternatively, the computer is amplifier of everything that matters to you.

By now I am placed somewhere toward the latter of those extremes, but not so far out as my harshest critics believe. Like everybody else, I have brought to the computer what I began with, which is a contradictory mass of pleasures, discontents, and yearnings. (While Eliot regretted our lost capacity to integrate mind and feeling, I was wondering why I—alone, I thought guiltily—held on to it, and could I explain it? I wasn't alone, and there were explanations, but about that, more later.)

But the machine of the century isn't merely a mirror, reflecting without comment. It's a dynamic medium, behaving intimately with us, changing with us moment by moment as we receive and respond, receive and respond some more. Surely the word *feedback,* despaired over by language purists as a shabby neologism, has crept into the vernacular just because it embodies that dynamism, that sense of reciprocal process, whereas earlier words—response, opinion, answer—do not.

"I always think of the computer as a medium," says Alan Kay, who has made many contributions to computing, such as the mixture of graphics and text, windows, and a mouse, that are just now showing up in personal computers* like the Macintosh. The idea was forced upon Kay as a graduate student that the computer is not a computing engine or even a representation medium but a communications medium, and not in the sense of the telephone or the Telex but as something more personal. "As with all media, you use it to communicate through and back to yourself reflex-

---

*Alan Kay is sometimes credited with both the idea and the term, personal computer. But such a good idea inevitably arises in many places. As early as 1948, John Lentz of the Watson Scientific Computing Laboratory at Columbia University completed the prototype of what would, eight years later, become the IBM 610 Autopoint Computer. He called his early vacuum tube machine a "personal computer" since it was meant to be operated by an individual user sitting at a keyboard control. The eight year lapse between model and production was caused by doubts about the potential market for a small, portable, so-called personal computer.

ively." But it must be human scale. "To me personal is like a pencil. If you can't use it at the beach, what good is it?"

In the early 1970s when Kay first described such a personal computer to me, it had seemed farfetched; ten years later they exist. They aren't as elaborate as Kay had imagined they would be, nor as easy to program as he had hoped. "I saw Seymour Papert's work with children and LOGO, and thought, that's it, that's the missing link: you should never do a system that's not engineered for children, and I vowed I never would again." But that ease of programming and the rich iconography will come, probably sooner rather than later. If Kay hadn't expected it would take so long, I continue to be surprised that it comes at all.

When he was chief scientist at Atari, Kay worked on a project (among others) that has intrigued him for years, the interactive movie game. "It has the dramatic content of a movie but the controllability of a video game." Calling on his own happy experience in amateur theatricals as well as his computing expertise, he and his team began to work on a game/novel/soap opera that allows the human participant into the action, to affect it in different ways that the player (in every sense) chooses. It's a staple of science fiction, but there we could only read about it; Kay hoped it would be part of our lives by the 1990s. However, as I have already reported, Atari's fortunes changed; long-term research became a luxury the firm felt it could no longer afford, and Kay left for Apple. But if not Atari, not Alan Kay, somebody will develop the interactive novel/game/soap opera. Others are already at work.

I muse on this: the implications for art, the implications for learning, the implications for entertainment. The implications for communicating through and back to ourselves reflexively and not only discovering, but transforming, our secret selves. The computer is to become a processor—and now, it seems clear, a shaper— of both our private and our communal symbology. What shall we invent, find inside?

Art and artifice, to be sure.

Chapter 11

The Venus of
West 53rd Street

Yet some practitioners of art and artifice, visual artists, have come late to the computer, the main reason being the high cost of doing computer graphics—only a few of the very lucky and persistent have had access to the best technology. Not enough to be open to the new medium; you had to be able to get your hands on it as well.

The history of computer graphics is a complicated and worthy tale in its own right, and someday I'd love to tell it in full, but briefly, it is the story of a technology struggling toward limits that are imposed by cost and human ingenuity. Since costs come down, and human ingenuity is nearly infinite, within the space of twenty years computer art has evolved from trite geometrical forms (one year my Christmas cards had a sort of squiggly Christmas tree badly reproduced from a plotter that had been fed simple geometrical transformations) to instantly recognizable but nonetheless novelty portraits of heroes,* to the first mature inquiries into

---

*I mean here Leon Harmon's experiments in the psychology of vision at Bell Laboratories in the 1960s. Harmon chose the very familiar face of Abraham Lincoln and eventually reduced it to a shaded matrix of about 250

the medium by artists trained in traditional fields of painting and sculpture. Trained artists see things differently from the engineers who first produced computer graphics and called it art.

Thus during the 1970s it took David Em, a southern California artist whose designs are haunting renderings of space, inner and outer, more than two years of steady effort to find somebody who would let him work at a computer. His eventual patron was the Jet Propulsion Laboratories, which agreed to let him use its computer graphics facilities so long as he worked the graveyard shift, when the computer would otherwise be idle. Shivering in the cold and dark, he recapitulated in twentieth-century Pasadena at least one experience of nineteenth-century Parisian artists, but the terrible hours and the inhuman surroundings were more than offset for him by access to the machine and to the brilliant transformational algorithms that had been designed by James Blinn for converting digital data from space vehicles into pictures everybody could see. Em, classically trained in painting and sculpture, continues to work in chemicals as well as electronics.

Lillian Schwartz comes from a large family that is both artistic and medical, and she trained in both fields. However, a few years after her marriage, while she was in Occupied Japan with her husband, who was a physician stationed there, Schwartz was stricken with polio. Bedridden for months, the only physical act she was capable of was holding a sumi brush. A Japanese teacher came to her daily in the hospital. When she was finally able to get up from her sickbed, she had chosen art irrevocably.

At a 1968 show at the Museum of Modern Art where she was exhibiting light sculpture, she saw her first computer graphics, and the new medium fascinated her. Among the other exhibitors at that show was Leon Harmon, who invited her to try out the computers at Bell Labs, where she began a long and fruitful collaboration with Harmon and Kenneth Knowlton, creating sculptures, computer-generated films, and other graphics.

squares, the minimum number, it turned out, of elements necessary for most of his human subjects to recognize Lincoln. This planar Lincoln image showed up a decade or so later in all the resort and hotel kitsch boutiques that specialize in such novelties, and Harmon was forced to take legal action to obtain royalties. Harmon's experiments in visual psychology were taking place at just about the same time Andy Warhol was (perhaps) testing the same proposition in his "deteriorating image" canvases, a series of regressions that eventually gave us a sort-of-recognizable image of famous faces.

I have the second piece of computer art Schwartz did. It's a man's head, bearded and bushy-haired, a suitable symbol for the 1960s when it was done. The primitive technology of the time was such that she had to work blind with the computer—there was no screen showing her the results of the program or her manipulations of it. She first had to sketch the piece, needlepoint style, on a piece of graph paper. Next, she assigned values to each of the squares and painstakingly keypunched those values onto cards to be fed, line by line, into the computer. She then designed specially hued icons for each value, which the computer printed out, and from that printout, she created a silkscreen. Almost predictably, when she submitted the result to a major museum as "computer art," it was rejected. The following year she resubmitted the piece as "silkscreen," and it was accepted.

By the early 1970s computer art had fallen into complete disgrace. The nadir might have been a New York exhibit when live gerbils in a computer-kinetic sculpture stopped everything, blocked by their own fecal matter, an event critics saw as symbolic of the trivial connection between art and technology. More important, and harder to argue with, were complaints that the first wave of computer art had only copied what could easily be achieved by conventional media. Things were so bad that Harold Cohen, who had switched from oils, where he had a significant international reputation, to the computer, wouldn't even tell museum directors what he was doing. When they called to ask what was new, he insisted on showing them his work before he revealed how he'd done it.

Schwartz, who also continues to work in conventional media even as she works with computers, was undeterred. She kept experimenting, and as a consultant at Bell Labs she had access to the rapidly evolving technology of computers. Tedious keypunching gave way to interactive graphics on a screen, where she could see what she was creating and change it immediately, using a keyboard or other input devices such as a joystick. There flowed from her an amazing variety of work, pushing the medium in every direction possible, pushing the engineers and programmers to provide more for her to play with, whether hardware or software, picking up computing techniques and adapting them for her own purposes. One of my favorite pieces from this period is called *Hommage à Duchamp*, which rephrases Duchamp's famous nude, rendered from algorithms normally used in program design or printed circuits. The piece itself is precious metals printed on copper plate, a jewel of symbolic resonance.

And then in 1983, a kind of political rehabilitation of the computer as a medium for art was signaled. New York's Museum of Modern Art commissioned Schwartz to do the poster that would announce its reopening after extensive remodeling, which includes an enormous apartment tower above the museum.

It seemed to me fitting that computer art, so referential in its symbols that evoke other sets of symbols, should be selected to capture this particular fin-de-siècle, a century whose artistic leit-motiv all along has been to deny the value of ornament—embellishment for its own sake—and instead regards everything, especially art, as objects of encoding and decoding, in other words, symbols.

Shuttling back and forth between IBM's Yorktown Heights research laboratory (which was underwriting the poster) and the museum, Schwartz began looking at paintings that would lend themselves to scanning and digitizing. Some favorites had to be left alone, since they were so dark that in the course of being scanned and digitized, their details disappear.

"Here I was with the problem of trying to put together all these great artists' work and make a new composition. How could it ever be as good as each of the individual pieces? I tried in many, many ways. First I wanted to look down into the museum and use Renaissance perspectives. Then I wouldn't have done anything with those paintings I was digitizing except hang them in unique ways. I rebuilt the museum itself—I made a little film out of that, building the museum out of its collection—because I was struggling with the question, What does the museum mean to me? It means the design department, the book department, all of the paintings, the sculpture. And so I kept trying to find ways to deal with this."

Those first renderings strike me not only as visually satisfying but also as a delicate reflection on the act of viewing within the museum itself. But the committee in charge of choosing the poster art, made up mainly of the different curators of the museum, rejected the idea, complaining that to reproduce and distort the paintings (as they must be to achieve the bird's-eye perspective) was a kind of desecration. Since artists regularly repaint each other's canvases, commenting, alluding, and paying homage to, this seemed to me odd and probably not the real objection.

Schwartz would later speculate that the curators had other

expectations. "They were used to the commercial computer graphics they saw on TV, all the things that fly around and sparkle and break up; they couldn't see anything, they said, as a still graphic that they thought was museum-worthy."

Schwartz worked on several more sets of ideas, which either she or the committee was dissatisfied with. She returned to the museum to feel again what it really meant to her. On one visit she was drawn to Gaston Lachaise's *Standing Woman* in the sculpture garden. "It's so powerful; I've always loved it. She's the Big Mama to me, Big MOMA. I had to use her. I put her hovering over the museum. Then I looked at her as a form for building with abstract shapes. In one of my earliest versions, she's just a series of abstract planes. Then I thought I'd use the paintings on those planes to give me some texture—my program didn't happen to give me texture. So I abstracted her, built on her, and then I needed her body back. Suddenly it just dawned on me that this is Big MOMA, I think of the Museum as MOMA, it's really a symbolic thing. I felt, I have to rebuild her out of the core of the museum. So I took the liberty of stretching the paintings to wrap them around the contours of her body. I didn't feel I was destroying the essence of the paintings—in the museum you see the paintings from different angles, different perspectives. I used paintings that meant a lot to me. I guess it's a new form, computer collage."

Big MOMA in all her 4- by 8-foot immediacy brings back the visceral shock of art to me again. She overwhelms. Once past the impact of her imposing presence, she seems a loving joke, containing jokes within jokes, such as the painting by Oskar Schlemmer of people climbing the stairs at the Bauhaus, which climbs appropriately up Big MOMA's calf, or a still from a Chaplin film wrapped around her thigh that gently kids the patron. The eye of Magritte's *Christina* stares out from her navel, Picasso's *Demoiselles d'Avignon* is repeated at each shoulder. Modigliani's *Reclining Nude* reclines peacefully across her right breast, a breast toward which Wyeth's *Christina* stretches painfully. Big MOMA's left breast has an impudent Miró egg yolk at her nipple. Henry Moore's sculpture of a family sits squarely in her womb, and then again at her feet between her legs; Warhol's Marilyn Monroe stares out dreamily from her crotch and again from her Achilles tendon; Johns's *Target with Four Faces* is precisely on her kneecap. Hands set easily on her generous hips, she stands firmly, almost insolently, upon Louis Lozowick's *Brooklyn Bridge*.

But Big MOMA is ultimately much more than affectionate visual commentary. She speaks of the complicated condition of being a woman and an artist, of fecundity and solidity, of experience—and experience denied. She is a woman of the 1980s, strong, funny, and deeply disturbing to our sense of what women have traditionally been in art, the passive models of artists. To be sure, her past is part of her, those wounded Marilyns and Christinas, those languorous (and anonymous) female nudes who recline, frolic, beckon, smile. She is of them but no longer one of them: part of the energy of the entire image arises from the tension between what woman has been and what she is becoming. She is not to be trifled with. She verges on the pushy.

Big MOMA was not for the museum in the end, although I wasn't the only one who loved her at first sight; each of the curators has a small reproduction of her, and a very limited edition of the big Big MOMA has been produced. The final design instead was a shaded New York skyline with the museum in the foreground and its tower fading away into the sky. The shading of the sky is from the palette of Matisse. It is elegant and subtle but lacks the impact—visual, emotional, or symbolic—of Big MOMA; and was not used as a general announcement of the museum's reopening, it has also been reproduced in a limited edition for friends of the museum. (The animated film based on it and the Renaissance perspectives Schwartz had done earlier won an Emmy in 1985 in the category of public service announcements for television.)

For Schwartz, the experience opened a new avenue for her own work: in the newest and most powerful equipment she was using at IBM, she discovered an exceptional tool for studying and elucidating the work of other artists. She had scanned and digitized scores of paintings and could study each artist's work—its color, design, and composition—in ways never before possible.

"First I would get rid of all color, and just look at composition. Then I'd put in only the reds, and then only the blues, and then only the greens to see what would happen with the palettes.

"I began to take apart Picasso's paintings. First I used his own palette, and abstracted more and more around it. Because of the way he handled the paint, I could actually pick out a color and then extrapolate between different colors to make up his palette and then paint with those colors myself. *Les demoiselles* was perfect for that because of the angles, and the table in the foreground with the still life that pulls you into it; I couldn't leave that painting alone. As I tried to redo it, the eyes of that painting were so haunting that every time I tried to repaint them I had to have them come through again. Using the computer, it was so fantastic because I could paint over them, and then have them come back again; I had all these choices. Eventually I got rid of his palette, but his figures, which were based on the African masks that he was so excited about, became of another culture for me; they became American Indian, so that the upraised arms became part of headdresses, and before I knew it, I was doing other things, using that as a source. But his painting was very strong, and even when I dropped his palette to use my own palette I could never get away from the fact that this was really, underneath, *Les Demoiselles d'Avignon*.

Analyzing Matisse with the computer was different. "I used Matisse's *The Dance* because the colors were blues and greens, the hair was brown, and it was simple to use. The first thing I did was abstract all around in the background. I found that what I was doing was cutting out his figures, just as later on he would do with his paper cutouts. Before I knew it, his dancers, which were based on Catalan fishermen dancing, which he had to change to women dancing because he got another commission, became sort of ceremonial. As I emptied out his figures they seemed ceremonial to me, and I put Modigliani's *Nude* in the middle, so that they danced around her in some kind of ceremony."

For Schwartz, this was a way to use the computer to understand creativity, as opposed to using technology for purposes of creative expression. Until then, the computer had been a medium, starting with the keypunched pieces I have a sample of and going into film, when she had only eight colors and such poor resolution on those ancient computer screens that she speeded up her films just to cover the flaws: "*The New York Times* called them 'drumbeats on the eyeballs,' but if you froze a frame it looked terrible." But now the computer is an analytical tool as well: a means of studying other artists' processes.

"I always studied old masters, I always studied Rembrandt, and here I have this machine that can let me analyze design and work from the originals. In the Matisse series, I changed all the colors and did different things to them, and even put myself into a painting looking at the painting. There's a fifteenth-century Altdorfer print that Picasso analyzed; in sketches he broke it down and simplified and simplified until he got at the very essence of what Altdorfer was trying to do; it's a nice progression. Well, I have a tool where I can do that same thing with great immediacy, and compare, and see what's going on. To study, to build, and begin another direction for myself and my work. Doing this is a learning process for me."

Process. The processes of others are revealed; one's own are made explicit and then amplified. The theme recurs everywhere the universal machine enters. In Schwartz's case, the artist is continuously involved with the process, hands-on at all times, seeing, editing, re-viewing, reworking, artist and medium in passionate dialogue together. This is what artists have always done but there is a dazzling pace, impossible until the computer, amplifying the artist's work (I think of Claude Monet, filling his London hotel room with scores of canvases, each meant to capture the Houses of Parliament at a given moment in the day, in a given kind of weather, and am saddened for the physical effort alone, never mind the interruption in dialogue).

Does more mean better? Yes, in the sense that it allows the artist to explore thousands, millions of more possibilities in a search for the exact expression. David Em once explained to me the differences he felt between painting on canvas and painting electronically, the freedom to explore every branch of possibility he felt moved to because there was no penalty; he could always come back to where he'd been, to dozens of where-he'd-beens, if he wanted, the computer's memory effortlessly storing any stage of a design for study, amendment, enhancement, abandonment.

And what emerges? From trained artists, wonderfully satisfying visual art, which is also a monument to human artifice, human processes.

Yet this kind of intense involvement with the production of a single piece of work, this change in quality thanks to a change in quantity (known, of course, as the order-of-magnitude effect), is not the only way the computer lends itself to the visual arts. In that complex symbolic process we call making art, the computer has allowed the artist to shift to a completely different level of abstraction, a level that no artist anywhere has ever had the means to reach before, as we shall see next in the work of Harold Cohen.

Chapter 12

AARON

On the wall in front of the desk where I usually work are a number of pictures. The largest is an abstract black-and-white line drawing that always engages me—I stare at it when I am woolgathering (and not staring out the window). Being unregenerately human, I insist on imposing a pattern upon the abstraction. In my view, it is a landscape, and a rather fanciful one at that, with Grand Teton–shaped mountains in the distance and a forest in the middle distance (or vegetation of some kind).

But the figures in the foreground are what inevitably claim my attention. They're a set of George Lucasian robots, the largest a creature with its back to me, staring off into the distance (ready to traverse the plain and scale the mountains?), its windup key clearly visible in its backside, its feet a variety of locomotive devices from treads to air cushions. This creature has an assortment of companions, ranging from the airborne to the slithery (by the time of the second movie in the *Star Wars* trilogy, Lucas's robot technicians understood that future robots would be specialized, which meant they would come in many shapes and sizes). My windup robot seems to be the only one enjoying repose; the rest are agitated. In any event, everybody is waiting for something about to happen. I like to assign personalities to them in my idle moments; someday I may even give them names.

None of this pattern finding I do is particularly surprising. It is only human to impose the familiar upon the unfamiliar: one wanders through the Luray Caverns in Virginia, say, and finds oneself in a wonderland of banality, the wonderland supplied by nature, the banality by humans who insist on naming those lime-stone shapes after the everyday: "Wishing Well," "Giant's Thumb," and the like.

The picture on my wall has not been supplied by nature, however. It is the work of a computer program named AARON. AARON itself was created in turn by the artist Harold Cohen, who has spent the last fifteen years trying to model some aspects of human art-making behavior and produce freehand drawings as a result. Before he became interested in AARON's art, Cohen did it on his own, exhibiting in international shows as a repre-sentative of Great Britain, including the Venice Biennale. He has had some fifty one-man shows in New York, London, and other cities, most recently at the Brooklyn Museum and the Tate Gallery in the late winter and the summer of 1983. To be absolutely precise, the Brooklyn and Tate shows were AARON's.

The landscape above my desk was done at the Brooklyn show. You could go to the museum and see AARON at work, a plotter that Cohen himself had built (one of four) and connected to a VAX, scribbling away to the amazement of spectators standing about. AARON could produce a drawing in anywhere from 10 to 40 minutes, depending upon the complexity of the drawing, not one identical to another, although they resemble each other in ways that might be expected of drawings from the same artist.

The drawings were sold for a token cost, $10 at the time. This raised a bit of a political problem, as it turned out, for the museum authorities were not predisposed to selling art, and Cohen felt very strongly that computer-generated art was a way for people of ordinary means to be able to have something that, although it is produced quickly and relatively cheaply by a machine, is never-theless unique. (In fact, the real cost is much higher: equipment costing $250,000, plus the cost of publicity, printing, and opera-tions borne by the museum, plus Cohen's own fee, works out to more than forty times the $10 purchase price. "I've really been playing Robin Hood," Cohen says. "The corporations give the equipment, the museums put up the money, I give my time and effort, and the public gets drawings at a nominal—one might almost say a symbolic—price.") Matters were somehow worked out, and one afternoon as I stood watching, I saw at least a half dozen people gladly pay their $10 and walk off with an original AARON.

"It's a lot better than monkey art," said one happy buyer to me. Harold Cohen's assistant happened to be standing nearby, and he responded: "That's because AARON knows a lot more about art than monkeys do."

Does it? In fact, just what does AARON know? The current version of AARON knows what Cohen calls some twenty or thirty "things."

> I think I said somewhere from this standpoint that the program wouldn't become really interesting until it knows four or five hundred things. I was simply trying to give some sense of how much development I thought would be required before things became combinatorially rich enough to achieve my purposes. Put to the test, I'm not sure I could say what a "thing" is. A memory item may be a conceptual item—"closed form," for example—or a member of the set "closed forms," or the specifications for constructing a figure from closed forms, or the specifications for constructing an entire picture from a variety of different figures. Then it knows some "meta-things," like the fact that closed forms (in most circumstances) stand for solid objects, and that solid objects occlude each other. You can't equate "memory items" with "things" because the items are built hierarchically from other items, and you can't count the meta-items because they're implicit in procedures rather than explicitly stated in rules.

AARON is not exactly hierarchical, although there are higher and lower levels to the program. Rather, it uses what in artificial intelligence is known as the blackboard organization, which as we have seen, is a way of representing hypotheses at different levels so that independent but cooperating sources of expertise can be used in parallel and adaptively, causing and responding to the main, or controlling, pattern on the blackboard and its changes.

"To the degree that a 'meta-thing' might be seen as the actions of experts in a blackboard model, the occlusion expert and the completion expert are watching all the time." (Though the blackboard metaphor is visual, this organization was first used in the automatic understanding of continuous human speech and has found uses in other disparate fields.)

AARON is a self-enclosed, autonomous entity, making up drawings as it goes along, without reference to input from the outside, relying instead solely on its internal rules. In this it is different from Lillian Schwartz's work, for Schwartz is always firmly hands-on, whereas Cohen has provided AARON with a patrimony consisting of rules and then sent it out into the world of art to see what will happen.

Out in that world, AARON makes drawings. "It builds an internal representation as it goes along," Cohen says.

> Obviously it deals with the internal representation rather than with the physical drawing, which it can't see. If it could, the act of seeing would generate a new internal representation, which it would use in place of the drawing. Thus it can learn, and it does have an archival memory, which the earlier AARON couldn't and didn't. It has criteria by which to assess its own performance—it wouldn't know when it had finished a drawing otherwise—and I suppose it could report on its assessment if required to do so. I've never thought it would be interesting. But presumably criteria imply critical judgment.

AARON has no ability to color at the moment, and so from time to time Cohen hand-colors AARON's work, and these colored images seem to me to have a different quality from the untouched AARON. In a curious way, they are simultaneously enriched and constrained by the addition of color. They are enriched because the colors are jolly additions to what is already a whimsical set of images; they are constrained because the figures take on Cohen's declaration of their space and importance, whereas the black-and-white figures allow more ambiguity and declaration by the spectator. This is not to say I prefer colored or uncolored. AARON makes thousands of drawings and there is room on my walls for examples of both.

Cohen's intention in designing AARON was not to invent a

machine that would turn out aesthetically pleasing drawings, though, in fact, AARON does so. At first he wanted to examine symbolism, or what he calls "standing-for-ness." What, he asked, would be the minimum condition under which a set of marks might function as an image? But as AARON has developed beyond minimum conditions, Cohen's ambitions have risen accordingly: now he aims to understand the structure of representations—images that express intent with respect to the external world—rather than the structure of images.

In the years that AARON has been drawing, distinct patterns of audience response have emerged. Europeans, Americans, and Japanese, in cities as different as London and Amsterdam, New York and San Diego, Washington, D.C., and Tokyo, first make the nigh universal assumption that each drawing has been made ahead of time by a human artist and then somehow fed into the machine. When this is clarified ("What human artist could possibly have made all the drawings to feed the hungry brute?" Cohen asks), viewers then talk about the machine as if *it* were a human artist. Audiences describe AARON's work as witty, even droll. (Cohen once told me—with some amazement—that he'd received a letter from a therapist in the Boston area who had taken a group of her depressive patients to the DeCordova Museum in Lincoln, Massachusetts, where AARON has some murals. The effect of the murals was so cheering to her patients that she brought back a second group, who were also immensely cheered.)

A majority of those in the audience find recognizable shapes in AARON's work, just as I do. A visitor to my study saw that the work above my desk had been inscribed "Brooklyn" and took my Grand Tetons to be the towers of the Brooklyn Bridge. *Chacun.* Museum-goers are always finding fish and birds and bugs and other creatures in AARON's work.

So then, is it art? Cohen says he has always been frustrated by that perhaps non-question and would certainly answer it if he could. "The last hundred years of art have been devoted to that question: I see AARON as carrying on the tradition," he once wrote, and the art historian Leo Steinberg would go further and argue that all important art since at least the trecento is preoccupied with self-criticism.

Recently, in fact, I've taken to replying, of course! as if I find it surprising that anyone would have questioned it. The more interesting question is, what PART of it all is art? And my answer is that all of it is. The black-and-white drawings function as black-and-white drawings, as you yourself have testified. The colored drawings function as more precious—rarer—commodities and are purchased as art by art collectors at appropriate prices. The museum installations function as extended performances, the purpose of which is to restore the status of intelligent conversation. Alan Kaprow saw the Brooklyn show and judged it to be terrific in terms of the social dynamics the event was generating, without ever looking at the drawings.

Well, what is art, anyhow? If Cohen finds the question frustrating, Arthur C. Danto, a philosopher, has written a splendid book to address it called *The Transfiguration of the Commonplace.* I must reduce a subtle argument (that is often hilarious—what a good time Danto has with art!) to its bare bones. Danto maintains that art is meaning, and hence a question of truth. Like Cohen, Danto declares that art has evolved in such a way that the philosophical question of its status has almost become the very essence of art itself. Over time, he goes on, standing for or denoting has come to be less and less an important thing for artworks to do— a transformation from being a part of reality into something *contrasted* with reality. Danto writes:

> I am trying to state that the "aesthetic object" is not some eternally fixed Platonic entity, a joy forever beyond time, space, and history. . . . The aesthetic qualities of the work are a function of their own historical identity so that one may have to revise utterly one's assessment of a work in the light of what one comes to know about it.

So, Danto asks, how do we distinguish works of art from mere representations? How is a Brillo box under the kitchen sink different from "Brillo Box" displayed at the Guggenheim? "Any representation not an artwork can be matched by one that is one, the difference lying in the fact that the artwork uses the way the non-artwork presents its content to make a point about how that content is presented." That would suggest that the landscape above

Then it's not assessment but reaction.

my desk is art, for it is making a very distinct point about how the content is being presented. Cohen continues:

> Whatever else art does, it has to feed into the ongoing discourse on the nature of art, or we will judge it trivial. I will make so bold as to claim that my work over the past few years has raised more than its fair share of questions about the nature of art and art-making, and on that ground has to judged to be non-trivial art. It isn't really surprising that the questions should be directed first at the work which raises them. Twas ever thus. But I think my work has held its ground against the questions it raises and its status is less in question now than it was a few years ago: witness the fact that by the end of this year I will have done eight major public works, murals and the like, in five years.

Danto goes on: "A work of art is the externalization of the artist's consciousness, as if we could see his way of seeing and not merely what he saw." But AARON has no consciousness, nor has it any visual contact with the real world, so cannot "see." In AARON's work we spectators are seeing—at a distance mediated by the artist's introspection and by the formalities imposed by the programming language he uses and by the machine itself—the artist Harold Cohen's presentation of an increasing number of rules of representation.

Cohen himself used to be puzzled by the emergence of the personal. "I have never been able to understand how there can be such general agreement about the 'personality' which AARON's drawings project, or why that 'personality' appears to be like my own in a number of respects. Personality has never been an issue on the conscious level of writing code, and I know of nothing in the program to account for it. To put the problem another way, I would not know how to go about changing the program to project a different 'personality,' " he wrote in 1979. Now he says, "I've concluded that what we call personality is to be regarded as the signature of a complex system, and that any system of sufficient complexity will exhibit something very like personality: though we should call it 'entitality' in the case of an entity. By the way, I've thought that the program's personality was *not* like my own."

I suggested to Cohen that one way to change the program's

personality might be to let someone else intrude into the rule-making and code, another artist, for example. Cohen has extracted all the rules AARON uses out of his own experience. The addition of another artist's sensibility would create a fusion of expertise, not unlike the paintings that came out of Renaissance ateliers of certain masters who only painted the faces and hands on portraits, leaving the draperies and backgrounds to other specialists. But since Cohen is uninterested in personalities, he isn't interested in trying to change whatever personality AARON seems to exhibit. "I don't think your analogy is sound," he added. "The first expertise required of van Dyck or Jordaens in Rubens's studio was an exact knowledge of what a Rubens looked like and how to make one."

Late in his argument, Danto reports:

Bach was accused of having a secret fugue-writing machine, something that ground fugues out like sausages. Of course there would in one sense be no Point in patenting such a machine. It would be like the goose who laid the golden egg, in that now anyone could turn out all the fugues he wanted to. That would be true but essentially uninteresting. What would be interesting is not some proof that such a machine did not or could not exist, but that if it did exist, the person who used it would stand in a very different relationship to the generated fugues from Bach's, and the mechanical fugues would be *logically styleless* because of the failure of that relationship defined exactly by the absence of mediational devices—rules, lists, codes— which the fugue-writing machine would exemplify.

Is AARON the fugue-writing machine?
Cohen replies:

I think this is all very confused: unnecessarily so. Within Western culture we have always afforded the highest level of responsibility—and praise or blame—to the individual who works on the highest conceptual level. We may hear a hundred different performances of a Beethoven quartet without ever doubting that we were listening to Beethoven. We remember the names of architects, not those of the builders who made their buildings. And, particularly, we value those whose work leaves art in a different state to the state in which they found it.

Now it seems to me that AARON—the program— stands in relation to the individual drawings the way a Platonic ideal stands to its earthly instantiations. It is a paradigm. The fact that I have found a way to work my will upon, and through, the paradigm, rather than upon its single instantiations simply means that my level of involvement is a great deal higher, conceptually speaking, than has ever before been possible for the visual artist. It is more like the way a composer writes a score instead of giving a performance, although in my own case the program is responsible for all the performances also: as if a score could play itself. And, of course, that has been the avowed aim of composers throughout this century.

Danto would not allow Cohen to evade responsibility for AARON's work, I think, even if, as Cohen truthfully states, he cannot predict how any given drawing of AARON's will turn out. Style is the man, and if AARON has any style, it is Cohen's, not AARON's, even if Cohen's own work, where he puts his hand to a paintbrush and that paintbrush to a canvas, bears no resemblance the artist can see to AARON's work—though others more familiar with Cohen's pre-AARON work claim to see similarities.

I have never tried to evade responsibility for AARON's work, obviously. My involvement with that work is a great deal more than normal, not a great deal less, notwithstanding the fact that AARON can be churning out drawings in London while I'm in Paris. The similarities between AARON's work and "my own" rests upon the fact that AARON is a knowledge-based program, and the knowledge is a subset of my own. Style? Part of style is knowledge, and part is the signature of a complex system. I am not a computer program. That part of AARON's style is AARON's, not mine.

And then he adds: "There are so many things we are going to have to get used to in the coming years. . . ."

Both philosopher Danto and artist Cohen are deeply interested in representations—representations in art, in the computer, in the artifacts of the twentieth century. Art, Danto concludes, externalizes a way of viewing the world, expresses the interior of a cultural period, offers itself as a mirror to catch the conscience of our kings. Cohen presents AARON as the begetter of images that are references to some aspect of the world, containing within their own structure a reference to the act of cognition that generated them.

AARON expresses some of the great themes of computing; namely, artifice, process, representation, complexity out of simplicity, and uniqueness within mechanization. They are, as Cohen says, some of the great themes of art as well. They are, as Danto says, the interior of our period, our century-long fascination with symbols *qua* symbols, symbols *of* symbols. AARON's drawings—how apt the word—involve us in whole new levels of art and reference, confirming Henry Adams's epochal intuition of 1900 that the dynamo's energy is connected in intimate and profound ways with the energy that built Chartres.

Interlude:
The Twilight of Heroics

There is a universal human fascination with heroes. They dwell in our myths, ancient and modern. The rise of the hero (or as we prefer, the maturing of the individual psyche) engages us at the deepest level, and no wonder. The hero risks much, braves great dangers, accomplishes high deeds, inspires everyone.

Two themes pervade these myths. First, heroics cannot be achieved without help. As the hero undertakes his task, help comes in a variety of ways—ancient crones bestow magical amulets upon him; goddesses cause natural laws to be suspended; enchanted animals disclose secrets that will help him on his way. These personages are a colorful and, by now, quaint way to admit our personal inadequacies in the face of life's trials. Second, heroes are activists. The gods help those who help themselves.

The good life is equipoise between the knowledge of our own limitations and our will to find the means of transcending them. Equipoise takes practice. We are ever in danger of leaning over too far. We topple, lose heart. So, though we've passed irrevocably beyond the magic amulets and enchanted animals, our new way of transcending life's trials, our individual reason, has proved a disappointment. We were each to be our own heroes, the wherewithal for heroics right inside our skulls, and we cannot.

Perhaps we only substituted a new superstition for those we outgrew. I don't mean the fashionable "exhaustion of Western rationalism" or the superiority of feeling over thinking. On the contrary, to deal with the enormous problems that face us now I think we need a lot more reason. The witty fifteenth-century monk Erasmus observed that while it might be wisdom to be governed by reason, there's half an ounce of reason for every pound of passion in the human body, and those few ounces of reason were "imprisoned in a cramped corner of the human head," whereas passion has the run of the body. We shall not much change what seems to be an evolutionary legacy, what psychologists now call the bounded rationality of the human mind. In that case, perhaps it is time to resume humility and look around for help.

In our new artifact called the computer, we have invented a helper for ourselves that is more appropriate to us and our times than the Ancient Crone, the Benign Goddess, the Magic Crow, whatever. This puts the computer in its place: helper—even wiser helper—but not the hero of the drama of life, who can only be human, if for no other reason than life was long ago stipulated to be a human drama and constructed by humans to be so. It isn't just that the computer can reason over bodies of information that would stagger the human mind, though that is true. Through its networks, the computer also allows the community of minds to function together, making not two heads but scores, even hundreds of heads, better than one.

Everybody agrees that the results of our technology sometimes exceed our abilities to cope with it, at times with terrible results. Heroics around the hospital bed are the Hippocratic oath to a fault. Though technology permits it, society balks at paying the enormous costs of kidney dialysis or organ transplants, which leaves hospitals in the uncomfortable position of treating only Middle Eastern sheikhs who can pay the bills. Even those with means, or with sympathetic neighbors who raise funds for them, must appear on prime-time television, pleading distraughtly for news of suitable donor organs before the imminent death of a loved one. (As a shy person, I wonder if I could do that for one of my own, and feel a little bit inadequate before I am even put to the test. A fraction of the money spent on such bravura performances could more usefully be spent on computer networks that would systematically put people in touch with help on a national or even global basis, and that is beginning to happen.)

If we have begun to be skeptical about heroics in the hospital room, more quietly we have begun to be skeptical about heroics in the criminal courtroom too. Heroics here, meaning absolute protection of a criminal's civil rights regardless of his previous record or the nature of his crime, have also proved in their way to be too costly for society to bear. Thus in the early 1980s the American criminal justice system began to practice what amounts to cost-effectiveness. That is, the cheapest and most lenient treatment went to criminals least likely to commit serious crimes again, regardless of the seriousness of their offense. The harshest punishment was reserved for those who repeatedly committed serious crimes and were most likely to continue. Never mind reform and rehabilitation, which is at present unpredictable. Never mind an eye for an eye.

Thus we move away from extremes and toward equipoise, chastened to learn that we cannot have everything, that civilization is a series of compromies among legitimate but conflicting demands. There is surely a lesson here in weapons and warfare, but about that, more later.

I have used *heroics* here with several meanings. Curiously, its original meaning is "protector" and that brings me back to my original point, which is that although we have fashioned a machine that has the potential for abuse, we may also have fashioned our next and best hope, an instrument with the potential for protecting us from our own natural but regrettable nearsightedness. We are free to be heroes in the sense of adventurers, but we have a useful ally.

We can breathe a little sigh of relief. We don't have to do it all by ourselves, after all. If the supernatural is lost to us, we have fashioned the artificial, and that promises an interesting change— an improvement, I believe—in human fortunes.

PART 3

The Vernacular Computer

Chapter 13

The Medical Microcosm

What illustrates the places occupied by computers in the world right now so well as medicine? Here, side by side, are the ordinary and the extraordinary, making revolution in ways both obvious and subtle. Professionals and clients alike view the computer's effects with deep ambivalence, embracing the universal machine dutifully, not always lovingly.

Thus computerized billing, hospital information systems, even decision support systems for administrators, instead of files and ledgers in folders, are commonplace, although most of this has happened only in the last decade. Communications networks are slowly being set up for, say, fast transfer of information about suitable donors and recipients of organ transplants; and statistics about the incidence of disease, whether geographical, occupational, by age, or any other characteristic, are being gathered and sorted for the tale they have to tell. These are mundane, familiar tasks, and yet their significance for our health and well-being cannot be exaggerated.

Routine laboratory work is undergoing great changes. The MetPath firm recently opened an automated laboratory in Des Plaines, Illinois, designed to serve the entire western United States.

It began by processing 2,000 specimens a day; when it reaches capacity, it will be able to process 45,000 specimens per day. A network of desktop terminals with displays allows physicians to receive analyses and test results without waiting for human couriers. While information will be more convenient, less error-prone, and perhaps even cheaper, the new laboratory will never employ more than 1,000 people. Many lab assistants will have gone the way of steelworkers, though with considerably less publicity. (A change in the structure of Medicare payments has suddenly made office tests more attractive than outside laboratory work, a political change that may have its extra-technological effects on this large laboratory.) The point is, similar "invisible" changes are happening in communications, entertainment, manufacturing, and large areas of business management.

Microprocessors implanted in the limbs of paralyzed human beings stimulate nerves and make muscles work again, after a fashion; heart pacemakers are now programmable, so that their functions can be changed—reprogrammed—without surgery. Personal computers serve as communication devices for people unable to speak and offer advice to parents of children with chronic diseases such as cystic fibrosis, leukemia, and diabetes.

For healthy people, Control Data Corporation has added to its PLATO self-instructional program a set of microcomputer programs that help people help themselves to stop smoking, lose weight, keep fit, and otherwise stay well (indeed, the series is known as STAYWELL). The programs are highly flexible and personalized, assuming that what works for one human being doesn't necessarily work for another in different circumstances. They present data in graphical and informative ways, helping users see how they compare with others in similar circumstances and how they compare with their own performance over time. Participants can communicate with one another, asking for help at difficult moments, and this, like the home advisors for chronically ill children, is prelude to medicine at home, the trend toward personal responsibility for health.

Each of these applications has parallels in other fields. Their effect is less dramatic than quietly cumulative, making things better, on the whole, for human health. I call these ordinary applications, though they are not at all ordinary to people whose lives they have eased and even saved. They also illustrate one of the most important changes wrought by the computer, the so-called order-of-magnitude effect, where a large change in quantity brings about a marked change in quality.

And then the extraordinary. Consider the changes computing has made in diagnosing disease. Ultrasound imaging, for one, is now widespread and is especially useful in correcting fetal abnormalities. The computed axial tomographic (CAT) scanner, for another, produces images of "slices" of the body; its data are so profuse that only a computer can transform them into images for clinicians to use in diagnosis. An experimental "surgeon's work station" permits surgeons to use the latest advances in computer aided design and manufacture to plan an operation, and design custom replacement parts, before cutting open the patient.

A newer and even more promising diagnostic tool is the nuclear magnetic resonance (NMR) scanner, a machine that resonates at the cell level, sending back great quantities of data that, again, are converted by the computer into images that clinicians can use for diagnostic purposes—it amounts to exploratory surgery without so much as a pinprick. One experimental NMR scanner at Columbia-Presbyterian Medical Center in New York City is so powerful that it can show sodium levels in cells, an important sign of cellular health. Since NMR scans can be done immediately after tissue damage occurs (rather than the 48-hour lag involved in diagnosis with CAT and radioisotope scans), such tools might help physicians locate damage that is reversible and thus improve treatment as well as diagnosis.

Still another kind of imaging, single photon emission computed tomography (SPECT), allows graphical representations of a variety of organs, including the brain, the heart, the lungs, the liver, and the skeleton, the latter at a level that conventional X-rays cannot reach. In the brain, lesions can be seen that other kinds of imaging cannot detect. But perhaps SPECT's most important contribution lies at the level of cell receptors, where clinicians can trace the course of neurological diseases.

All these new tools, with their images so graphic and, for those trained to read them, easy and quick to understand, would be unthinkable without the computer to gather and convert such torrents of information into pictures that humans can usefully comprehend. The same techniques that turn masses of medical data into images for physicians to diagnose are also found in engineering and design, in the monitoring of global resources, and in the latest special effects in movies.

In the early 1970s complaints were raised about the cost of CAT scanners, and the U.S. government allowed funds for only a limited number of such machines so that they would serve whole communities instead of individual hospitals. But the CAT scanner has become such a valuable tool that no large hospital feels it can offer good medicine without one, any more than it can do without an X-ray machine. Government studies have since concluded that despite the large capital outlay, the CAT scanners ultimately save money. The same will probably prove true of the NMR. As it happens, the price of these machines is coming down as the cost of computing drops, but they are still expensive.

Perhaps the most extraordinary (and controversial) application of computing to medicine is its role as expert assistant to physicians. As medical knowledge has grown in the last few decades, individual practitioners have been overwhelmed by the sheer amount they must know. Medicine has fragmented into more and more slender specialties, and while patients are happy to have remedies to some of their most exotic illnesses, they also complain that they are too often treated as a "case," an incidence of a given disease, instead of as the sick and sometimes troubled human beings that they are. Though some efforts have been made to reverse that, the most successful, ironically, has been the introduction of still another specialty called family practice. In providing primary care, the family practitioner must often call in an outside consultant (and would be remiss for not doing so) when the patient's problem falls outside the expertise on hand.

That consultation generally involves a dialogue between the two physicians, with the consulting specialist offering advice and the practitioner questioning points he doesn't understand or concur with. Though this is extremely time-consuming for both, the primary physician simply must know why things are being suggested: he makes the final decision and has ultimate responsibility for the patient's well-being.

Recognizing all this, physicians and computer scientists at Stanford University sat down together in the early 1970s to see if a new idea in artificial intelligence, an idea that had proved its usefulness only in chemistry, could indeed be transferred to the realm of medicine. That idea was the expert system, a related collection of computer programs that acted as an advisor to an expert in an extremely narrow field, whose principles I have described in Chapter 3, "Technologies of the Intellect." If the success of the system in chemistry—where it was performing at the level of a Ph.D. in the interpretation of mass spectrographic data—could be repeated, then an enormous burden could be lifted from physicians and better medicine could be offered to patients.

The first problem the medical and computing specialists tackled was deciding which medicine to prescribe for a patient with an infection. This pioneering program, called MYCIN, accepted data about the patient—temperature 102, heavy drinker, weight 145 pounds—and in return gave the inquiring physician advice and, if probed, information. The advice included a tentative diagnosis and a suggestion of appropriate therapy. In test trials, expert physicians rated MYCIN as performing as well as, or better than, human physicians.

MYCIN was an attractive idea, and soon expert systems began to be devised for many diseases, including arthritis, glaucoma, and all of internal medicine. A highly specialized grandchild of MYCIN called ONCOCIN assists physicians at Stanford University Medical Center in the extremely complicated problems of chemotherapy for patients with certain forms of cancer. Along with programs that help manage a patient with a specific disease, there are programs that help the physician use statistical methods to assess the likelihood of a patient's having a particular disease, given statistics on disease incidence in a certain population. Those same statistical methods can also help with prognosis.

Though expert systems using the same design principles have been adopted in manufacturing, with provable cost benefits, their medical cousins have had virtually no impact outside the experimental laboratory. (This is a remarkable contrast to diagnostic imaging techniques.) The reasons for this lack of impact seem to be, first, that limits now exist on the kinds of expertise that can be stored in computers—anatomical information, which involves complex spatial relationships, has been difficult to capture and process. Second, there is a question about the cost-effectiveness of AI techniques in medicine. Expert systems are expensive and time-consuming to construct. It may still be cheaper to train human physicians. Finally, physicians themselves have been reluctant to use expert systems, partly because they fear upsetting the traditional doctor-patient relationship, partly because of a general mistrust of, and discomfort with, the infernal machines.

I have said that medicine is the world in microcosm with regard to computing, and I mean that in both positive and negative ways. It is easy—nearly irresistible—to get enthusiastic about the wide range of applications, the novel diagnostics and therapies, the leverage that more and better information gives any professional.

But the problems are enormous. There is, for example, the problem of incompatible standards. After I saw a demonstration of the ONCOCIN program at Stanford, I asked to be taken from the computer laboratory to the clinic to see the system in action. My host seemed puzzled, but happy to accommodate me. In fact, I wasn't sure why or what I wanted to see.

As we entered the reception area, a physician was coming out of her consulting room to make handwritten notes on a patient's chart, copying the information from a central monitor. At the Stanford hospital, some records are on a central system, but despite great efforts, the ONCOCIN researchers have been unable to tie their system into the central system. Thus the physician must physically fetch information that ought to be automatically available and, worse, used to be, on an old-fashioned written chart. She must enter that information through a keyboard into the ONCOCIN system so that it can be considered in the diagnostic process (although the Stanford installation has a human information manager who helps there; the institution also has been experimenting with specially designed keyboards and graphics that are relatively easy for physicians to use).

These two incompatible systems at Stanford are by no means unique; on the contrary, they are typical of a rapidly evolving technology, which is almost always awkward. Identical problems can be found in nearly any computer installation of even modest complexity, and they frustrate the best intentions. On the other hand—and the reason people endure the frustrations—ONCOCIN performs a job that human physicians simply cannot do with the same accuracy and speed.

Another set of problems arises from the fact that medicine, even as the rest of us, faces a changing population. In the next fifty years, the numbers of people in the United States sixty-five years and older will increase, and the biggest increase will be among people over eighty-five. Such people need disproportionate amounts of health care, not to mention help at home. In time, we shall have no choice but to pay attention.

Then there are costs. If nobody is certain who should pay for NMRs and CAT scans, let alone aspirins and bedpans, where to allocate the cost of computing is even more vexing. Without very persuasive cost benefits, it is difficult to justify the outlay for new systems and to ask workers to endure the headaches such new systems inevitably drag along with them, especially if matters seem tolerably under control without change. At the same time, the search for cost-cutting might very well accelerate computerization. (This touches upon the different perceptions different workers usually have of the computer's role: the physician is less interested than the hospital administrator in containing costs. The physician's interests lie in treating individual patients, improving their care, reducing their risks, and providing themselves with scientific bases upon which to make decisions.)

A researcher from a major national hospital telephones me to ask about the role of the computer in medicine: she is preparing a report for the hospital trustees. I'm baffled, for that's like asking about the role of the book or maybe science. Where to begin?

"The doctors here don't think they need computers," she says at last. "They have a first-class hospital as it is. Why do they need to change?" My first impulse is to tell her to leave them alone. Computing as it is now is so difficult (the user interfaces are so ragged, in the field's jargon) that nobody who doesn't absolutely need it, want it, or long for it should be exposed to it. But then, on the book analogy, I recall that many medical schools at the turn of the century in the United States had no libraries. Why did they need libraries? they asked. They had physicians, where knowledge resided, and they had patients, where problems waited to be solved. What advantage did books have?

They were right, I say, given the level of medical knowledge of the time. But they were wrong in the long run. And it was a fatal misperception; none of those medical schools without libraries survived into the next century.

And what about the legal ramifications of computers and medicine? The Food and Drug Administration (FDA) has already declared that, under the Medical Devices Act of 1976, it has the right to regulate software that controls devices such as pacemakers and insulin pumps. But industrialists fear that the FDA may also assert authority over expert assistants, thereby slowing development intolerably. If the FDA wants to control expert assistants, it is argued, then by the same logic it will have to control textbooks and lectures in medical schools. But others who favor federal regulation believe that the sensitive problems of human health care must have such go-slow and well-monitored development, since human lives are being risked. We should no more allow unregulated expert systems into health care than we allow unregulated drugs. No one, so far as I know, has taken both a physician and his former professor of medicine (or a medical journal) to court for redress, the law of torts drawing limits to liability; but an expert system, a device that contains dynamic knowledge and advises a physician as he is in the process of treating a patient, is perceived as different from a textbook or a lecture of some years past. The medical example is more dramatic than most but embodies the problems every field faces as knowledge becomes dynamic instead of static; some Solomon-like decisions will have to be made about dividing up responsibility in the realm of knowledge. Finally, when malpractice is charged or liabilities for misdiagnosis are being assessed, and advice from an expert system plays a role, who will be responsible, the attending physician, the human expert who supplied his knowledge to the system, or the programmer?

As everywhere on the planet, American medicine takes in computing piecemeal and at different levels, depending more on social than on technical circumstances. "Medical computer projects are undertaken to fulfill particular goals," Bonnie Kaplan writes, "they reflect particular values, and have political and social implications. Because there are always more projects than resources to do them, it is necessary to evaluate and select from potential projects those that are *worth* pursuing."

The words are unintentionally ironic, surrounded as her essay is by a wild mixture of the commonplace and the compelling that can be found not only in collections of reports about computer applications in medicine but in nearly any other realm, from fashion to finance, entertainment to education, that we thrust the computer into.

Chapter 14

Flatland:
The Micro Universe

The June 1983 issue of *PC: The Independent Guide to IBM Personal Computers* was, as it happened, the largest monthly magazine in the history of consumer magazine publishing up to then, pushing aside the former champion, the September 1981 issue of *Vogue.* (I should say at once that by largest is meant heft: at 642 pages and 2.8 pounds, *PC* was 22 pages longer than the old *Vogue.*)

PC is a magazine for owners of IBM personal computers, and it aims to sell products that such people—130,000 subscribers to that particular issue—might like to know about and buy, from software to dust covers for the hardware.

The appearance of the championship issue of *PC* is daunting: it looks like nothing so much as a catalog. Catalogs can be wonderfully useful, the Sears Roebuck catalog being one example of structured information, an orderly access to goods, and not incidentally, with written descriptions of products so complete yet concise that any writer can profit from studying them. Moreover, behind those admirable descriptions and their no-nonsense photographs stands the Sears warranty, which allows you to return anything you find unsatisfactory, regardless of your reasons, and get your money back.

PC, however, is not a firm but a medium, and its catalog-like qualities are less attractive: old-fashioned, cluttered graphics, vague and insubstantial descriptions (there is nothing significant to be discovered about a piece of computing equipment by looking at it; all the worse for looking at a picture of it). Few warranties are offered, fewer implied.

Caveat emptor would be difficult enough, but in fact poor *emptor* is utterly befuddled—how are you to get through 642 pages that, except for some (but not much) pagination, are arranged at fiendish random?

A spreadsheet program? Ads for those appear on pages 1, 3, 5, 8–9, 16, 17. This suggests a pattern of odd-numbered pages (give or take a little noise). But no: page 11 advertises something called PC Pal and PC Tutor, an on-line explanation of your system, which the manufacturer might have thought to supply but didn't; and page 13 advertises a game that, commendably, encourages your children to negotiate with aliens instead of killing them. As for attachments, such as modems, printers, and sound synthesizers, they're here, there, and everywhere. But you never know quite where.

Here's disorder that some would cherish: endearingly human, and perhaps it is. I have already claimed that the computer is the most human machine we have ever invented. Surely all this bears me out, and only a grouch would object. Call me a grouch.

There may be subscribers to the magazine who have time for a complete search in the hope that some treasure will surface, but I am not among them. Nor am I certain I'd know a treasure if I saw one. Every hawker's line sounds the same: believe me, little lady, this here is the best, the cheapest, the most powerful, the most reliable.

Captured between the covers of *PC* is nothing less than the carny atmosphere of the microcomputer shows, where prices are posted on blackboards, to be changed the moment a competitor's do. There's fun at such a volatile bazaar, and history too, if you think of markets as the original human exchange. But there is not dependable information. Sniff the odor of sawdust and snake oil rising from the pages, hear the unmistakable shuffle of take-the-money-and-run. It couldn't be more human.

I think I am not singling out *PC* unfairly. The primitive graphics and copy that dominate the magazine's advertising pages are typical of computer magazines. Many factors account for that, I suppose, beginning with the vast amounts of money to be made in building better computing mousetraps, hence the engorged proportions of advertising, which all but obliterate editorial text. Then there might be some dilettantish legacy from hobby and electronics catalogs. But the conclusive business, understood at some level by editors and advertisers alike, is this: for most readers, reading the magazine is its own reward. That piques my interest.

As it happened, that particular issue contained a profile of the typical reader, who is male (97 percent) and well-educated (96 percent have been to college, 82 percent earned a bachelor's degree, and 40 percent have graduate degrees, including 14 percent with Ph.D.'s). The same survey claimed that 80 percent of the subscribers read nearly every ad. If this admittedly self-serving statistic is at all accurate, then I am not only in a sexual minority among the magazine's subscribers but also in a reading minority. Here am I, meditating on the irony that a magazine devoted to a processor of information should be so poor at that task itself when, clearly, that is irrelevant. Something else is going on.

To examine the ads is to enter a relentlessly literal universe. A preponderance of them are nothing but large (often full-page) listings of items and prices, pure text aligned in columns of small-point type. Practically speaking, the comparison shopper must not only flip back and forth through the 642 pages but also have sharp eyesight. (Images in the ads with pictures suggest one explanation: nobody in the microcomputer universe is over age thirty-five. And, for the record, nearly everyone is overwhelmingly white, male, and dressed for business, usually in a three-piece suit. This magazine is, after all, for owners of *IBM* personal computers. Violations of those canons signify, as we shall see.)

But this approach is much too practical. Let me imagine the contented reader taking sensuous pleasure in those tidy columns, not longing to *have* every item so much as comforted by signs of their abundant existence, a feeling I understand from, say, window-shopping on Madison Avenue or the Place Vendôme: I don't covet those endlessly sumptuous silk scarves or hand-cobbled shoes; it simply gives me pleasure to think we exist on the same planet. Perhaps *PC* is the something of the same for the reader.

And yet, despite my best wishes, the literalness of the micro-computer universe persists in ads that go beyond agate and into images. For example, the next batch of ads are nothing but pictures of equipment (a little innocuous text, a trade name). Again, there is nothing substantial to be learned from a photograph of a computer or its peripheral equipment, but there they are, page after page of printers, modems, expansion boards, IBM PC look-alikes (at slightly lower prices than the original). The pictures testify that such equipment exists, but they cannot say anything authentic about its performance, which is what really matters.

But only to me, and I am missing the point. Let me at least allow that these are the pictorial equivalent of the lines and columns: there to give pleasure, not information.

Curiously, there is practically no use of computer graphics in these ads. Television, for example, has a regular repertoire of computer-generated icons. This absence may have to do with the static medium of the printed page as opposed to the dynamics of television images, but it seems remarkable. Among thousands of images, I noted only three that seemed to owe anything to computer capabilities: a crude reproduction of a Northwest Indian motif, complete with jaggies (the computing term for the rough edges caused by discrete picture elements—what might be called the needlepoint effect); three stylized human heads with data wrapped around them conforming to facial features; and finally, an ad for a real-estate investment program, a stylized boot on a computer screen (a small visual pun here) with overlaid drawings that convert it to a dwelling with such details as a Mexican tile roof, sliding glass doors opening on to a deck, the heel made into a garage. Its caption: "We could show that old woman what to do with the shoe."

"I call our world Flatland, not because we call it so, but to make its nature clearer to you, my happy readers, who are privileged to live in Space," wrote Edwin A. Abbott, a turn-of-the-century English clergyman who fancied a two-dimensional world where "straight Lines, Triangles, Squares, Pentagons, Hexagons, and other figures, instead of remaining fixed in their places, move freely about, on or in the surface, but without the power of rising above or sinking below it, very much like shadows—only hard and with luminous edges."

The Flatland narrator's tragedy is to visit the three-dimensional world and return to face disbelief and martyrdom at the hands of his fellow Flatlanders. From prison he writes: "Yet I exist in the hope that these memoirs, in some manner, I know not how, may find their way to the minds of humanity in Some Dimension, and may stir up a race of rebels who shall refuse to be confined to limited Dimensionality." Alas, those rebels aren't to be found among the ardent readers of *PC*. On the contrary, it is Flatland they seek, ad by ad.

To wit, the dominant theme of the human images is men coping with stress. Anxiety and despair are signaled unambiguously: the loosened tie, shirtsleeves, hand to the brow, face furrowed. More often, the stress has been overcome before we see him. It's a familiar before-and-after drama, simple in concept, simpler in execution, the happy user saved from whatever misery he once endured, smiling at us now over his keyboard in blessed relief, perhaps even tossing no-longer needed equipment into a wastebasket, assuring us that a remedy is not only possible but can be had at once. (These are coordinal with ads that appear in certain women's magazines, where the problems are expressed in the same gestures but the remedies are headache pills, cake mixes, and bathroom cleaners.)

In my favorite ad, perhaps because it contains some ambiguity, readers are invited to compare two users, photographs side by side. Which one has the product? The first picture shows a jacketless man, shirtsleeves of his (significantly) blue shirt rolled up, tie loosened, posed in exasperation at his printer, waiting for data. His surroundings are an exercise in minimalism; white walls, drapes, carpet, furniture, all save the chair he sits in, which is red (the hot seat, we can suppose). Outside a crescent moon pierces the dark sky, and an office clock on the wall tells us it is 7:43 p.m., certainly no time to be sitting around waiting for a computer.

Next to this is a picture of a man at a table, smiling out at us, holding up a glass of white wine, perhaps a toast to his own providence. He wears a white shirt, sleeves buttoned, tie knotted neatly. His plate is piled high, a basket of rolls is just beyond his place setting, a large cooked fowl (goose? turkey?) in the lower left corner reposes in a veritable forest of parsley; a chocolate-and-vanilla cake is in the lower right; the wine bottle lower center. He too has a window behind him with the dark night and the same crescent moon; he too has a large clock on the wall (in his dining room—odd, but high-tech isn't entirely passé as a decorating style), which for some reason is a minute ahead of the clock in the adjacent picture. Nevertheless, a message of leisurely cheer seems to be intended.

And yet . . . What's in the glass beside his plate? Brown liquid, looking suspiciously like Coca-Cola. Maybe the glass is really a cup, and he's only drinking coffee with his wine, eccentric but not a capital offense. But why is he eating so much off such a tiny plate? Who allowed those cafeteria tin-top glass salt-and-pepper shakers on the table? Once started, I can't stop: what shall I read into that cooked fowl?

Abundance and grace may have been intended, a happy ending to the story, but the impression is something else: careless attention to detail has comically sabotaged general intentions. That is interesting only because readers of this magazine are expected to be inhumanly attentive to details; a misplaced comma can crash a program.

In some ads, other technologies are a point of reference. A favorite is the sportscar, especially the Porsche. One ad imposes "Supercharged communications for your high-powered 16-bit PC" over the image of a Porsche; Volkswriter, a text-editing program, invites you to "test write" it, and pictures a Porsche-like car in the ad's center; a hard disk you can add to your personal computer bluntly calls itself Targa and of course features a picture of a Porsche. More generally, a spreadsheet program announces that you can go from "zero to Multiplan in 5.2 minutes" with a stopwatch and a racing car driver's glove at the bottom of the ad. In a curious mix of technologies, one manufacturer claims "supercharged access to Visifile," but the image is a laser beam slicing through a floppy disk. An unpleasant ad features a pistol aimed menacingly over the reader's left shoulder: "Microsynergy takes aim with the Sixshooter."

This is a masculine universe, simple and direct—boyish, I am compelled to say—devoted to the symbols, though not necessarily the reality, of power through technology. It reminds me of the lower middle class suburbs of America, where driveways are full of motorcycles, campers, pickup trucks, supercharged and over-sized American cars: horsepower in inverse relationship to real power.

What little humor there is, is schoolboy obvious and sometimes carelessly cruel: "We can help your little IBM PC" says an ad for the language "C," illustrated with a cartoon figure of a PC made to look like a blind man, dark glasses, a cane, and led by a floppy disk on a leash.

While this universe is not utterly free of women, they play a nearly inconsequential role. "Our Women are Straight Lines. Our Soldiers and Lowest Classes of Workmen are Triangles with two equal sides . . . they can hardly be distinguished from Straight Lines or Women . . . Our Professional Men and Gentlemen are Squares."

There is hardly any sex in the microworld (like science fiction, that). What there is remains decorous. A man and woman snuggle cheek to cheek: "Let Shoebox tidy your affairs." "Software for mature audiences" is the slightly naughty come-on for a stock analysis program.

An interesting exception is an ad for IRMA, a hardware link between PCs and mainframe data bases. In a brilliant marketing stroke, IBM chose the Little Tramp, a character we can both empathize with and patronize, as a theme for selling its personal computer, and of course the industry that is nourished by the PC has been quick to follow. The ad for IRMA shows a full-color picture of the Little Tramp's grubby hand on the waist of a well-groomed and formally dressed woman. Her back is to us. "Irma and Charlie were made for each other" reads the caption, but everybody understands the truth, that this blonde goddess is inaccessible to somebody as ordinary as the Little Tramp.

Willy-nilly, the ad has dipped into all the poignancy of masculine deprivation that Charlie Chaplin succeeded so well in portraying (perhaps exploiting). Here is hopeless yearning by an average man for a highly desirable woman who, being desirable, can choose instead of waiting to be chosen. And despite the Little Tramp's goodness of heart, he is only an average guy. Or less. A creature like Irma always prefers the handsome hero (in other words, the adult), leaving the Tramp to hide his disappointment manfully and wish them happiness together, the outcome of many a Chaplin two-reeler. But: the aloof Irma can be bought, the ad implies; dreams can come true, happy endings are possible. Lurking beneath: every woman has her price.

To be sure, *PC* magazine's ads show a handful of women in suits—to be taken seriously—smiling over their spreadsheet programs or their high-speed printers, but they are so unusual they arrest attention. And there is one telling exception to the rule that nobody in the microcomputer universe is over thirty-five years of age: it is a picture of two white, elderly (that is, gray-haired) office charwomen, standing in wonder at a terminal that is communicating with other terminals late at night.

As it happened, the championship issue of *PC* also contained an article by Lindsy Van Gelder, a contributing editor, that examined the topic of women in computing. The reasons she cites for the underrepresentation of women in computing generally are unarguable and well-rehearsed to any feminist: women's historical lack of seriousness about a career; female "math anxiety"; social conditioning ("I see an awful lot of parents running out and buying a home computer for 12-year-old Jeremy, but not too many buying them for 12-year-old Jessica," she quotes Katharine Davis Fishman saying).

She goes on to point out some fallacies women still adhere to: that they have no experience using anything like a computer—though they use microwave ovens, digital watches, and preprogram their VCRs with ease; and though, news to me, the skill that seems to correlate best with potential in programming is musical training, not mathematics. (I can imagine why: music is, among other things, abstraction and process, which are central to computing.)

Women complain that computers don't make their jobs easier but instead less fun (if you're stuck between earphones in a word-processing pool, with an electronic boss counting your keystroke speed, you're no better off than your nineteenth-century sisters were in the textile mills of Lancashire and New England).

Unlike men, women worry that video terminals may be health hazards, and while the statistical evidence isn't conclusive, surely common sense suggests that sitting and staring at a small screen for hours on end is, at the very least, hazardous to your composure. Women are repelled by the typical shoot-'em-up video games (but so, by now, is everybody else, it seems).

Van Gelder airs each of these issues with brisk directness, and while she has counterexamples and strategies for remedying some of the problems, she puts the responsibility for educating themselves squarely back upon women. With that I agree.

But what a shock it must be for the woman (or any other adult) who takes the first tentative step toward computing by buying a magazine such as this. Fresh from a world of ambiguities, texture, difficulties that evade solution, systems that have depth as well as breadth, nuance and indirection, zest, she encounters a fundamentalism so arid and simplistic in its rules, so petty and cramped in its ambitions, so stubbornly resistant to large concerns, that she might well imagine she has tumbled into the pages of a 1950s housewives' slick, a species of reading matter she has learned to deplore and even be ashamed for. Micro indeed. If nothing else, such an encounter must confirm every ungenerous thought she ever had about computer specialists.

As for me, I have already been through all this, when I started by reading the complex and quirky Tales of the Brothers Grimm and then had to switch to the intellectual malnutrition of approved children's literature. I have let my subscription to *PC* lapse. To ramble each month through the Flatland of adolescent boyhood was a peculiar diversion but not rich enough to bear repeating often. I call my friends for advice.

Chapter 15

War

The computer and I are cohorts, born within months (and in one instance, miles) of each other in the early part of World War II, children both of that heartbreaking time. Perhaps this circumstance of birth is why the computer is irrevocably connected in many people's minds with war and weapons, especially nuclear weapons. The connection exists, of course; the two technologies are also cohorts, born about the same time and in the same circumstances.

The first general-purpose computers were used in World War II for code-breaking in England and for ballistics calculations in the United States (a third project in Germany at the same time, considered useless by the German Government, had no applications of any consequence). And then a primitive computer—with less power and speed than the computer on my desk that I write with at the moment—was used to calculate the implosion method used to detonate the plutonium bomb, first at Alamogordo and then at Nagasaki.*

*The computer was the ENIAC (Electronic Numerical Integrator and Computer), built at the University of Pennsylvania's Moore School of Electronics.

156

As computers have grown smaller and cheaper in the forty-odd years since those detonations and as weapons have grown more powerful (the two technologies exhibiting almost eerie parallels in their declining costs and expanding power), it is deeply tempting to conjecture that if computers were banished, many of our troubles would be banished too. In some limited sense, that is true, or at least a tenable point. But like literacy in Western Europe by 1300—a century and a half before the introduction of the printing press—computers in the Western world are here irrevocably. They're here because we believe their advantages outweigh their disadvantages, just as Europeans wanted literacy, drawbacks and all.

I have already mentioned the Japanese government's ten-year research project to produce a version of Everyman's intelligent computer, the fifth-generation of computers, that can talk and translate in natural human languages, understand, see, draw pictures, reason, plan, and so forth—a cheap, robust appliance to transform our lives. The project's sponsor is the Japanese Ministry of International Trade and Industry, leading a consortium of eight private firms and two national laboratories. And while the product is intended to transform the lives of everyone, it is also intended to give Japan technical and then economic dominance in information processing in the 1990s.

Two years after that 1981 announcement, almost to the day, the U.S. Defense Department's Advanced Research Projects Agency (ARPA), announced a five-year plan to produce similar machines, meant to transform the lives not of Everyman but of the militia: the Strategic Computing Project is to produce intelligent battle management systems, intelligent pilots' assistants, intelligent robotic vehicles (this child of World War II shudders: buzz bombs with brains). The department also intends the technology to spin out rapidly into the commercial world.

It's a plausible response to the Japanese challenge. Yet it was melancholy to me that the American announcement came from the Defense Department while the Japanese announcement came from the Ministry of International Trade and Industry. The fault, it must be said at once, lies not with that particular agency of the

It contained more than 18,000 vacuum tubes, weighed 30 tons, and occupied a room 30 by 50 feet.

Defense Department but with a set of national myths that do not permit Americans to spend such large sums of money on anything for the common good that isn't in the name of national defense. It is not fault but default: we have shoved the Defense Department into the role of long-range technological planner for the nation because no one else is there. We have National Institutes of Health but no National Institute of Economic Health, much less an Institute of National Technological Health.

Yet—and it troubles me to admit it—this is the American way, since at least the Lewis and Clark Voyage of Discovery under Thomas Jefferson's presidency. That expedition was as strong and supple an alloy of geopolitics, literature, commerce, and science as can be imagined, the fifth generation of its day. Jefferson intended that mixture, knowing therein lay its strength. He foresaw that when the purposes of one part of the expedition were frustrated, purposes of the others would keep the project going. And so they did. Congress, beset by Revolutionary War debts, saw no point in appropriating much money for something so risky and nebulous as exploring the new Louisiana Purchase. So Jefferson, blessed with (or driven by) his vision of the long-range value of the Louisiana Purchase in its every aspect, took matters into his own hands and made sure that the army added between $15 and $20 for every civilian dollar allotted. Moreover, the expedition itself took a military form, co-captained by Lewis and Clark and run, more or less, with military discipline. In retrospect, its failures (and they occurred only afterward) were civilian, not military.

The brilliance and vision that informed the Voyage of Discovery, not to mention the sheer human adventure of it, make me pause. My longtime wish has been that science in the United States be "purer," untainted by military or commercial considerations. But the lesson embedded in the Lewis and Clark expedition compels me to wonder if what I've called hypocrisy—our reluctance to pay for what we really need as a nation, whether it's building the interstate highway system, educating college students, or doing the important business of science, except in the name of national defense—is instead a strategy for succeeding after all, in ways much richer and more varied than a single purpose would permit.

Surely the connection between science and defense needs continual examination. Its most conspicuous failure, atomic weapons, must make us very leery. But it would be dishonest to deny that this connection, this mixture, has had its successes too. Long-range scientific planning in computing has been a vacuum in the United States until now, save at the Defense Department's Advanced Research Projects Agency. This agency has taken on a multitude of essential tasks that might more properly belong to, but were ignored by, the National Science Foundation, the Department of Education, and the Commerce Department. The private sector has neither the resources nor the justification for taking the risks that long-range research requires, though it has been glad enough to share in the benefits. And yet.

Part of that continual examination of the connection between science and defense at present has to address the final tragedy— in every sorrowful sense of that term—of the liaison between computing and war, a set of strategies entertained by some members of our military and government that is conceivable only with the computer. It is the launch-on-warning idea that was proposed, dropped, and once more revived in the late 1970s and early 1980s. What this means is that any sign of an adversary's aggression will trigger massive retaliation. Whether the sign is true or false— whether the adversary meant this as the beginning of Armageddon or whether a solitary lunatic has somehow managed to launch a single missile—is immaterial. The philosophy is street-gang bravado: mess with us, and you'll be sorry. But of course we'll all be sorry. Launch-on-warning invites catastrophe upon the planet. Moreover, if the nuclear winter scenario is correct, mutually assured destruction has been transformed into assured self-destruction, national suicide. The "surgical" preemptive strike becomes a dagger at the self's own heart. It is derangement, not policy, owed to unexamined passions, not rationality. (Some scientists argue that even a miniature nuclear winter on one continent will be ruinous.)

A group I belong to called Computer Professionals for Social Responsibility (CPSR) has published a paper pointing out some of these dangers; regarding the ARPA's Strategic Computing Project, the paper points out that the limits of computer reliability include not only the obvious troubles of equipment failure but also the less obvious troubles of design failure: "Unfortunately, except in trivial cases, we cannot anticipate in advance all the circumstances [computers] will encounter. The result is that, in unexpected situations, computers will carry out our original instructions, but may utterly fail to do what we intended them to do."

Moreover, all complex systems, including AI systems, have to evolve for a substantial period before they are flawless, and they never truly are. "No amount of testing under simulated conditions can replace the testing that comes from embedding the system in the actual environment for which it was designed," the CPSR paper continues. "The reason is quite straightforward: simulated tests exercise exactly those circumstances that the designers expect the system to encounter. . . . But all experience with complex systems indicates that it is the circumstances that we totally fail to anticipate that cause the serious problems."

True. These arguments are even more germane to the Star Wars undertaking (known officially as the Strategic Defense Initiative) than to the Strategic Computing Project. The aims of Strategic Computing are more modest and are testable without resort to war—at least the pilot's assistant and robotic vehicle are, if not the battle management assistant, which, indeed, is planned as an important part of Star Wars. The pilot's assistant and robot vehicle also seem to me less destabilizing than the battle management system, and in a terrifyingly unstable world, this matters. If all the other arguments against Star Wars weren't valid (its cost, its technological unfeasibility in the first place, its perfect functioning still admitting enough destruction upon us to be devastating), its sheer provocation should be enough to nullify it. But in weaponry, reason has not been much evident.

The connection between war and computing is deeply troubling to me and many others, because it is complex and impervious to easy answers, particularly easy personal answers. Each of us faces a question: are we ready—am I?—to give up all the good I see in computing if only I could, by that sacrifice, ensure that I also eliminated the possibilities of catastrophic button-pushing? Hard question; they always are when they're only hypothetical. Starting out as a young writer I was confronted by a European journalist. "You're writing fiction?" he said icily. "Make-believe? Don't you know about the tin miners in Bolivia? *That's* what you should be writing about!"

Luckily, I could take the question to an older and wiser writer, who told me she'd faced the same interference when she was beginning, only then the great problem she was urged to give up her writing for was Trieste. "Trieste," Hortense Calisher laughed softly. "Who remembers Trieste as the world's greatest problem now?" This is not to belittle the anguish of humans caught in whatever crisis Trieste caused once upon a time (though it happened within our forgetful lifetimes) or to belittle the unspeakable misery of the Bolivian tin miners; it isn't even to equate those miseries with the horror of global annihilation, which is surely, by anybody's measure, infinitely worse.

Instead, it is to admit that I live in the real world and have not only finite but very limited personal powers. I would rather think about the possibilities for solving the problems than about making splendid, empty gestures of self-denial. (Or worse, pontificate.) There are intelligent, earnest, even wise people working on the problems of disarmament, and I wish them godspeed. They range from Nobel laureates and other distinguished scientists who have the ear of the very powerful to ordinary computer professionals willing to do the decidedly unglamorous but essential tasks of computerizing mailing lists for activist groups on the sensible premise that public attitudes are as important as military or political attitudes.

Though I've announced my pleasure in the technological fix, smart weapons coupled with brutal force aren't a fix. (I don't think much of dumb weapons attached to brutal force, either. It even enters my dreams: I'm on a medieval battlefield, horrified to see men hacking at each other's limbs with swords that are so dull that only pain, not death, is inflicted. An overwrought metaphor, as dreams often are, it corresponds to a hack editor who took a magazine piece of mine and chopped out all mention of the computer and war, among other important issues, and substituted happy talk about the vacuum tube era instead.)

Across the electronic networks, graduate students and professionals in computing debate the issues electronically. How can the Japanese offer to make the world better for humanity with their artificial intelligence machines, when all we can offer is to make it better for warriors? A message even comes across the network from a stranger asking me where I stand.

Where I always stand, slightly apart. Japan and the United States play different global roles, whether they like it or not. In part, this is conditioned by past events (I am reading a history of the Pacific war as the message comes, so cannot quite take seriously the idea of the Japanese as being inherently peace-loving). Our global role has also been conditioned by the size and immense wealth of the United States. We cannot change the fact that the United States is a global power, although we could certainly change the nature of that power. I add to my correspondent that I have no problem with national defense, as such; all the enemies of the republic did not perish in the Berlin bunker, and the republic is eminently worth defending from its enemies.

What could be changed in all this is, first, strategic reliance on weapons of mass destruction and, second, the national attitude that holds that nothing is worth spending public money on except weapons. This is what I have called hypocrisy, although I now admit to uncongenial second thoughts about that.

exagg.

My network correspondent's question has put me in mind of that young student of literature who was able to study the classics of the English language thanks to the largesse of the National Defense Education Act, a congressional solution to the problem of insufficient numbers of well-educated people (while the adversary, who had just put a tiny satellite into outer space, was well known to educate all its students at no direct cost to them). I remember no debates about whether it was ethical or unethical to accept money in the name of national defense to study literature. In those post-Sputnik and pre-Vietnam days, our innocence—or our cynicism—was different.

It may be something more. We humans have a very hard time grasping abstractions. Asked to make sacrifices (and taxes are a sacrifice), it is easier to imagine we are saving our skins from the marauders than to sacrifice for something as curiously intangible, at least to most Americans, as more knowledge. We can understand and are prepared, for the most part, to pay for a cure for cancer and heart disease. We cannot quite understand—or we are less willing to pay for—the research that leads us to the nature of the universe.

I shouldn't wish to imply that the hypocrisy is limited to ordinary people. With my own ears, I have heard a prominent scientist and leading anti-war activist concede that, yes, he took money from the Department of Defense; he may even have told them that it would eventually be useful in some kind of weaponry, but he knew it never would. These were Vietnam days, and I was shocked. Nowadays, it only makes me a little sad, both for him and for us.

The report of Computer Professionals for Social Responsibility criticizes artificial intelligence researchers for a "growing appetite for research funding which has led to promises that can't be kept." Yes, AI budgets have grown, but to lend some perspective, a single satellite lost in a space shuttle launch in the early 1980s cost the same as the aggregate funding of all AI by the Pentagon up to now, about $200 million. (The Strategic Computing Project, however, would increase budgets dramatically. So did the Japanese project, and so did European responses to the Japanese, all civilian programs.) To attack the researchers themselves is to aim at too easy a target. A more intellectually demanding task is to face up to our several legitimate goals as a nation, understanding, as Thomas Jefferson did, that singularity of purpose is not only inhuman and impossible but is even undesirable: a multitude of purposes lend strength to each other at critical moments. What makes such a facing up so personally demanding is that it can never end.

A few years ago, the director of the Advanced Research Projects Agency of the Department of Defense went to the community of artificial intelligence researchers and told them he wanted a machine smart enough and small enough to land a bomb on Brezhnev's lunch plate. They all laughed; it was scientifically absurd and strategically bizarre. When I heard about it, I laughed too.

Now I am not so sure. In a way, it relieved me to know that somebody in the Defense establishment could think in such simple, concrete terms. His request implied that there really is a moral difference between, on the one hand, assassinating a national leader and, on the other, destroying a city of millions of people or even an entire nation. It is not a pretty difference. It gets personal. We imagine a real Brezhnev (then an elderly man) at his blinis, not the faceless, impersonal foe. To accomplish such an act of political assassination requires stealth, cleverness, and a high degree of consciousness. It is not the impersonal brutality of mass destruction, disguised in the jargon of war strategists. We can grasp it. It brings us out of Flatland and face to face with what war is all about.

With some exceptional good luck (for we weren't wise enough

to plan it that way, I think, though there may be planners in the Pentagon who would show me that it was planned and sought), we have opened a possibility for the mitigation of world catastrophe. Largely unnoticed by the public, the arms race has changed. I quote Freeman Dyson:

> The central paradox of the arms race is the discrepancy between public perception and reality. The public perceives the arms race as giving birth to an endless stream of weapons of ever-increasing destructiveness and ever-increasing danger. The reality is more complicated. In the nineteen-fifties, there was indeed a race to produce weapons of mass destruction—to assert technological superiority by exploding the largest possible firecracker. But that race came to an end with the Soviet fifty-seven-megaton explosion in 1961. Since then, the arms race has been running strongly in other directions—away from weapons of mass destruction and toward weapons of high precision. While bomb technology has stagnated, there have been three successive revolutions in the technology of computers and information-handling. The computer made possible the accurate delivery of small weapons, non-nuclear as well as nuclear. One consequence of the computer revolutions has been the replacement of big hydrogen bombs by the MIRV and the cruise missile. Another consequence has been the appearance of accurate non-nuclear missiles. The computer revolutions are not yet over. If the arms race continues in the same direction, toward cheaper and more capable non-nuclear technology, then there is a chance that we may see not only hydrogen bombs but nuclear weapons of all kinds gradually becoming obsolete.

It is mitigation of catastrophe, not its elimination. It may be the beginning of what Dyson calls the David and Goliath deployment, the invention of smart little weapons whose only purpose is to find and destroy big dumb weapons. If matters turn out as Dyson hopes, it will mean that the Department of Defense really was engaged in defense after all. Or, in any event, is returning to the business of professional soldiering and individual political assassinations instead of global destruction. Everyone can breathe a little bit easier, the world will return to a level of morality it once enjoyed, which is far from perfect but preferable in every way to the amorality and suicidal irrationality of the nuclear age.

Those who long to bring about the New Jerusalem will find this cold comfort. It requires no change in human nature (which the New Jerusalem would) but only attention to a rationality beyond facile passions. It is something realistic to hope for soon. To be sure, human beings do change; accepted behavior becomes unacceptable, limitations are understood and acknowledged. We can hope for this too, but it will take longer. Meanwhile, the computer-directed David weapons offer a substitute for the Goliath weapons of mass destruction. In Dyson's words, such weapons "allow people to defend their homeland against invasion without destroying it."

There's another role for the computer in keeping the peace. In February 1984 a resolution was introduced in the U.S. Senate calling for the establishment of two Nuclear Risk Reduction Centers, one in Washington, D.C., and one in Moscow. Computers would be central to their functioning.

More than a year earlier, alarmed by the growing dangers of nuclear confrontation through misjudgment, miscalculation, misunderstanding, and terrorism, parochial or national, a group of senators and their colleagues had quietly established a nonpartisan working group to examine various means of reducing the risk of nuclear war.

The working group included experts in national security and intelligence, men of experience and skepticism. They soon concluded that even the improved communication links between the United States and the Soviet Union, approved a year earlier (and then still under negotiation), were welcome but insufficient.

More comprehensive and systematic answers were needed to lessen the dangers of accidental nuclear war. Thus they proposed establishing nuclear risk reduction centers in Washington and Moscow that would maintain a 24-hour watch on any events with the potential to lead to nuclear incidents. "These centers would be designed to reduce the danger of nuclear terrorism, to build confidence between the two sides and to avoid the buildup of tensions that could lead to confrontation."

The dangers of nuclear confrontation do not come merely

from the antagonisms between the two superpowers, the group argued, but increasingly from third-party provocations, including, of course, terrorists. Thus the two centers, though independent in some sense, would have to be linked directly—both through communications channels and organizational relationships—to political and military authorities. Their staffs might include liaison officers from each side, and if that proved successful, perhaps they might eventually be managed by joint groups. (An alternative the group envisioned would be a single center staffed by military and civilian representatives of the two nations at a neutral site.) The centers' missions might be narrowly defined at first, expanding as they gained experience and the confidence of their governments. In short, the centers would replace the limited and ad hoc responses on the part of their governments with systematic and comprehensive procedures.

Among their first tasks would be to plan steps to be taken during incidents involving nuclear weapons—for example, the unexplained explosion of a nuclear bomb, a terrorist threat to explode a nuclear weapon unless certain demands were met, the discovery that a nuclear weapon was missing, and similar scenarios. The working group conceded that such scripts might not be followed should an actual event occur, but the very existence of such routines might make appropriate action easier.

Should terrorists provoke a nuclear crisis, the two centers would maintain close contact, providing ways of defusing the incident and avoiding the danger that it might lead to a nuclear confrontation between the superpowers.

The centers would exchange information on a voluntary basis about events that might lead to nuclear proliferation or to the acquisition of nuclear weapons or the materials necessary to build them by subnational groups. They would also exchange information about military activities that might be misunderstood by the other party during periods of tension.

Finally, they could be the partners in a dialogue on nuclear doctrines, forces, and activities, including discussions of strategic practices, and even establish a data base on the strategic forces of the two sides, which the working group felt was a necessary precondition for virtually any strategic arms control agreement.

The working group predicted reasonable success for the centers. Precedent exists in more than twenty bilateral and multilateral treaties and agreements to which both the United States and the Soviet Union are parties, establishing requirements for exchanges of information, prior notification, special communications links, and other negotiations. One example is the 1972 Incidents at Sea Agreement, which has all but eliminated what used to be frequent and dangerous confrontations between the two superpowers. A 1975 Helsinki Agreement requires notification of certain military maneuvers within 150 miles of East-West borders.

Senator William Bradley said:

The establishment of nuclear crisis centers is so clearly in the interest of both the Soviet Union and the United States that agreement ought not to be difficult to achieve. Unlike many bilateral negotiations, this agreement is readily perceived as a positive sum game: both parties win. If the negotiations on nuclear crisis centers succeed, they might set the stage for superpower agreement on other nuclear nonproliferation and confidence building efforts, now stalled.

The Nuclear Risk Reduction Centers would rely on computers for communicating and interpreting the vast amounts of data that such monitoring bodies must have to function properly. But in the longer run, the computer has a rather different role it could play: an aid to rational reconciliation, which is the subject of the next chapter.

Chapter 16

The Computer and Conciliation

It seems a childlike wish: that adversaries be transformed into collaborators to work together on problems common to them both. In my primary school we celebrated the opening of the new United Nations Building with catchy songs of joy that the nations would be friends, multi-hued boys and girls holding hands around the globe and smiling.

Everybody in the fourth grade was assigned the flag of a U.N. member to paint on butcher paper (mine was Brazil's, bringing back the fourth grade every time I pass the Plaza Hotel in New York City and a Brazilian dignitary is in residence). The best painter among us, June Yoshida, not so long out of a California detention camp for Japanese-Americans, was permitted to paint the U.N.'s own flag. Perhaps she painted as we all did, with hope for better things to come. Understandably, our hope obscured a certain reality, that the fourth-grade pupils of Santa Fe School, Oakland, California, could hardly manage a 10-minute recess without squabbling in the schoolyard. If anybody had pointed out that contradiction to us, I suppose we'd have said, ah, but that's different. *They* have Mrs. Roosevelt: who'd be naughty around her?

To grow up and leave the school grounds of Santa Fe was sadly, and sometimes frighteningly, to outgrow any hope that reconciliation was possible among peoples with such widely disparate assumptions, resources, hopes, and goals as the sovereign nations of the earth. Goodwill and reason seemed quaint anachronisms, superseded by the more urgent realities of short-term self-interest.

Yet some modest experiments in computer-assisted negotiations have begun to suggest that the transformation of adversaries into collaborators, pursuing solutions to their common problems, isn't solely a schoolchild's dream. Groups of people with widely differing perceptions of a problem, its solutions, and compromises, both possible and impossible, have met in conflicts as varied as the correct site for power plant, or a multinational treaty for the equitable disposition of the mineral deposits in the seabed, and have come to reconciliations that were acceptable not just to a minority but to nearly every one of the participants.

Donald B. Straus is a past president of the American Arbitration Association and now heads its research institute. Since the early 1970s he has been interested in the computer as a tool to help decision making among varied participants who are trying to solve very complicated problems: international commercial arbitration, disputes over the delivery of health care, transborder environmental issues, and, most recently, international treaties for mineral rights.

The problems he and his colleagues address are different both in size and complexity from those they were called upon to mediate in the past.

> Environmental energy disputes are less often the distributive kind, which is what you find in labor-management controversies—here's a dollar, and who's going to get how much of it?—and more often caused by the frustration of parties with conflicting interests who cannot fully comprehend the interdependence of the complex issues involved in a planning or a regulatory process.

Thus we take inflexible positions that nearly foreclose constructive solutions. The zero-sum mentality, that any win by you must result in a loss to me, prevails, while the idea that both of us might be winners in the long run is obscure and incredible. We are at an impasse.

Enter the mediator, who is in fact a facilitator; his job is not just to help settle a conflict but to assist all the parties throughout the entire decision process. Whereas in earlier, simpler disputes, certain details could be left to common sense, or precedent, the complexity of these new problems requires constant information, what-if scenarios played out to their plausible conclusions, values and assumptions made explicit, variables factored and re-factored, data validated. Only a computer is capable of doing such a massive task and doing it quickly. Negotiations can't simply stop for a few weeks while statisticians calculate their stochastic models or hydraulic engineers solve their partial differential equations. What can be known must be known now. The rapidity of feedback is one key to the success of the entire process; the interactive nature of the modeling process, which allows participants themselves to sit down and fiddle with the model on the spot, is another. But the most important part of a model's success is that it has been built by the participants.

"One point has to be made over and over again to participants in such a process," Straus says. "The model we use is not a decision-making tool, but rather a tool to support the decision process. The model can't think, evaluate, or make independent selections. It simply applies the decision rules that it has been programmed to use by the participants' prior agreement."

The model doesn't favor one party, because information and assumptions have come from all parties: instead, it provides a consistent framework for all to validate their data and compare results with those expected by others.

Straus and his colleagues warn potential users that the tool can produce results that are damaging to one or another side unless all parties agree that the model is not an oracle but a means to consensus. And effective consensus can come only when humans have confidence in their tools. A best compromise solution can be produced only through the process of human deliberation.

After some pilot tests, computer-aided negotiation was given an early test in a two-day workshop in 1980 under the auspices of the National Power Plant Team of the U.S. Fish and Wildlife Service. Experienced representatives of three states (New Jersey, Maryland, and Pennsylvania) and three special interest groups (utilities, state and federal governments, and environmentalists) participated in the make-believe selection of a power plant site, but they brought their real-life predilections and points of view with them, including a decided preference for things as they'd always been done. As it happened, the numbers of the facilitating staff about matched the number of participants—nearly twenty in each group.

Despite their experience, and despite their preference for doing things in traditional ways, the participants soon discovered, rather to their surprise, that they were all genuinely interested in investigating a common problem. In a major dispute, it was possible to build on limited areas of agreement in order to find other components for further consensus, until the parties themselves agreed that they had pursued the matter to achieve the greatest possible agreement.

The transformation from adversary to collaborator in the problem-solving process is psychologically subtle. At an early stage in the dispute, one of the facilitators brought the various factions together in a room to examine preliminary outputs of the model and to explain how the elements could be changed to produce different solutions. Conflict was muted as people's attention focused on the possible solutions that nobody had seen before. A comment or suggestion from one was followed up and piggybacked by another, without regard to their previous allegiances. For the first time, adversaries realized that they had common objectives, objectives that could be achieved better through collaboration than through conflict. The tool had become nothing less than a vehicle for inducing a change of behavior. From these informal encounters, new bipartisan task forces formed, which triggered the invention of a whole new range of solutions.

There was no magic. Straus's computer-aided mediation offers a workable method to arrive at solutions that are intellectually satisfying, emotionally gratifying, and participatory. How is that accomplished?

In the first place, the nature of computer modeling forced participants to be explicit about data, assumptions, and implicit values. This focused deliberations on major constraints, which, in turn, often uncovered new solutions, alternatives that the participants might not have discovered for themselves. The model could quickly accommodate any condition imposed by the parties at any stage of the negotiations and spell out its implications. It could (and did) serve as a framework for providing a consistent dialogue over various issues. It revealed reasons for changing from one solution to another. In short, it was a fast-moving vehicle to reach agreement on the best compromise solution.

All this was done interactively: sometimes the programmer/analysts provided data on an overnight basis; sometimes the participants themselves sat at computer terminals and with the help of computer graphics saw with their own eyes how variables changed outcomes. The computer converted massive volumes of data and complex interrelationships into terms that humans could deal with.

Though the process could examine more possibilities and accommodate more of the participants' concerns than other processes currently in use, it finally succeeded because the people most directly concerned had participated in producing the model and thus understood what it was doing.

In the final moments of the conference, solutions had been found to all the problems except for 5 gigawatts of disputed capacity. Everyone agreed that the best way to tie up the loose ends was to ask the programmer/analyst team to run the model again. It was agreed that new solutions should include all plant sites that were already part of the consensus solution and that, in addition, the remaining 5 gigawatts of disputed capacity should be located according to criteria that all the parties had already agreed to build into the model. And so it was done.

Never mind that a solution was found within two days to a difficult set of problems with many aspects and legitimate interests to be represented, though that's a happy outcome. The interesting part to me is that the model had so won the confidence of all participants that no question existed in their minds at the end that this was the fairest way to find a lasting compromise everybody could agree on.

But while Straus and his colleagues concluded that the method was promising, they also saw that better methods of introducing and training participants in complex decision-making processes are needed. So are technical capabilities in computers that are better suited to the negotiating process. If every decision maker cannot be trained in computer techniques, then the facilitator team must be more adept at explaining the computing tools and their potentials, must act as intermediaries and communicators. Straus and his colleagues also discovered that they had greatly underestimated the participants' resistance toward new techniques and technology under live or simulated conditions. There was a final problem that emerged writ large when the method was put to its first test in a real, not a laboratory, situation. That was the problem of communicating with constituencies.

The Law of the Sea is a complex set of negotiations sponsored by the United Nations to equitably assign, by treaty, the profits to be made from deep-sea mining. Negotiations began a few years ago in good faith but bogged down immovably over contrary views held by the developed and the less developed countries as to how profitable deep-sea mining really would be, the developed countries claiming that such mining wasn't going to be very profitable at all and the less developed countries concerned that this claim was merely self-serving and ultimately selfish on the part of the developed countries.

As it happened, nearly a decade earlier the World Bank had asked Daniel Nyhart and his colleagues at M.I.T. to provide a model of the potential for profit of deep-sea mining so that the bank could be informed regarding loans to entrepreneurs. James Sebenius, an assistant to Elliot Richardson, who was the U.S. ambassador in charge of negotiations on the Law of the Sea, knew about the Deep Sea Mining Model from his own work at Harvard and M.I.T. and thought that the conflict between the developed nations and the developing nations over the potential profits to be realized from deep-sea mining might be illuminated by this model. He suggested this to Richardson, who was interested, and they approached Singapore's Tommy Koh, chairman of a working group charged with trying to resolve the issues then generally referred to as "financial arrangements" of the Law of the Sea negotiations.

Koh, an urbane and witty man who holds a Harvard Law School degree, had already come to realize that two interrelated problems must be addressed by his working group. One was the tax system, which would be negotiated so that royalties would be paid fairly to the international community; and the second was how the first international public mining venture would be financed. The tax system seemed to him an insuperable obstacle. The seabed mining industry did not exist: how were revenues to be estimated when nobody had any idea how the venture might go?

The M.I.T. model was serendipitous. Koh quickly saw that,

in principle, it could help overcome the many intellectual, political, and psychological barriers that had deadlocked negotiations. He coaxed a number of leaders from the less developed countries to examine the model, sometimes at M.I.T., sometimes at quiet retreats where the model's designers came to explain their assumptions, the model's utility, and its shortcomings. The world leaders were intrigued but skeptical. This had been, after all, an American model, built for the United States Department of Commerce.

But matters were at an impasse and the negotiators were ready to try almost anything. Representatives from the LDCs spent a year tearing the model apart, going into every aspect of it—data, algorithms, assumptions, just as Straus and his team had suggested. That the model was as good and objective a model as anybody was likely to build began to take hold of the skeptics, especially as they saw it criticized by the mining industry and the European Economic Community (in its own computer model, which had been offered, the assumptions were impenetrable). At the end of the year the negotiators had confidence that at least they understood how the M.I.T. model worked and that it was probably as close to reality as they could make it.

Based on that, they returned to the negotiating table, where, among other things, Koh persuaded negotiators to shift away from royalty or fixed payments to profit-sharing, a move he says could never have happened without the information provided by the model. In another case, the Indian delegation, which had insisted on financing the project one way, quickly changed their minds as the figures came from the model showing that their scheme wasn't reasonable. Other negotiations moved very quickly, and an agreement was soon reached that everybody felt was fair.

"Now that's the good side of the story," Straus says, "and I think that's an excellent example of how these things could be used. Richardson, his assistant James Sebenius, and Tommy Koh all have said that this might be one of the most powerful instruments that we've ever seen for international negotiations. The bad side, as you well know," he said to me, "is that the United States, in the Reagan administration and then in the Senate, turned down the treaty because they didn't think it was workable, fair, or economically reasonable."

Straus is a genial man, and his long years of labor mediation have left their mark: he strives to be fair.

Now—I'm speculating—it seems to me that in the use of computer modeling for this purpose, everything that was done by Ambassador Koh and Ambassador Richardson and the M.I.T. group was correct for the *negotiators*. Missing was the link between the negotiators, as they moved along in understanding, and their constituents. Ideally, you would have had interim repetitions of the negotiations back to the U.S. Senate, back to the governments of the other nations, so that as this went along, all the decision-makers were brought up to speed.

In my experience, the analogy with labor relations is apt: very often negotiators come to an agreement and the labor movement (usually it's labor that lacks those close communications) moves further than they thought they would when they stirred up the troops, and so they can't sell the agreement. They get repudiated. That's precisely what happened in the Senate. And so somehow or other, when you use a powerful tool like the computer to manage complexity and help the negotiators come to a greater understanding of their problems, you've moved away from normal intuition and come up with some counterintuitive thinking. If your ultimate decision-makers haven't been brought along, you're out ahead of your troops.

In a panel at the New York Academy of Sciences where most of the principals discussed their experience, Straus was asked whether equal access to data by all parties changes the very nature of negotiations. Yes, he believed it did.

It can have the effect of moving the adversarial attitude of the parties more towards collaboration, more towards what the academicians call a positive-sum result rather than a zero sum. One of the newer skills that all of us are going to have to learn as we broaden our skills from dispute resolution to the management of the entire decision cycle is to be sensitive when parties are ready to become more collaborative. In these large-scale and complex issues there are times when the parties can see an opportunity, for their own best interests, not for altruism but for their own best interests, to move towards a collaborative study of a problem rather than withholding information and being purely adversarial. Decision-cycle facilitators must be alert for such opportunities and must be ready to encourage them. Mr. Richardson touched on one aspect of this and so did Ambassador Koh—and this was the *quality* of the agreement that was reached. An agreement, *any* agreement, used to be the only thing that mediators were interested in. But it is increasingly the quality of the agreement that is important as the issues addressed become more complex and far-reaching in their impacts. The interactive and joint use of the M.I.T. model indeed changed the nature of the negotiations, but it has been suggested that the quality of the eventual agreement was also better than it might have been without it. I think this is an essential point to emphasize.

At the same panel, Elliot Richardson talked about other possibilities for international computer-aided negotiations. Like M.I.T.'s Daniel Nyhart, who had already addressed the question, Richardson agreed that the problems most amenable to this kind of negotiation were those where numerical values could be assigned—economic problems being one obvious example, agricultural commodities, pollution liabilities and compensation, and transnational uses of science and technology being some others. But he added that one further essential factor was recognizing those issues that turned on, or were significantly affected by, a question of fact that, once established, would contribute to consensus on a policy or choice.

Second, he went on, the problem must be of a kind that can be handled by computer, which means that it must have quantifiable variables, numerous enough—and the data involved voluminous enough—so that it's worthwhile to do it by computer rather than by some simpler mechanism.

These limitations are surely significant, he went on, and yet committing a problem to this kind of exercise has the added advantage of insulating it from the more emotional and value-laden factors surrounding other elements of the debate, thereby contributing to a more rational process. "I think that this can be a secondary value of the use of computer models in multilateral negotiations." On the one side, such limitations make it possible to deal with the rational issues that directly concern the model; on the other, they allow "an approach to the resolution of other issues in an atmosphere of rationality and increasing trust."

And then there are the special conditions of a democracy. Straus was recently invited to spend a half year in Vienna at the International Institute for Advanced Systems Analysis to share his ideas on computer-aided negotiations with representatives from all over the world. "When I talk to my colleagues at IIASA about the necessity for participation of all the negotiators, many of them, especially my colleagues from the socialist countries, think it's the most ludicrous, funny, archaic aberration on the part of Americans talking theoretical democratic policies. How do you expect the average citizen, or even a non-technical person, to understand these models? they say. What we do is put faith in our scientists."

Whether because he is an American or because he isn't convinced specialists have all the answers, Straus isn't prepared to put his faith in scientists alone. Within IIASA, for example, Straus found what he called tribal warfare between all sorts of specialists. The builders of small-scale models were ignored by the builders of large-scale models. Among the large-scale builders, the large-scale clean-air model builders ignored the large-scale forestry model builders.

"And when I suggested that maybe clean air had something to do with forestry, that the two models might be able to supplement each other, they first pooh-poohed the idea; then they said that even if it was a good idea, they were too far along in the modeling process ever to be able to talk to each other." When Straus suggested that at least talks be started between large-scale model builders and the builders of highly interactive smaller models, "everybody was so intent on saying my model can beat your model that it required more mediation than I was capable of doing in my short stay in Vienna!"

The idea of bringing in nonexperts to participate early in the model-building process offended nearly everybody. "The scientists themselves felt under too much pressure to spend time with the nonprofessionals, explaining things to them, while they were doing this hard work of programming; it was a distraction for them; they didn't see the value in it. It was also a tremendous threat to the Soviets. When I finally gained their confidence, they said to me, in effect, if you expect us low-level political people to come to a place like IIASA and work on a model that comes to conclusions that might differ from those we were sent to support, and then go back with these different conclusions, this is a one-way ticket to Siberia. You're not going to get people like us to do such things, because it's suicidal, *unless* people at the very top tell us to do so."

Straus shrugs. He is a man used to the facts of life. "Out of this came my flight of imagination, maybe the most unrealistic thing I ever thought of, which is that we will probably not, either domestically or internationally, make maximum use of the computer as the powerful tool it can be until there is—and here I borrow Thomas Kuhn's phrase—a paradigm shift in attitudes, which says, in effect, that for my self-interest I had better first understand how the system works before I try to win a presently perceived but perhaps erroneous victory. That is counter our culture, counter our intuitions, and would be a very hard sell. It may even be wrong."

But I sense Straus doesn't really believe it's wrong; he is merely acknowledging the obstacles to bringing it all about. The obstacles are large, but I don't believe they're intractable. More important, the ideas might be counter to our cultures and even counter to our intuitions, but they take their energy from something deep and precious in the human spirit. When such negotiations have succeeded, as they did with the energy negotiators and almost did with the 120 nations involved in the Law of the Sea Treaty, I think they have done so because they rely on an appealing and highly adaptive set of human qualities. We like to solve problems. Puzzles delight us, mysteries charm us, games intrigue us. To put it another way, excessive tension distresses us and demands resolution. Curiosity drives us.

Computer-aided negotiations have helped orchestrate—and the word is chosen deliberately—an ensemble. The thrill here is not in individual performance (which certainly has its pleasures in other circumstances) but in being a part of something transcendent. Whether Straus and his colleagues intended it or not, in computer-aided negotiations they have tapped into a deep and powerful human capacity to cooperate, to fashion a whole greater than the sum of its parts.

Perhaps he has intended it. Straus is the exemplary American aristocrat. Family privilege would have permitted him an idle life;

instead, he has worked through a long and productive life to bring
reason to human affairs, whether in labor-management relations
(his official career) or as a member of enormous numbers of boards
and committees, ranging from population control to systems design. No human meanness, folly, or weakness escapes him (nor
at this stage can it possibly surprise him) and yet he harbors hope
and good humor.

Once I remarked on his serene and unflagging imposition of
reason upon human conflict. "That's a real insult to a lot of people,"
he said evenly. I agreed, but said I meant it as a compliment, and
expected he knew that and moreover had taken it as praise. Then
he laughed heartily and conceded the point.

On the issue of computer-aided negotiations toward arms control, he said with considerable feeling: "I wish we'd stop talking
about arms control. I think it's counterproductive and a no-win
situation. How you're ever going to work out with the adversaries
a package that consists of everything from rifles to Star Wars, and
say now we're equal, seems to me to be a no-win goal. I go back
to my early days in labor mediation: if the parties were talking
about nothing but strikes and lockouts and how long they could
withstand a work stoppage, I would say to them, look, this isn't
what you're really concerned with, you're concerned with wages,
hours, and working conditions. Unless I can get you talking about
wages, hours, and working conditions, you're going to have a
strike. And they would."

What would be the equivalent of wages, hours, and working
conditions in arms limitation? "The way I put the question is, what
are the issues that you're willing to risk a war with Russia over?
Are they territorial? Economic division of the Middle East oil?
Environmental concerns? Human rights? Control of the deep-sea
mines? Political control of El Salvador? It seems to me these are
issues you can talk about. Bite-size chunks of war-peace issues.
The peace movement may have moved into a tragic dead end by
making us sit down in all these little enclaves and ask whether we
are on par with each other in missiles and MIRVs and whatnot.
You can never make an even bundle of that. But you can negotiate
simple, concrete things."

The computer has demonstrated its possibilities as a powerful
tool to shift people from being adversaries to being collaborators.
Used skillfully, it can illuminate motives and goals and redirect

dialogue away from rhetoric and argument and toward the task of inventing new solutions, increasing flexibility, and starting to find solutions that are agreeable to a broad spectrum of concerned individuals. Used unskillfully, or without the participation of many different constituencies, computer-aided negotiation degenerates to nothing more than what Straus calls "the battle of the print-outs."

"If we can turn these computers into aids for finding a solution to problems we have, then they can be a great force for good," Straus told me. "The difficulty of talking about arms is that there's no way we're going to share data to build a model on arms that's designed to do anything except obfuscate. But we might be able to sit down and build a model of pollution, or the flow of Middle East oil, or the trade between Latin America and the Soviets, or any of these other issues. In such cases, we might just be able to sit down and model together."

Chapter 17

Computing in Senegal

The West African republic of Senegal, which lies on the outermost tip of Africa, nearest the New World—and so once served as an infamous depot for humans who were to be transported into slavery in the Western Hemisphere—is these days a worldly amalgam of indigenous cultures, the French colonial legacy, and, perhaps most fortunate of all, the vision of a single man, Léopold Sédar Senghor, who served for twenty years as the nation's first president until he retired voluntarily in 1981.

Senghor, a distinguished poet as well as an accomplished statesman, held a dream for his Senegal. It was a dream of African socialism based on African realities, which is to say theistic (Senghor is a Roman Catholic; a majority of his countrymen are Moslem) and free of excessive materialism. It would be an open, democratic, and humanistic socialism, leading in time to participation in a planetary civilization of peace and harmony among all humankind.

The dream endures, but the African realities are harsh.

Senegal's annual per capita income is about $320, not unusually low compared with those of other emerging nations (although the figures are a bit misleading, since the discrepancy between city dwellers and country people is very great). Only 5 percent of Senegal's adults are literate, and its population grows at the rate of 2.6 percent a year. Over the past decade, persistent drought has pushed the Sahel (an Arabic word that means the border of the Sahara) south at the horrifying rate of 3 miles a year, causing the pastoral peoples who live in the northern part of the country to push south themselves in search of arable land to cultivate. Famine has appeared. Thus rural people have fled to the capital city of Dakar, whose population grows at 6 percent per year, and 60 percent of the city's inhabitants live in slums and squatter settlements. Unemployment, as much as it can be measured in Dakar, has increased dramatically. Unlike its West African neighbor Nigeria, Senegal has no petroleum. Some phosphate deposits exist, and the French government has encouraged investments by French manufacturers. A free trade zone that takes advantage of low labor costs has been created to attract still more foreign investment. But Senegal's main product is peanuts, and attempts to diversify have not been altogether successful. The West African franc, tied to the French franc, has rapidly been losing value against other world currencies. Those are the African realities.

Yet Senghor's dream is nowhere more alive than in a brave, almost quixotic project that the national government is sponsoring under the auspices of the École Normale Supérieure, the National Teachers College, to bring computer literacy to the schoolchildren of Senegal.

I have asked to see this project with great curiosity and not a little skepticism. I do not know what I will find. My major worry is what might be called the boom box phenomenon, my own shorthand for that depressing tendency developing countries have of picking up the most meretricious pieces of Western trash, confusing gadgets with substance. (On a long air trip around Africa I have watched those enormous radios debark at every stop and said a silent prayer of thanksgiving that each one in Africa represents one less to assault my ears on the streets of New York.) The boom box phenomenon is hardly limited to radios; in East Africa, an entire class of the indigenous wealthy are known, in Swahili, as *wabenzi*, the tribe of Mercedes-Benz. In fairness, it must be said that the inverse also applies: the tourists go home with equally meretricious trash to mark their contact with African cultures. The question is, Will I see computers playing the same role?

The morning I am to visit the installation, I awaken thinking for the first time in years of *triage*, the old battlefield medical tactic, which says forget about those who have no hope of making it, forget about those who can make it on their own, and concentrate care on those you can really help. So much of west and central Africa seems to fall into the first category. I am apprehensive that the Senegal computer literacy project will fall into that first category too.

And so I taxi out of central Dakar to the École Normale Supérieure, where I will meet my host, Mme. Fatimata Sylla, a young woman who is in the process of earning a master's degree at M.I.T. in computer education, and who is, luckily for me, home in Dakar for the holidays and willing to show me around. I wait for her in the school's computer laboratory, which looks like any school's computer laboratory, with perhaps ten Apple IIe's connected to a variety of screens, wires here and there, instructions on the blackboard, motley scuffed chairs and tables.

As is usual in Africa, I am warmly welcomed by everybody, the Africans I meet both here and in East Africa being wonderfully tactile people who touch and kiss each other easily and, given the least encouragement, will include visitors in their tactile greetings too. For myself, I gladly encourage.

I have only spoken to Fatimata Sylla on the telephone, and so I am charmed to meet her, a strikingly handsome woman dressed in the Senegalese national gown called *le grand boubou*, a sumptuous set of draperies that, as the afternoon goes on and we move through school yards ankle-deep in sand and dust, I admire more and more. (I have come from two weeks in the bush, and look it.) Her hair is in tiny braids, elaborately massed in a high chignon. She might not soon be taken for somebody who can tear down a failing Apple IIe, diagnose its problem, and repair it on the spot, though that is one of her many accomplishments.

I am taken to meet the director of the school, Mr. Sega Seck Fall. After a few pleasantries, I ask him how it is that his country has decided to undertake a computer literacy project, given its other very obvious and surely more pressing problems. Politely he answers me: "When there is a tool that can be used by mankind, we must do our best to master it. I am convinced that computers are one of those tools." It is during the same conversation that Mr. Boubacai Kâne, head of the research center of the École Normale Supérieure, observes that with the computer, for the first time in the history of civilization, we are all starting at the same time. It's a provocative thought, and I come back to it again and again.

On the grand scale of human civilization, he is quite right. While the United States, for example, is slowly pursuing computer literacy, the effort is probably comparable, once scaled for the size of the two countries, to Senegal's project. Moreover, Senegal is not recapitulating the experience of the United States or other developed countries, starting out with vacuum tube machines, say, and moving then to transistors: many a first worlder is coming to computer literacy on the same machine at the same time and, indeed, using a dialect of the same language, in this case, LOGO, a language specifically designed to allow novices (especially children) to gain mastery over the machine as soon as possible.

Europeans achieved widespread literacy enough to matter centuries before Africans did, which changed the histories of both continents. Nobody wants Africa to pay the penalties of such a long lag in computer literacy. In a sense Kâne is correct: we are all beginning together. Still, I am troubled by other problems, such as how a nation like Senegal will ever provide the ordinary prerequisites of computing, such as a reliable source of electricity or a clean, well-lighted place to work in.

There are immediate financial problems too. In principle, the Senegal government is very enthusiastic about this project—it was originally the brainchild of Jacques Diouff, the former minister of Scientific and Technical Research, and in late 1981, he and a delegation from the École flew to New York City to seek support from the LOGO Corporation for the novel idea of bringing computer literacy to a country where ordinary literacy is a luxury. Only later, with the formation of France's Centre Mondial Informatique et Ressource Humaine, did the Senegal project begin receiving some help from there as well. Jacques Diouff's successor as Senegal's minister of Scientific and Technical Research, Balla Moussa Daffe, also takes a special interest in the computer literacy project. But the project is funded only from year to year, its finances dependent on the nation's revenues, which are unreliable.

There are other kinds of problems. The software provided by Apple LOGO cannot be translated easily into Wolof and other indigenous languages and, in any event, is often inappropriate for the purposes of the Senegal project. The small group trained at the Centre Mondial in Paris works on these problems as they can, but their main purpose, as they see it, is to train teachers in the primary schools; the job of training teachers and producing new software at the same time is a taxing one.

Indeed, at the laboratory, I have noticed a computer-generated cartoon on one of the Apple monitors that shows a stick figure of a farmer plowing his field, crops coming up, rain coming down from the sky, and the harvest. One of the staff members at the École has designed it, intended for teaching children not the principles of agriculture but the notion of *process* in ways they can relate to.

The time comes to visit the schools. Four primary schools have been selected as pilot projects, all of them in the city of Dakar. They represent a cross section of society, for they include, at one extreme, the elite Franco-Senegalese School in the suburb of Fann, which is for the children of Senegal's government officials and for children of foreign nationals posted to Senegal; two more middling schools; and at the other extreme, the Dakar equivalent of a ghetto school, Ouagou-Niayes School #1, where 1,200 students are squeezed into 14 classrooms (which works out to about 86 children per classroom and teacher). Each school has been given four Apple IIe's, and key teachers have been chosen to receive instruction in LOGO at the École so that they can go back and instruct other teachers and, of course, the children.

At the Franco-Senegalese School, a Richard Neutra-like set of buildings that might be found anywhere in California, we are welcomed by the principal, M. Roux, who himself is a computer enthusiast, and bought himself an Apple IIe for his own use on his last trip to France. He leads us into the school's computer room, explaining to us that half his pupils are French and that the other half are a mixture of Senegalese and thirty other nationalities. Ten specially selected children each receive four and a half hours a week on the computer, and after some initial instruction in LOGO, they are left alone to do what they wish, an instructor standing by for consultations if needed. (In theory, this is how it should work in the other schools too, but as we are to see, there are some obstacles to that.)

As we talk, and the dust cover is removed from the computers (one long cover for the four of them, oddly reminiscent of the dragons in a Chinese New Year's parade), four boys come tumbling in—three black and one white—and sit down immediately at their machines. They are obviously veterans; they ask for their favorite software and get to work immediately. LOGO allows children to write programs that can display interesting and entertaining graphics, and in no time the usual stars and wheels are appearing on the monitors, though one child has written a program that answers questions about arithmetic, and is pleased to show it off to the visitors. In short, we might be in any good primary school in the developed countries.

Fatimata Sylla suggests it is time to move on to one of the Grade B schools, and so we do, through crowded streets that have not only motor vehicles but donkey carts, merchants with live chickens, women carrying cargoes on their heads. Along the way we happen to pass an outdoor class of some twenty absolutely still four- or five-year-olds, crouched on the ground in front of an old blackboard on a tripod, where the caftanned instructor is teaching in Arabic.

At the two Grade B schools, the degree of shabbiness seems extreme; we sink in sand as we walk across the school yards (my eyes as much on Fatimata's delicate negotiations in her gown and pretty shoes as on my surroundings). The school buildings are in need of paint and sometimes repair. We are always ceremoniously introduced to the principal, by now men in caftans and skullcaps, men with great presence and sense of the dignity of their positions and, by extension, the importance of education. Like Jews, Moslems revere study and the book.

One of those principals, an elderly man getting on to retirement, and with far fewer teeth in his head than he must have had in his prime, beams proudly when it is explained to me that he too is taking instruction in LOGO. I am frankly impressed at his intellectual courage, and say so.

Because of space problems, because of electrical current problems, not all four computers can be set up and running at either of the Grade B schools (two seem to be working at one location and only one at another), but the machines that are working are being put to use. I stand behind a schoolgirl who is doing her first LOGO program that very day, squealing with happiness when the machine does what she has instructed. We can't help but share her joy. The room where she works is in reality a dilapidated alcove; with the visitors and the instructor, there is barely room to move.

At last we move on to the poorest school, for me the most

moving place of all I see—as I said earlier, 1,200 students jammed into 14 classrooms with 14 teachers (plus 2 Arabic teachers and a handful of substitute teachers). The children in the classroom we visit are squeezed three to an old-fashioned two-pupil desk, but they politely rise as we enter and are seated quietly and orderly again moments later. Here as much as anywhere is the sense of the truly serious undertaking that learning is. Despite inconceivable conditions, the children are clean (as is nearly everybody, though the dust is thick in Dakar and blows incessantly), attentive, and eager. Face to face with those fresh and hopeful youngsters, mindful of the famine that afflicts this country and the lepers we have passed outside the school-yard gate, I also confront the paradox of computing here and elsewhere in poor places: it cannot be done; it must be done.

The sad news is that there is no space in the overcrowded tumble-down classrooms at Ouagou-Niayes School #1 to set up the four computers the school has received, though the instructors are eager and ready. Funds have been promised from the government for a special shed for the machines, but nobody seems to know exactly when those funds will materialize. Meanwhile, the Apples, wrapped tenderly in plastic and unused, are stored in flimsy cabinets.

Is this boom-boxery? I am unsure. In a discussion with the brave and gallant little band of six or seven at the École who are training teachers and adapting the software, I ask them what they see as the purpose of this project beyond the immediate goals of teaching forty (or twenty or only ten) lucky pupils to program. They discuss this with great liveliness for a few moments and arrive at a consensus. The main purpose of the project, they say, is to see how they can adapt this new technology to their culture, so that their children will be prepared to use it. "We are experimenting in different ways," they remind me, "and this is research. We do not know which way will prove to be best."

As they see it, there are four groups they must answer to. First are ordinary citizens. Those who are educated and understand that computers are important are still skeptical, worried that this computing project (especially if it expands) will cause reductions in other important parts of the Senegalese national budget.

Second are teachers. Those who are exposed to the technology are enthusiastic and understand that the task must be done regardless of the difficulties. But the majority of teachers, who, of course, haven't been exposed to computing, are highly skeptical: is this going to be the same as audio-visuals, which were touted as a panacea and weren't? (I laugh, and tell them that the same debate is going on in the United States.)

Third is the government, which is trying to sustain and renovate the entire nation, using computing in different sectors of the bureaucracy, such as the Ministry of Finance (I am told that IBM has donated a number of PCs to train users in the government). As I have been assured before, in principle the government is *for* this project in the schools, but finances do get in the way.

Finally, there are the children, who love the project and show no resistance whatever; indeed, the computer excites and engages them.

"To the first group who object, the ordinary citizens, we tell them that we have no choice," one of the project leaders says to me. "We must do this. To the second group, the teachers who worry that this is just one more piece of silly technology, we say no, that the language of computing teaches children to learn by themselves, creating their own tasks, solving their own problems. We also tell them that unlike books, unlike films and records, there is a degree of interactivity here that makes the learning process qualitatively different from anything else. To the government—well, what can we say to the government?"

They express some ordinary longings: how useful a network would be in Francophone Africa for exchanging ideas and information; how they hope to introduce other languages, such as BASIC and Pascal; how they would welcome help from American experts to adapt this Apple technology to their own culture, especially translations of programs into Wolof and other indigenous languages; how, if this project is at all successful, they hope to move on to kindergartens, to handicapped children.

I admire their dedication in the face of what seem monumental impediments and tell them so. And to myself, for all the doubts I have, I wonder if what is happening in Senegal is after all any more improbable than what happened in a garage in Cupertino, California, a few years ago, when two post-adolescents brought the computer home in every sense. The world is full of such stories; little is downright impossible, no matter how farfetched it might seem.

Chapter 18

A Wider View of
Third-World Computing

After my visit to Senegal, I called on my old friend Professor Raj Reddy of Carnegie-Mellon University. In addition to his professorial duties, Reddy heads the university's celebrated Robotics Institute and, in addition to all that, has quietly and pro bono taken on the job of chief scientist at France's Centre Mondial. He flies from Pittsburgh to Paris once a month and virtually single-handedly has rescued the Centre from its early political and personality-clash morass and turned it into a going concern.

"Raj brought order and structure to what was utter chaos," says his friend Edward Ayensu, a highly respected biologist at the Smithsonian, who is originally from Ghana and who also advises the Centre. Gone are the grandiose plans for special technology, the exclusive use of LOGO, the enervating personal disputes of the earliest days of the Centre. These days, once every six months, groups of about thirty representatives from countries all over the world are brought to the Centre for an intensive five-week course in computing. During those five weeks they learn not only five different computer languages but also some applications programs, like spreadsheet analysis and word processing, and they learn how to maintain and repair a variety of personal computers including Apples and IBM PCs. The representatives are then sent back to their own countries with twenty to thirty machines (and selected spare parts) to use as they see fit.

Among the criteria for choosing those who will attend perhaps the most important is that a representative's own nation be willing and able to cover local expenses—housing the machines when they arrive, distributing them around the countryside, and paying for their maintenance. This is one of the ways the Centre has of measuring a country's dedication to the proposition that computing is important. Other expenses, including the cost of the machines and the cost of training the delegates, are covered by the Centre, which at present is funded by the French government at an official level of about $15 million per year (since half of that goes for taxes, the working budget is actually $7.5 million).

"Is this the right way to go about it?" Reddy asks. "Nobody knows the correct solution. But if we wait around for the correct solution to show up, it may never come."

I murmur worries about boom-boxery, about cultural imperialism, about the heartbreaking impossibilities.

Reddy laughs, the laugh of a man who's been through it all, since he himself was raised in a village outside the southern Indian city of Bangalore, where the school was so poor the children weren't three to a desk but had no desks at all, nor slates either, and so he learned to write in the sand with a stick. I can see I am about to learn a few things.

"Do you know what priorities in the third world are?" he asks gently. "You may not like this but here's what they are: first and foremost is entertainment. Have you any idea how *boring* village life is? As a friend of mine puts it, for most people, the only form of recreation is procreation. And we all know how bad that is for the world. In countries where the per capita income is a hundred dollars a year, a peasant will spend ten dollars of that income on entertainment, and he'd spend even more if he possibly could. So people come to the Centre with the idea that they're going to have a wonderful entertainment medium in the computer, and they're right."

I make some objections, citing the integrity of the old cultures as opposed to the chaos of the new, and detect, even as I'm saying it, a certain condescension in my attitude that I hadn't been aware of before.

"Change, change, change is here to stay. And I say that's good. I say send out *Dallas* and *Dynasty* and any old thing you want that will shake people up and make them question the way they've always done things. Resurgence—and oh, the third world needs resurgence—only comes from dissatisfaction. It doesn't come from exhortation or from being patronized by outsiders. Culture isn't necessarily spoiled or homogenized as a consequence of technology. The European cultures have all enjoyed the same technologies for years, but they're very distinct from each other; they do things their own way. It will be the same in the third world. People say, why are you doing this when half the machines will end up in the hands of bureaucrats? I say, good, the other half will get out to the villages. People say, why are you doing this when the witch doctor or some other local despot will hold on to that knowledge and use it to consolidate his own power? I say better the witch doctor than nobody. Sheikh Yamani of Saudi Arabia took me aside at a conference a few years ago and told me what terrible effects television had on the Bedouins in his country. Now they weren't working eighteen hours a day but stayed up watching TV until midnight. People were getting divorces. What on earth would the effects of computing be? Good, I said, would you rather people worked eighteen hours a day and stayed unhappy? Maybe he would; I wouldn't. And we each face change ourselves. If somebody had told me twenty five years ago that I would have a daughter who would insist on arranging her own marriage and, what's more, that I'd go along with that, I wouldn't have believed it for a moment. But that's a change I've had to deal with. At least, I'm trying to!"

Reddy went on to say that he had no interest in forcing the technology on anybody. For example, he doubted the new Islamic theocracies such as Iran or Pakistan would seek computing. It didn't matter to him; he was too busy thinking about those nations that wanted the technology. He didn't even care why they wanted it. That was up to them; with this technology, there were many paths to follow. Each nation would have to decide what was best for it, molding and melding the technology into its own culture as it saw fit. Then he resumed talking about third-world priorities.

"After entertainment, the next priority is health. Well, we can make a difference there too. We're just putting together a little computerized first-aid advisor that we'll send out with a medicine chest, a kind of medicine by the numbers. A villager can come to the paramedic who has this program and report his symptoms— 'I have this headache.' The paramedic, who by the way needn't have more than a fifth-grade education, reports this to the program, which then inquires how long the headache has been going on. If it hasn't been too long, the program advises the patient to take three capsules out of the box labeled number 71 and come back the next morning. If the headache persists, the program can give further advice—'stronger medicine in box 76'— or even 'this is serious enough to go and see a doctor.' Of course, the program can keep medical records automatically, so that it can identify persistent symptoms that might be signs of something more serious, and tell the patient that he gets headaches so often and so regularly, even though his ache isn't unbearable, that maybe he'd better see a doctor. It isn't a very complicated program, and pretty soon the person who's using it won't even need it any more, because he'll have memorized the tree structure that makes up the program's set of questions, and, all of a sudden, we've trained a paramedic. Great. That will be out in the field by the end of 1984. It's going to Chad first. Want to go see it in Chad?" I say thanks anyhow.

"The next priority is agriculture. People don't understand that the way they've been farming for hundreds, even thousands, of years isn't any good any more. Climatic conditions change, the population grows, all sorts of things happen. But farming doesn't change. What the computer can do is create learning by example. Suppose we distribute little expert systems in aquaculture, how to get lots of protein by farming fish instead of hunting and gathering them. Okay, says the one entrepreneurial fellow in town, I like that idea. The computer says great; I can teach you how to do this, and I can negotiate a loan for you from the government so you can get started. And I can get the raw materials purchased and delivered to your village, all right? And the dynamics of village life are such that as soon as one person is making a hundred rupees more than his neighbor, then his neighbor is going to want to follow his example.

"Or what about arid area agriculture? The Israelis are experts at this; they can make things grow with a tiny fraction of the water that most agriculture requires. Well, that expertise ought to be spread, and it can be by means of the computer. If we're talking about my real dream, which is a village information center in every village that includes not only a computer but also videodisks and a dish to communicate via satellite, then we're talking about communicating information like that to the world: no two-, or five-, or ten-year lag in knowledge but instant dissemination when and where you need it. That's a very expensive proposition right now, maybe $30,000 for a two-way satellite link, but we could bring it down to $1,000 with economies of scale, and then such a village center could be self-supporting, with people paying maybe four cents for access to information. However, we're starting on a much smaller scale."

He comes at last to education. "What we need in education is the microversity. We want to bring quality education to everyone who wants it. The first priority in the third world is vocational education. Okay, we conceive of a place where you can train, working not only with an intelligent computer program but also with a human tutor who knows something about the subject. When the student asks a question that neither the program nor the tutor can answer, the tutor has access to the next-higher level of human expertise and so on up the line. The advantage of the computer is that it can give *experiential* learning in the form of computer animation, slides, what-if problems and so on, and we know that experiential learning penetrates and sticks in the human mind the way book learning just doesn't. So instead of an expensive laboratory, we have an electronic laboratory where a student can perform all sorts of simulations of experiments, including things he'd never be able to do in real life because they're too expensive or too dangerous or take too much time or whatever. We've also got an electronic library project starting up at the Centre so that we can really carry these projects out."

I express concern about the problem of infrastructure: the villages he speaks of have no electricity, and even a fifth-grade education is rare in many places. "True," Reddy agrees, "but those problems all have technological fixes"—Reddy too has been John McCarthy's student—"if we're willing to push a bit. The technology is within our grasp to make very rugged, self-perpetuating computers—maybe through solar power, for example—that you can speak to in any human language. And that wouldn't be good for only the third world, by the way; space exploration has the same needs."

When I ask him why he is doing this, expecting some reference to his own third-world beginnings, he just laughs. "I don't know. I suppose I should tell you how important it is for the poor people of the world, but I don't think that would be enough to motivate me. I'm interested in the problem, and this looks like a good way to solve it. It may not be. As for the French, they're doing it in their own self-interests too, and I think that's just great. I don't trust excessive high-mindedness."

I tell him how moved I have been by the Senegal project, the collective courage people show in the face of high challenge, high risk. Is there any way I can help? "Help begin the debate," he says promptly, "the debate about the right thing to do. How can we conduct as many experiments as possible? For we aim to teach people to solve problems for themselves, not to give up when the going is hard. And we do that because we know that knowledge is power, and we're trying to find a way to communicate the right knowledge, whatever that might be."

With variations—some of them frankly profound—the Senegal experience is being repeated all over the planet. UNESCO and other United Nations groups have funded major projects that encourage developing countries to computerize; some nations have bilateral agreements with other nations; in some countries individual scientists are pitching in to help; some firms, such as IBM, donate equipment and help train users. The Centre Mondial is but one such effort to bring about computer literacy in the less developed countries.

Julian Bogod has described the enormous gaps that exist between the developed and the developing countries (a group that, as he points out, is far from homogeneous). These include the systems gap, which is to say the systematization of software, hardware, and social organization that is taken for granted in developed countries and not at all for granted in the rest of the world.

Then there is the education gap, which Bogod sees as the principal barrier to successful development. Most developing countries lack a level of general education that will permit the population to participate in a system-based culture; they lack a sufficiently large pool of trained minds to form a source of computer practitioners; they lack a level of higher education to mature the nation's computer scientists, professionals, and teachers and provide "a level of excellence to which the computer professionals may aspire" (a problem not unknown in developed countries, I should add) and a level of technical training for such people as systems analysts, programmers, operators, and engineers to support the growth of applications. The less developed countries also usually lack a level of management sophistication where computer methods can be successfully introduced.

Next is the technology gap, a thicket of experience and expenditures that are beyond the means of most developing countries. (Even when money is available for licensing arrangements, some countries face intense political opposition to trafficking with multinationals, as Nathaniel Leff has pointed out; and promoting local electronics may impede the growth of other important development objectives, such as domestic food production.)

There is the applications gap, which is the difference in priorities between advanced and developing countries. As we have seen, entertainment, food, health care, and education are simply different matters in the developing countries than elsewhere.

Finally, Bogod mentions the political gap, that tension between the developing countries' desire to increase their own competence and self-sufficiency and their need to import expertise from the developed countries. Many in developing countries worry that the information gap will be like petroleum, an instrument for dictatorship by the haves to the have-nots.

I do not know how to bring Léopold-Sédar Senghor's dream to reality—nor even the more modest dreams of Fatimata Sylla or the somewhat less modest dreams of Raj Reddy. But I believe they are worthy dreams for the human race, and hope against hope for their realization.

Chapter 19

Computing in the Soviet Union

Like a tale from Chekhov, computing in the Soviet Union is complex, oblique, and not always what it seems on the surface. By turns, it's comical, bittersweet, and perturbing. Interpretations abound, seeming to contradict each other, when in fact they reflect facets of a many-sided whole. For if computers are making a revolution everywhere else, in the Soviet Union, champion of revolutions, the effects are more ambiguous.

There are Western authorities who assert that the computer revolution is simply bypassing the Soviet Union, because the Communist system is incompatible with the decentralization of information and power that computers introduce—in a political system that registers typewriters and forbids photocopying, the computer might pose the ultimate threat to the established state.

"It appears that George Orwell was simply wrong in *1984* when he indicated that modern technology would allow the state to become a 'Big Brother' checking every activity of its citizens," writes M.I.T.'s Loren Graham after a recent visit to the Soviet Union. "The new computers demand voluminous, accurate data and the decentralized utilization of that information in ways that mean that citizens will be following 'Big Brother,' not the other way around."

196

George Kennan raises the question more mildly and courteously in a letter to a Soviet friend: "I have also not mentioned the profound doubts I have always entertained about . . . the inadequacy of your form of socialism as a means of confronting the demands of a modern, technologically highly developed industrial society."

Perhaps. But as we have already seen, the protean machine adapts to many styles. If this is true of individuals, it is just as true of organizations, whether firms or nation-states.

Seymour E. Goodman, a professor of management information systems, management and policy at the University of Arizona, who has spent many years studying Soviet computing, writes:

"The Soviet vision of using computing as a means of implementing more effective centralized control on a national scale is neither hopelessly ill-conceived nor unattainable (to some extent at least) by the end of the century. Furthermore, this goal could possibly be achieved concurrently with a considerable amount of politically acceptable economic decentralization."

American scholars who follow Soviet affairs closely report debates, dissent, voices that suggest computers can save Soviet centralization, not destroy it, and at the same time push the Soviet Union into a position in the world economy more fitting to that nation's size and importance, if only the machines are allowed to function properly. Other voices in the Soviet Union argue that releasing such control, decentralizing, is much too risky and invites bourgeois individualism and other un-Soviet behavior.

These are the two extremes, and no one can predict where between them the Soviets will choose to go. At present the Soviets have no clear idea what implications computing technology has for them—nor, for that matter, does anybody—but as Goodman points out, Western capitalist societies and the Japanese have various mechanisms, markets as an example, for effective control, whereas the Soviets, although they have means for control too, are at present moving very conservatively, waiting to see.

"Here's one of the most interesting controversies to come along in the Soviet Union in a while," says Marshall Shulman, former undersecretary of state and now head of Columbia University's

Harriman Institute of Soviet Affairs. The debate is not merely technological, Shulman adds, but stretches across ideological, political, and cultural lines and may end up having some of the profoundest effects on that nation since World War II.

But whether the computer will save or destroy Soviet society (surely neither extreme) or have any effect at all depends first upon how well the Soviets develop their computer industry.

"How well are the Soviets doing in computing?" Goodman asks. "It depends how you measure it. The Soviet Union is the only nation besides the United States that can afford to support a full-scale computer industry. It has a large enough population, and economy, enough natural resources, and a large enough military establishment to support the entire spectrum of computing from top to bottom, from software to hardware. They don't depend on anybody else to supply them. They may not cover everything as well as we do, but it's worth noting that they *do* cover everything.

"So then, if you look at Soviet computing compared to what it was in the past, they're doing very well. If you look at milestones achieved, the Soviets are also doing well. In the early 1970s, they reproduced the entire IBM 360 line, and then a few years later, the IBM 370."

Moreover, indications are that some new IBM-like mainframes are in the offing, although Westerners haven't seen them, only signs of them. A nascent fifth-generation effort has been announced, but this might be no more than an effort on the part of the Academy of Sciences to reestablish the priority in computing it has lost to Soviet industry over the last few years.

"All of these are nontrivial accomplishments—in fact, they could only be accomplished in their breadth by three countries in the world: the United States, Japan, and the U.S.S.R. So by those measures, the Soviets have built a respectable computer industry. If, however, you measure Soviet accomplishments against Western standards generally, then they're not doing so well."

That the Soviet Union lags behind other industrialized nations in computerizing all segments of its economy seems indisputable. How far behind is problematical, for as Goodman points out, the diverse nature of the different technologies involved in computing makes an average figure—three years, ten years, fifteen years— meaningless. In certain hardware areas, the gaps are closing, but in software they are not, and new gaps are appearing, such as the spread of computing and digital communications across a broad spectrum of private citizens and small organizations.

Recent reports suggest that a debate is going on about the use of personal computers in the Soviet Union. Unfortunately, the debate is somewhat academic, because the home-grown Agat (a copy of the Apple II) is only produced in the tens annually. Thus a computer literacy project in the schools, strongly urged by leading Soviet computer scientists such as Anatoly P. Aleksandrov and Andrei P. Yershov, languishes: two schools, one in Novosibirsk and the other in Moscow, each have twenty personal computers. Though 150 schools are expected to have programs by 1986, the West African country of Senegal compares favorably, at least on a per capita basis.

There are many reasons for the Soviet lag, some of them ideological, some historical, others economic. For example, socialist doctrine holds that heavy industry is the key to economic success, so it is often claimed that Soviet planners have invested in steel mills and hydroelectric power complexes to the detriment of smaller, lighter industries.

But Goodman suggests a more subtle analysis. Soviet military, industrial, and academic leaders saw the value of computing very early, and by the late 1940s research and development in computing was under way. In the early 1950s, the Soviets began modest, serial computer manufacture. At the time, both the United States and the Soviet Union used computers almost entirely for scientific and engineering computations. Thus compared with the rest of the world, computing was doing reasonably well in the Soviet Union at the time Stalin died. By the late 1950s the Soviet public was even feeling what Goodman calls a "pro-cybernetic euphoria," expressed in popular articles and calls for computerizing Soviet society, but in fact that euphoria was not translated into far-reaching research or applications.

This was an important lapse, because by then computing in the West had moved out from science and engineering into government and business data processing, which would provide a sensitive feedback mechanism in the form of customers and users who would insist on convenience, ease of use, and general flexibility, demanding good service, good programming, large and cheap memory devices, and improved input/output devices.

Since such customers and, more significant, competitive vendors did not exist in quite the same way in the Soviet Union, Soviet computing remained cloistered in its original installations, lacking the service, support, and improvements Westerners took for granted. Machines arrived at Soviet sites and were virtually abandoned by their manufacturers; Soviet programming continued to be done mainly in machine or assembly code, which meant only highly trained specialists could program (high-level languages did not become widely used until the early 1970s); memories and I/O devices were primitive and flawed.

After a reassessment in the early 1960s, Soviet planners began to develop a family of upwardly compatible machines, which allowed data and programs designed for one machine to be run without modification on more powerful machines in the series, permitting organizations to grow up from one computer to another without undue effort. At about the same time, IBM announced its own upwardly compatible machines, the 360 series. The contrast is stark: by 1970 IBM had built more than 35,000 units of its System 360 models; by 1973 the Soviets had built about 1,000 of their models and then abandoned them.

In a new attempt to build up their computer industry, the Soviets now copied the original 360 series, and in a partnership with Warsaw Pact countries (not all of them equally willing partners) produced a unified system of computers known as Ryad. It was an eight-years-later version of the IBM System 360, and its development is almost a case study of the strengths and weaknesses of computing in the Soviet Union.

Since, as Goodman observes, the Soviets were determined to succeed with the Ryad project, its plan was very conservative. "No effort was made to try to attain or surpass the world state-of-the-art in any technical sense. The primary objective was to get a large number of respectably modern computers into productive use in the U.S.S.R. national economy as expeditiously as possible." Additionally, the development and distribution of software, a chronic Soviet weakness, all but dictated the choice of which machine to copy, since IBM and its customers had spent billions of dollars on software for the System 360, an investment the Soviets could avoid by "borrowing" the 360 software.

In many ways, Ryad succeeded. By 1980 it was second only to the IBM 360/370 series in the numbers of installed mainframes, which makes it a best seller. Manufacturing problems of the Ryad system have not all been solved, and installation and maintenance remain uneven. Production rates are very low, compared with those of the American models when they were in their heyday, and the distribution of hardware is generally hampered by institutional problems. However, customer service and hardware reliability have improved (although they are still a serious problem), and an upgrade in the form of a version of IBM's System 370 has been introduced. Most important, Ryad's very existence is strong evidence that the Soviets are committed to spreading the use of computing throughout the economy. (The Ryad project is not the full story of Soviet computer manufacturing: other efforts go into military systems, scientific computers of all sizes, including supercomputers, and other special-purpose machines.)

Still, nothing about Ryad's hardware can be described as really innovative by Western standards. Despite a large, mathematically oriented engineering community, which might provide something exciting, software continues to languish, since its success depends so much on shared effort. Though official ideology says otherwise, sharing beyond a small local group is not part of day-to-day Soviet customs. To fall back on copying Western hardware and borrowing software must have been a bitter expedient for a nation obsessed with national pride and self-sufficiency. *[margin: stealing / Why the taut?]*

Circumstances beyond the technology have had an effect. Much in the Soviet bureaucracy, and for that matter, the culture, works against innovation. There is not only the Soviet obsession with secrecy that keeps scientists and technologists from sharing ideas with each other: even the statistics necessary to plan a centralized economy are state secrets. Infant mortality rates have not been published since 1975, and grain production has been secret since 1981. Other public statistics are unreliable, meant to camouflage and not enlighten.

So despite rhetoric at the highest levels about the importance of computing, Soviet managers farther down in the hierarchy* resist the innovations it would bring about (indeed, the Soviet system has distinct disincentives to innovation). Goodman sees a disparity between the technical literature on, say, automated production and the reality. Much praised on paper, "the number, distribution and quality of installed systems in the general economy appears to be fairly unimpressive for a country with the

sympathy for the bosses

resources and aspirations of the U.S.S.R." And if unemployment doesn't exist as a serious issue in the Soviet Union the way it does in most of the West, Goodman believes stress can be expected as computer-aided design and manufacturing are introduced into the manufacturing process. Rumors already exist that workers are sabotaging robots in certain Soviet factories.

There is enduring evidence that the Soviet economy is poor. Grain must regularly be purchased abroad; consumer goods, when available at all, are shabby. An active black market mocks ideology. Advanced technology is influenced by the West and, once in place, often disappoints: the turnkey plants introduced by Western industrialists founder when nobody has been trained in Western managerial methods, and founder too on the country's notoriously poor infrastructure. Even the late Konstantin Chernenko, accepting his election as general secretary, said to the Central Committee: "The system of economic management, the whole of our economic machinery, needs a serious restructuring," a sentiment expressed even more strongly by his successor, Mikhail Gorbachev.

Is the answer to this in computing? Loren Graham suggests that the Soviets' problems have been aggravated by the evolution of the international computer industry. When computers were big mainframes, so expensive that only an organization could afford them, and thus controlled them, they suited Soviet ideology. But the proliferation of micro- and minicomputers, not to mention computer networks, is antithetical to centralized control and planning. While measures can be taken to control the use of micros and minis, for example by requiring any printing to be done centrally, where it can be monitored, the Soviets will pay such a high price for that control that they will severely impede the growth of the computer culture—not to mention tempting Soviet whiz kids to flummox the system.

But Goodman argues that the technology available, coupled with various management practices and controls, makes it easier to design and implement information systems that centralize rather than those that distribute. He agrees that this not only will impede the technology, but that the control the Soviets will doubtless wish to impose on that technology will cost the economy dearly.

Goodman believes the centralized vs. distributed systems debate is moot.

The USSR will have a difficult time getting *either* into wide-spread and effective use throughout the general economy. By comparison, improving the volume and quality of computer and telecommunications hardware production will be easy. Some of the reasons for this are technical, for example, the miserable state of the telephone system. The more important reasons are behavioral and organizational. Computing and telecommunications can get into the fiber of an organization more broadly and deeply than other technologies. The Soviet enterprise environment is poorly suited to the use of computing and telecommunications above the automated systems of control and management, or at least it is poorly suited to many of the uses that are becoming pervasive in the U.S. So far, the Soviets do not seem to have come up with imaginative and practical alternatives. Adjustments that would fundamentally relieve these problems are not likely to be forthcoming soon.

Shulman and others suggest that this is a matter of time, that many among the younger generation of managers in the Soviet Union understand the value of computing and are ready and eager to implement it whenever they have the chance. Shulman especially talks about the changes that have been made in the Soviet Union over the last century, observing that perhaps no nation has changed more, ideology to the contrary.

Seymour Goodman is more doubtful. "A matter of time is too easy an idea. The rate of change, and the quality of change, matter much more. On this, the Soviets aren't doing so well."

Confounding Western prejudices about the Soviet monolith, recent reports suggest that maverick Hungary is moving ahead much more briskly, at least with smaller computers. After East Germany, Hungary is the Soviet bloc's most important computer manufacturer. Moreover, personal computer shops are appearing in Budapest, and 1,200 personal computers have already been placed in secondary schools, at least one for every school, with a plan to have at least one in every secondary school classroom. Hungary feels driven toward pervasive computerization by its reliance on exports, which generate more than a third of the gross national product. In world markets, Hungary faces onrushing computerized competition and simply cannot afford to dally.

In certain respects, s. eg. payroll, S.U. is too decentralized.

Though the restrictions imposed by the United States on advanced high technology of its own has hampered Hungary's efforts to bootstrap, it has also forced the country's technologists to be more imaginative and resourceful.

Chekhov's tales end ambiguously. Outcomes shimmer beyond our understanding, for nothing is really resolved. Things are funny, and at the same time sad. But self-satisfaction eludes us in the face of such pretensions and follies, resistance and subterfuges, for they're too much like our own.

Chapter 20

Work

In the year 1887 in the pleasant town of Bath, England, which is celebrated for its exceptional waters, elegant architecture, splendid gardens, and its rich literary heritage, an eleven-year-old child by the name of Eliza Agnes Thomas left her parents' crowded household and took her first job. She moved into the cellar of a five-story townhouse where, daily, she rose before dawn to haul buckets of coal to every floor, laying fresh coal in each fireplace and lighting the fires so that the family who employed her would later waken in warm rooms.

As jobs for eleven-year-olds went in 1887, it wasn't bad. She was sheltered, clothed, and fed, considerable advantages in a time so economically uncertain that, until the next one came along in the 1930s, it would be known as the Great Depression (1873–96). It was a time of severe economic dislocations, as we'd put it today. Government commissions reported that mass starvation (and consequent national anarchy) threatened Britain because the country could no longer feed itself. Paradoxically, it was cheap wheat from abroad —the United States and Russia, primarily—that was wrecking the financial structure of British agriculture, and cheap goods from abroad—the Empire, mainly—that was wrecking the financial structure of British industry.

Whatever the struggle to carry a coal scuttle up five sets of stairs in the dark and cold and damp might be for an eleven-year-old girl, it was surely preferable to working in a factory, though the worst abuses of child labor had been corrected some twenty years before. Eliza even had the chance to better herself: she'd been educated (after a fashion—she could read and do sums, and her mother, an aristocrat who had impetuously run off with a handsome young gardener, had taught her refined speech). All this permitted Eliza to hope for eventual work in the nursery if she proved her diligence and obedience.

Eliza Agnes Thomas was my grandmother, and I often think of her and her struggle up those dark staircases when I hear about the dehumanizing effects of technology in the workplace. She was, to repeat, better off than most children of her time and place. Only two years before she went to work, a journalist had been put on trial in London for purchasing a twelve-year-old girl in order to expose "the ease with which depravity could be catered to," as one historian puts it. Thus, at the same time the middle-class Victorian woman was the "angel of the hearth," vice was an economic necessity for the poor: contemporary studies shocked the Victorian public by revealing that the proportion of those living in abject poverty—with income insufficient to satisfy the barest physical needs—was 30 percent of the British population as a whole, a proportion that rose to 43 percent of the working population. So not only was Eliza fortunate to be fed, clothed, and sheltered, but she was also fortunate enough to earn her living honestly.

She enjoyed the added blessings of good health. Having survived all her childhood diseases, Eliza would live, of course, to have her own family (though she buried two of her children). As it happens, those blessings were conferred on her by technology and by luck, the luck of having been born at a time when massive reforms were under way.

It does not diminish the earnest and dedicated crusaders of the late nineteenth century, who tightened the child labor laws and brought about public health reforms, to say that they might not have succeeded in their reforms without the technology that allowed more productivity from each worker and thus diminished the need for children's labor. They most certainly would not have succeeded without the knowledge of disease prevention and control made possible by scientific research and technological development.

It may seem odd to think of clean housing, pure water, and effective sewers as technologies, but technologies they are, and their introduction had a dramatic effect on limiting the spread of infectious diseases, humankind's major killers in that era. The drama came not in the birth rates, which were slowly falling, but in the numbers of people who survived beyond childhood to reproduce. According to statisticians, little change occurred in the distribution of deaths between 10,000 B.C. and A.D. 1850. But beginning in the second half of the nineteenth century, something new happened: more people began living beyond childhood than ever before, and deaths, which had been pretty evenly distributed across age groups, were now clustered in childhood and old age, which itself, statistically speaking, edged upward.

When we come to address the complaints made by the anti-technologists, especially as they complain about the computer, it is salutory to keep my grandmother—and the grandparents of most of us—in mind. For at the heart of all complaints about technology is an often unstated nostalgia for the past. We are in danger of "losing" something we must once have had, whether it is privacy, autonomy, control, individuality, security, or whatever.

Well now, surely it isn't the late Victorian period that the nostalgics long for. If Eliza was better off than many and had much to be grateful for, I doubt she would have described herself as having privacy, autonomy, control, individuality, or security in her life (which is not to say she was unhappy, on the whole). In any event, we know that the situation was considered unsatisfactory just then by some, because at the same time children were struggling up the stairs of their relatively benevolent employers, William Morris was leading a small group backward toward the time before the painter Raphael (hence their name, the Pre-Raphaelites), which was Morris's particular choice for the Good Old Days. (A careful scholar could surely construct an unbroken chain of Good Old Days reaching back to, say, the Greeks, who also believed that civilization was in decline.)

There is much romancing about preindustrial work, how integral it was with life (meaning that people had time for little else) and how its goals weren't the accumulation of goods but the perpetuation of the family unit. This pastoral and familial idyll is

usually contrasted with the rigidity of the factory system, alien
and inhuman, imposed upon the unwilling masses and tearing
apart the family. I intend no argument on behalf of the factory
system: dull jobs are dulling to the human spirit and dangerous
jobs are lethal; the sooner we can eliminate them, the better. But
uncritical nostalgia for what emerges as a different kind of tyranny
holds few attractions either.

Perhaps anybody sentimental for pastoral idylls, the perpetuation of the family unit, and organic connections between life
and work ought to read Alice Thornton's autobiography, written
by an ordinary English gentlewoman of the preindustrial seventeenth century. Alice Thornton writes cheerfully, full of thanks
to God for delivering her from great evils, but her tale is a melancholy concatenation of illnesses, miscarriages, stillbirths, dangerous childbirths, and other calamities, including the threat of
rape by Scottish marauders. (A surprise perhaps to those who
long for the law, order, and tranquility of the past.)

Having endured all that, she had then to make a final desperate scramble to keep body and soul together in widowhood,
which required her to plead with (and, against her wishes, flatter)
brothers, male cousins, and brothers-in-law to keep her and her
children decently, by administering her late husband's estate, which
of course she herself was not allowed to do. This is security, loyalty,
and mutual trust as it really existed in at least one preindustrial
family, dismal for nearly everybody but landed adult males.

Mrs. Thornton leaves us her life story because she could write;
she makes no claims to being extraordinary: we can believe her
life was typical. As for the lives of illiterate women and men and
the work they did, we can only guess.

In short, the family of the past wasn't quite the benign economic unit and provider its most ardent admirers like to pretend.
We see this not only from documents left by women like Alice
Thornton but also from other evidence. Simone de Beauvoir, in
her study of aging, observes that once laws were passed in
nineteenth-century France requiring middle-aged children to pay
an elderly father a life annuity in return for taking title to the
family farm (laws conceived as protection against the harshness
and neglect of offspring) that he all but signed his own death
certificate. Just as superfluous infants were dispatched from a
hard-pressed, even greedy, family, so were the superfluous el-

derly. The situation is not uniquely European nor specific to private property: tribes living as far apart as Africa and the Arctic have traditionally practiced infanticide or parricide for economic gain. Not mere survival, but gain. Marxists may argue that wages for work is debasing, but not everyone would agree (including, I think, Mrs. Thornton, and others like her, who had no alternative to flattery—at the very least—to secure a roof over her head for herself and her children).

Whether we like it or not, the nature of work has changed in industrialized nations over the last two hundred or more years, and we can expect it to continue to change. In the United States alone, the numbers of agricultural workers have dropped since the turn of the century from 25 percent of the work force to 3 or 4 percent; labor statisticians suggest that the same drop will take place among factory workers, who now account for about 25 percent of the work force but will presently account for something like 5 percent. If we welcome computer-controlled robots to take over the dull, repetitive jobs that everyone agrees are awful, what do we do about those whose jobs have been automated out from under them?

Harley Shaiken, a research associate in the Program in Science, Technology and Society at M.I.T., has studied these issues and reminded us in several reports that no matter how beneficial a technology—any technology is, there are potential problems, and "while some people may benefit, others may lose."

Automation by computers and microelectronics, he further reminds us, is qualitatively different from the automation that we have known in the past. It extends over a much wider range of technologies, and its rate of diffusion is much faster than past kinds of mechanical automation. The American experience of automation in the 1950s was on the whole a happy one: people were displaced from jobs, but the net number of jobs grew. (Those numbers nevertheless mask real human misery, as a study of the introduction of automation to the printing industry in New York City shows: few who made their living as well-paid printers were able to retrain for comparably paid jobs, and many interviewed ended up in early retirement or even on welfare.)

Shaiken also notes that our earlier experience in mechanical automation happened to take place at a time of worldwide economic expansion. But the new and powerfully labor-saving electronic automation is being introduced at a time of worldwide economic stagnation, indeed, sometimes as a remedy to it, which could have profound effects on the net number of jobs.

We have two scenarios here. One, presented by Nobel laureate Wassily Leontief, suggests that labor will grow increasingly dispensable, with subsequent unemployment and socially undesirable effects on the distribution of income.

A contrary view is presented by studies from SRI International. Economists there studied California, which isn't a perfect model of the future but is probably the best one we have. If California were a nation, it would have the sixth largest GNP in the world. Its economy is based on a mixture of information services, agriculture, aerospace, forest products, electronics, financial services, and various retail and wholesale services. Each of these sectors in California has a large component of electronics and information technologies, including areas most people wouldn't think of, such as lumber mills that have become sophisticated cellulose conversion and processing plants, highly automated and computerized.

From 1973 to 1980, California added nearly a half million new jobs, net, to its work force, which in 1980 numbered 10 million people. Of those half million new jobs that were added, about 60 percent were created by the new technologies. Few of them were in the electronics/computer/telecommunications industry, which grew rapidly but has relatively few jobs. The jobs came instead from other industries adopting the new information technologies: a distinct ripple effect. New techniques create new services and products requiring new workers. When computers were introduced in banking, say, twenty years ago, it was widely predicted that many jobs would be eliminated. Since 1973 the number of bank employees has grown at better than 10 percent a year because the new technologies allowed banks to offer new services to their customers and to serve new classes of customers at a faster rate than paper-handling jobs disappeared.

The California model suggests that the information technologies are modestly job-creating, not job-destroying, and that has certainly been true of all past technologies throughout history. Thus my own answer to the question I am usually asked about automation is that in the short run it probably will be a painful transition, but in the long run, there will be jobs, and the fact that we don't at present have the imagination to predict what those jobs are doesn't mean they won't exist. (Nils Nilsson, an eminent researcher in artificial intelligence, demurs, believing that such a hope gravely underestimates the effects of AI.)

Jobs might come in a number of ways. We might move into nonessential activities such as space exploration; we might reduce the workweek. We might begin government programs to improve energy and transportation systems and other public services and restore the environment. The unsatisfied demand for goods in the less developed countries is likely to keep manufacturing all over the world occupied for the foreseeable future, if those less developed countries have some means for paying for goods.

Even supposing our new experience mimics the happiest aspects of the past, and the result of the new automation is a net increase in the number of jobs, will those jobs be accessible to the unemployed? This is meant in two senses. First, will those new jobs be in the communities that have suffered the most from automation, such as the heavily industrialized cities of the American Midwest, Alsace-Lorraine, or the Ruhr? Or will they be somewhere else? The shortage of programmers in Boston is meaningless to the unemployed steelworkers in Pittsburgh. Second, even if the steelworkers moved their households to Boston, they cannot soon (if ever) be retrained as programmers.

Shaiken asserts that we cannot afford the long-term unemployment and worker dissatisfaction that a rapid and thoughtless introduction of such technology would cost. The alternative, he believes, is not between new technology and no technology but between a foolish introduction of technology and the development of technology with social responsibility, which he defines as shorter work time and the planned development of new industries in areas of declining employment. "Finally, the participation of the people affected by change—the workers and their unions—is needed to ensure that workers become the beneficiaries and not the victims of the new technology."

William W. Winpisinger, the ebullient president of the International Association of Machinists and Aerospace Workers, has suggested that there be a Technology Bill of Rights. It says:

1. New technology must be used in a way that creates and maintains jobs and promotes full employment.

2. New technology must be used to improve the conditions of work.

3. New technology must be used to develop the industrial base.

4. Workers and their trade unions must have a role in the decision-making processes with respect to the design, deployment, and use of new technology.

The translation of such well-meant generalities into effective social and industrial policy isn't easy, and we aren't very good at it yet. When superior Japanese production techniques allowed Japanese autos to capture between a quarter and a third of the United States automobile market, causing massive layoffs and near bankruptcies in the American auto industry, a compromise was eventually worked out in the early 1980s that imposed "voluntary" quotas on Japanese imports until the Americans could catch up. It seemed a good and fair way of solving the problem, saving jobs and giving the industry a breathing space to become more competitive, and only a few disgruntled consumers complained.

But the Brookings Institution has reported that the quotas have led to price increases of at least $1,000 per Japanese and $400 per U.S. auto, for a 1983 cost to consumers of $4.3 billion. The number of jobs saved by the quotas was, at most, 46,000. Each job saved cost Americans nearly $100,000 per year, which seems like economic heroics in the extreme. Even higher estimates are made of the cost of saving jobs in the steel industry by protective laws. Consumers not earning as much as the workers whose jobs they are paying to save (never mind the astonishing salaries earned by management) have a right to be skeptical.

But another answer to whether such generalizations can be translated into effective social and economic policy is that equally woolly ideas have found their way into our laws, beginning with our Constitution and stretching up through the affirmative action and anti-pollution laws of the 1970s. We are committed as a nation to justice, and that is a good thing even when we misstep or fail to achieve it.

We shall need to hold on to that larger commitment as we move into the new world, for perhaps the most profound changes must come in the minds of everybody who participates in the economic process, employer and employed, consumer and law-maker. Those changes will be forced upon us by certain facts.

First, the computer is changing the nature of work, which grows steadily more information-intensive, or abstract, with concomitant demands on worker preparation and skills. (The present alternative to those information-intensive jobs is low-paying service jobs, but that won't always be the case.) Little in our schools is preparing us for what we can reasonably foresee, and we simply do not know what to do about the unforeseeable.

Second, the computer is changing the social dynamics of work. In principle (though not necessarily in practice) a computerized work force is more easily monitored and controlled by its managers than the mechanized work force once was. Collective action by workers, such as a strike, is impotent in a workplace where a flick of a switch can reroute work from one location to another, hundreds or thousands of miles away. This seems to shift power drastically toward employers. But at the same time, high-skill workers—very high skill: inventive, flexible problem-solvers—are essential to an economy whose value comes in the knowledge added to products instead of their simple production.

Traditional categories of worker and manager suddenly become blurred to the point of meaninglessness. Traditional antagonisms serve nobody. Traditional assumptions are beside the point, even counterproductive. We need a new set of measures, and if not a new ethos, perhaps a refined definition of justice.

In the new economy, we shall have to redefine the terms of work. Raj Reddy, the head of the Robotics Institute at Carnegie-Mellon University, puts it this way: "The old dogma of 'labor-value' theory is no longer relevant. It must be replaced by a 'knowledge-value' theory based on a symbiotic relationship between man and his personal computer providing access to the knowledge of the world. The value of a person or a society will be *directly proportional to their ability to master the information resource to achieve their goals.*"

Shaiken's cautions and Winpisinger's Bill of Rights are imperfect guides toward our well-being. Is that so surprising? Life is one long social experiment, and we're not likely to get it right the first time or even the first ten times. But we have the obligation to try.

Equally compelling, we won't survive economically or probably any other way if we don't bring imaginative action to bear on all this. Peter Unterweger, a research analyst for the United Auto Workers, has pointed out that the failure to automate more quickly in steel, and to a lesser degree in autos, is responsible for at least some of the current difficulties of these industries. "It is an unfortunate paradox that the greatest job losses will most likely occur in industries that fail to automate."

Work is changing because the economy—and the world—is changing. The best way to meet those changes has no tidy answers. It demands a comprehension of the human community as far more interconnected and interdependent than we have ever before needed to believe.

For most of us, it is a new world view, though we have been prepared for it by the ecologists and owe them thanks. Now we must turn that holistic view of physical systems, all delicately interdependent and balanced, toward symbol systems, specifically economies and governments, which we understand even less well than physical systems. About all we can anticipate now is that, first, we shall all be in a perpetual state of learning the new, because that will be our personal and national currency in the new economy, and that, second, a new kind of cooperation, not competition, will be demanded of us and, what's more, be in our own best interests.

The instrument forcing us toward this view is, as it happens, the best means for realizing the view as well. In a later chapter, I shall report research in computer science on complex systems that might give us insights into the symbol systems we are all part of, the computers that have always been our companions. But there are no guarantees. We are already faced with demands that transcend immediate self-interest, employment, and even national economies; they are sibling to the demands made on us by the computer in war and peace. No hero in the myths of our childhood was ever more exquisitely challenged.

For whom? to meet them?

goo.

* There is no advice to the reader on how to meet the changes he faces.

Chapter 21

Aiming at Computer Literacy

In a recent television commercial a proud and adoring family sees eager son off to college; next scene, hangdog son returns, having flunked out, we are informed, because his parents neglected to buy him a personal computer. The whole episode takes place at a train station—the point being, I suppose, that anybody old-fashioned enough to send their son to college on a train is also too old-fashioned to realize the importance of computing to his intellectual growth.

Thus computer literacy, it has been charged, is a term made up by manufacturers to sell unneeded personal computers to the rubes who are being gulled into fearing that without such skills their offspring will be unable to compete in the new world out there.

True, commercialization proceeds apace (and many a personal computer sits neglected in trendy closets), but this is beside the point of computer literacy. The term was probably first coined by Arthur Luehrmann in 1972 when he was director of computing at Dartmouth College. In those days, Dartmouth was in the lead of undergraduate institutions that encouraged scholars to use computers. John Kemeny, who would later be Dartmouth's president, and Thomas Kurtz had invented BASIC (Beginners All-purpose Symbolic Instruction Code), which was intended to be very simple to learn and cheap to implement and use, so that large numbers of users could be accommodated.

In a 1972 talk, Luehrmann invented a parable about "writing-aided instruction" and "computer-aided instruction" and thus made explicit the power of computing as a fundamental intellectual resource. "Mass literacy is an educational mission about which few of us have doubts today," he said. "Yet that consensus among us seems to vanish when one substitutes 'computing' for 'reading and writing' and 'CAI' for 'WAI.' " Those few educators and federal policymakers who looked ahead were primarily interested in computers as a tool for instruction in math or remedial English. That was commendable, he continued, but there was a higher goal.

"If the computer is so powerful a resource that it can be programmed to simulate the instructional process, shouldn't we be teaching our students mastery of this powerful intellectual tool?" Mastery, he said, was the ability to get information in the social sciences from a large data-base inquiry system; to simulate an ecological system; to solve problems by using algorithms; to acquire laboratory data and analyze it; to represent textual information for editing and analysis; to represent musical information for analysis; or to create and process graphical information. Such uses would make students masters of computing, not merely its subjects. He outlined objections that might be made, but concluded: "How much longer will a computer illiterate be considered educated? How long will he be employable and for what jobs?"

The world has adopted Luehrmann's view so wholeheartedly that it is hard now to see how radically visionary it was at the time. Moreover, computing technology, both in hardware and in software, has changed enough so that many of Luehrmann's specifications for computer literacy can be met in a few hours' instruction, in large part because those very firms that the critics scorn for pursuing profit have been working hard at creating that ease of use. The most successful at achieving user-friendliness, as the phrase has it, was probably the Xerox Corporation, which, for reasons mysterious to many, decided not to press its advantage in the early 1970s. Its clever icons, windows, menus, and mouse, which allow almost anybody to sit down at a computer and start doing things immediately, turned up ten years later in the Apple Corporation's Lisa and Macintosh.

Critics might prefer computer designers and manufacturers to have taken the same attitude as atonal composers, which is to say that the public must overcome its antipathy toward the atonal and learn to like it regardless, for the responsibility is the public's. The public, so far, has not learned to like atonal music, however agreeable some of us have been to *trying* to like it or at least admiring it when we couldn't feel affection.

On the contrary, from earliest times, computer designers and manufacturers were at pains to make computers as easy as possible for people to use (although at the beginning that wasn't so very easy). A cynic would lay it all to economics, and a cynic would be partially correct. But even those unconcerned with the market, such as Luehrmann, and computer scientists in general have been missionary-like in seeking converts and continue to strive to make conversion easier and easier.

Such accommodations don't sit well with everyone in the field. I've heard computer scientists complain that certain obstacles should be retained—the piano analogy, which says that nobody expects to play a Chopin étude the first time at the keyboard. Why should computing be different? But most of them prefer the automobile analogy: you don't need to know what's under the hood to get into any automobile in the world and drive off. The important thing is the journey, not the vehicle.

I think the missionary spirit is healthy, even if, from time to time, the missionaries neglect some obvious things. Computers ought to be easier to use, even right now, and there ought to be ways of learning to use them that don't require strenuous mathematical conditioning, an inhuman attention to detail that frustrates all but the most dedicated, or a lack of standardization that introduces endless error.

For example, I do most of my own work using a word processing program. If I move over to my networked computer to send and receive messages around the country, another set of commands—to accomplish the same tasks of manipulating text, so far as I am concerned—is required of me. However, sometimes I wish to write a program. In that case, I have to use still another editing system, with commands that are just different enough from the editing commands I use regularly to introduce odd little errors that discourage me from writing too many programs. I get short-tempered at the arbitrariness of it all and consider it no part of intellectual growth to memorize three (or more) different sets of editing commands. Designers would retort that it is too early to standardize, and perhaps they are right. But I don't believe it.

Psychologists make more sense on the topic. Why, they ask, when interaction between humans and machine could be so smooth, even elegant, is it often so rough, even hazardous?

First, interaction with computers is just emerging as a human activity. Previous styles of interaction with machines had people *operating* on machines in limited ways with limited means (wheels, levers, knobs). But a computer user is not an operator. He communicates with the computer to accomplish a task.

Second, the radical increase in both the computer's power and its performance/cost ratio has meant that an increasing amount of computational resources is available for the interface. This exacerbates the novelty of the area, since more computing cycles allow novel styles of interaction, new interfaces, even more ragged than before. Opportunities for good interfaces increase and are irresistible.

So it seems computer literacy is a moving target. At Carnegie-Mellon University, a school committed to computing for everyone, a report of a recent task force for future computing on campus says:

> Computer literacy is not equivalent to learning to program, but is different in at least the following ways: First, using a computer often means not programming, but using available tools—editors, electronic mail, statistical packages, simulators, computer-aided design systems, data base systems and so on. Using these tools intelligently requires skill, together with knowledge of when to use them appropriately. Second, using a computer effectively involves more than just local skills for using particular languages or tools. It requires understanding the fundamental nature of the computer, what kinds of things it can and cannot do. Third, if the role of computation is to increase qualitatively at CMU, computer literacy must include competence in the local computational facilities. This part of computer literacy is in fact an important part of good access.
>
> Computer literacy is not a separate educational objective. If computation becomes more intensive in our envi-

ronment, then we must convey to our students, as part of
their education in all areas, the difference between intelligent and inappropriate uses of the computer.

More than a decade after coining the phrase, Luehrmann
refined his definition: "Computer literacy means more than an
appreciation of the role of computers in society. Mathematical
literacy allows translation from verbal codes, and invites opera-
tional manipulation through algebra or calculus. Computer literacy allows a different translation, into a code that permits general
and realistic representation of a process, which is easily adapted
to new circumstances."

That key word: process. But we must begin simply. For most
people, what's needed in the beginning is the computing equivalent of driver's ed. To be sure, driver's ed can take many forms.
Nearly any normal adult can learn to drive a car, although we do
it with varying degrees of skill. Despite the relative ease of learning
the minimum, knowing how to drive well can be a matter of life
and death. Simplicity is not triviality. Complexity is not depth. My
Polish friends laugh about the six months of driving "theory" they
are required to complete before they can sit behind the wheel of
an automobile and start to learn the practical business of driving,
but that's no more bizarre than the story I heard from a young
landscape architect.

It occurred to him that a computer might be very helpful in
his business, cataloging the plants and their characteristics, keeping track of soils, mixing and matching seasonal flowers. He signed
up for the beginning computing course at his community college
but dropped out in despair after three weeks of the theory of
binary numbers.

I do not know if he had already tried to learn computing from
a book, but if he had, he would have been no better off. Most
manuals and handbooks that now come with personal computers
and their software are a scandal of obfuscation. The whole situation is causing a resurgence of oral culture: people turn to each
other in terminal rooms or call each other up on the phone. *How
do I get it to do this?* The drawbacks of oral culture are well-known:
ephemerality, lack of leverage, lack of precision, ad hockery, wasteful
duplication of effort, and so forth. Crossing the barrier is still
worthwhile to many, so they endure the hardships, but it's cold

comfort to know that some of the hardships are unnecessary and will eventually disappear.

I heard the young landscape architect's story in a sunny garden he had created in the Montclair hills of Oakland, California. The garden belongs to William Gallagher and Deborah Wright, who run what they call an adult computer camp. The landscape architect had decided to give computing one last try with Dr. Gallagher (the doctorate is in linguistics, which turns out to be significant to Gallagher's success, I think). He had taken Gallagher's two-day course, had soon been able to write exactly the software he hoped for, and was now about to begin a modest marketing effort to sell it to other landscape architects.

Bill Gallagher is a bouncy, athletic man in his early forties who came to the computer by an indirect route (as nearly everybody over forty has). He was trained as a linguist, with a specialty in teaching English as a second language. In Hawaii he taught English to Koreans (and wrote a textbook for that); in Israel he taught English to expatriate Soviet physicians (who had to learn it to read Western medical journals and bootstrap themselves up from what Gallagher called "the paramedic's education" they had received in the Societ Union); and he taught English to Spaniards in Barcelona. Each of these experiences has contributed to the format of his adult computer camp.

For example, in teaching English to Koreans, he soon came to the conclusion that what linguists use to describe a language isn't necessarily very useful for teaching a language to someone else. Thus he argued for a distinction between language "learning" (the rules, the grammar, the vocabulary irregularities) and language "acquisition" (getting along in a new language). Gallagher had his adult students act out skits, interviews, and dialogues that forced them to speak English to each other in real-life situations. Compared with a control group taught by traditional methods, the skit-playing group made significantly better progress. In Barcelona, where he was teaching English in a social club, he discovered that drinking alcohol had an effect on people's skills. Too much and you wouldn't learn anything, but a glass or two of wine seemed to loosen adult inhibitions and ease language acquisition markedly.

Finally, in teaching the Soviet expatriates, Gallagher was exposed to PLATO (a computer-aided instructional system devel-

No mention of this in the continental chapter on the S.U.

oped at the University of Illinois and now marketed by Control Data Corporation) and sensed that here was a pedagogical tool that would become more and more important in the future. It was his introduction to computers, and he would soon teach himself much more.

Thus one Saturday morning I joined six students in Gallagher's home in the Oakland hills to observe a class. It was a comfortable setting: family photographs, floor-to-ceiling bookcases with an enviable collection of dictionaries in many languages, a large, friendly house cat. Strung out across the front wall of the living room, facing the eucalyptus trees in the garden, were simple collapsible tables that held four Apple IIc's. Gallagher had begun his courses by giving every student his or her own computer, but it was soon apparent that students learned more quickly with the buddy system, talking problems out with each other, reminding each other of procedures, and so forth. If I had any doubts about that strategy, I was to find that working with someone else later that day was much more fun than working alone.

The group was obviously middle class, male except for another woman and me, and white except for another Bill, a Chinese X-ray technician, who had won the course in a drawing at a recent computer fair. Don was an executive in charge of the San Francisco mayor's energy office, Jim was an attorney and a starting principal in a new savings and loan company, Wayne was a real estate specialist in marinas, and Steve was in commercial real estate. Elizabeth mentioned that she handled her own investments, both real estate and securities, but that she had really come to take the course because her grandson was beginning to learn computing in school and she had decided she didn't want to be left out.

We began with an icebreaker: each of us was supplied with two nametags. On one we were to write a true statement about ourselves; on the other, a false statement. We would be left to stare at those statements on the shirtfronts of our colleagues all morning, and try to decide which statement was true, which false. Gallagher's own were the most intriguing: one said *I speak fluent Eskimo*, and the other, *I have five children*.

As soon as we had each told why we had come to the course ("I own a personal computer," one said, "but the instructions are so confusing I can't even run it." "I need computers in my office," the lawyer said, "but every sales rep who comes through the door tells me something different." "Yeah, just like talking to a lawyer," the marina man laughed). Gallagher began. First he described the computer as "something like" a human brain, speaking simply but accurately about various theories of human memory, comparing them to various kinds of computer memory. To drive home his points, he had us play games or make up metaphors; he would present each concept, he told us, in three different ways. So it was; as we worked our way through memories, bits, bytes, and buffers, using plastic tubing and plastic balls to demonstrate the on-off capabilities of the computer, and always in the context of some situation: we were sponge divers being attacked by sharks and needed to signal to the folks on board ship that we wanted to be hauled up; we were castaways trying to signal to a plane overhead that we weren't friendly natives having a luau but victims of a shipwreck who were in trouble. I was amused to hear, very softly in the background, music from the *Star Wars* soundtracks to inspire us. Gallagher, a firm believer in New Age pedagogy, was leaving no sense untouched.

We broke for lunch outside. We quizzed each other on our true-false name-tag statements to demonstrate that old computing truth GIGO: garbage in can only lead to garbage out. (From the dictionaries I guessed that Gallagher's true statement was that he spoke fluent Eskimo and quizzed him as best I could; it finally emerged that he spoke Eskimo badly and really had five children.) We sipped our wine or beer, were briefed on the etymologies of numbers and, in particular, the binary system that underlies digital computers.

At last it was time to go inside and sit down at the computer itself (normally hands-on experience comes before lunch, but our group had begun late). We are all soon into demonstration programs that prompt us to do and say things. When the program begins addressing a user by his name, saying encouraging things like *Great, Don,* Don says, "That's a little scary." We play elementary video games (to learn to move the computer's cursor) and shift into music, horse racing, and a program that asks for ten nouns, five verbs, five adjectives, and a female name. The program will then produce a choice of stories: a western, a letter home, or a classified ad, using the words supplied in strategic locations.

Since the wine has had some effect, the marina man and the

lawyer, who are partners at an Apple opposite me, supply words that border on the lascivious, and the female name they offer to the program is mine. Soon somebody named Pamela is starring in a lewd but hilarious tale of western derring-do. This is, after all, an *adult* computer camp, and the idea of camps is to have fun. We are all having fun. What a wonder Gallagher and a glass of California Chardonnay have performed. Here are people who, a few hours earlier, have expressed all degrees of computer phobia, now having the time of their lives at a computer. And learning. By the end of the day, they'll have written their first program in BASIC, played with word processing, and gone into good-natured competition with each other and their spreadsheet programs. (The following day, which I cannot attend, the students will learn how to introduce computers into their own offices, calm computer phobia among their colleagues, build and use personal files, use a word processor, a spreadsheet program, and even how to buy the best microcomputer for their own needs.)

The fun recalls a conversation at lunch. Wayne had told us that he mentioned to his daughter, a student at the University of California at Davis, that he would be coming to the computer camp. She wished she could come too. "You're crazy, I said to her. You go to one of the best schools in the country. Get it there. But she said, 'No, I can't. There's too much pressure for grades.' " I hear that afternoon laughter and think that Wayne's daughter has summed up much that is wrong with conventional education.

Gallagher is doing driver's ed. He shows students how to get where they want to go but doesn't give them more than they need to know to get there. The best way to learn to drive is to sit in the driver's seat: brake too soon, pop the clutch, lug the engine, oversteer, but do it. The best way to learn computing—for most people's needs—is the same. Gallagher has recognized that we do not need to be linguists to acquire the language of computing; we need merely open our mouths and give it a try.

It is not exactly literacy, although it begins to satisfy some of the CMU computer literacy criteria: learning to use appropriate tools for tasks, an acquaintance with the fundamental nature of the computer and what kinds of things it can or cannot do. Still, to the many firms that bring Gallagher in to train their employees, driver's ed is sufficient to the purposes of getting started. (I should add that many of their client firms disapprove of the idea of official fun, never mind wine, so Gallagher and Wright have spent some time wracking their brains to dream up synonyms that will soothe corporate America: "stimulating," "challenging," "gratifying." Well, to be sure. But fun most of all.)

So where does this leave computer literacy now? Luehrmann's refinement of his own term is robust (but perhaps not final either— for so it must be in this fast evolving field): computer literacy is the ability to translate verbal or mathematical codes into a new code that permits a general and realistic representation of a process, easily adaptable to new circumstances. It seems to me to admit many levels of literacy, which is true of the conventional kind. And its acquisition has been made easier, on the whole, not only because of the courses like Gallagher's that have sprung up all over the country, from the Grand Tetons to Key West, but also because special-purpose courses address special constituencies: the Women's Computer Literacy Project, based in San Francisco, conducts courses all over the country for women only; there are courses for doctors, farmers, real estate brokers.

Combine these opportunities with the technological breakthroughs, such as Apple's Macintosh, that allow a novice to start working alone almost immediately (thanks not only to the technology but also to the best manufacturer's manual I have ever used), and the hesitant beginner can move confidently into the new world, a bit at a time.

But in coining the term computer literacy, Luehrmann meant students in school, and that is a story in its own right.

Chapter 22

Computing in the Schools

Why should computers be in the schools? If, to continue my analogy, it's all a matter of mere driver's ed, isn't that just the kind of frill that has intellectually impoverished American education since the end of World War II? No. The purpose of analogies is to illuminate differences as well as similarities between objects and ideas, so let me argue why computers belong in the schools and why they are different from driver's ed (or audio-visual aids, as teachers like to call movies) or even paper and pencil, essential as all these are.

Unlike any of those implements and skills (but like a human teacher), the computer is interactive. It can respond to students when they address it, illustrating with text and animation, adapting itself to an individual student's curiosities, pace, and style. Moreover, it can deal swiftly with large quantities of information, sorting and sifting in ways none of the others (especially humans) can. These are truisms about the computer, but consider the potency of those capacities at work for a student in a classroom.

Perhaps the most advanced use of computers in the classroom is at Brown University. In the Gould Laboratory, a tiered classroom-laboratory, each of forty students faces a personal computer

display but can also see the instructor at the head of the room—
who also has a computer. The student learns both from the instructor's lecture and from the scene that is unfolding on his
personal screen. (I watch enviously as a concept in programming
I've been struggling to understand, using only a book and my old-
fashioned text display, is illustrated by a combination of text and
cartoon that makes the concept suddenly and utterly clear to me.)
At Brown this experimental laboratory is used mainly to teach
programming (why shouldn't the computer scientists use it to
make their own lives easier?), although at least one other course
has been designed for teaching color theory in the studio arts
program. For the first few weeks of the course, everybody's computer is synchronized with the instructor's, but after that, the more
gifted or swifter students can go ahead, while others keep a slower
pace.

The Gould Laboratory embodies a promise of nearly two decades, but aside from Brown, and a handful of other exceptions,
the promise has not been very well kept. The main reason is that
for such applications to work well, more intelligence on the part
of the computer—not the student—has been required than we
have had. Moreover, restructuring a course to take advantage of
computing cycles that are growing cheaper and cheaper is an
enormous undertaking, and not many educators can do it. Restructuring entire classrooms, schools, or school systems is even
more precarious.

We must return to first questions: what are the purposes of
school? It's a place where children learn, we answer impatiently;
we hope they'll learn the basics, or the fundamentals, or the three
Rs, or whatever we want to call them; we hope, in addition, that
they'll learn something about the culture they live in and its values,
its history, its language. We hope the kids will learn to get along
with each other, learn to lead and to follow, as everyone must.
We hope they'll stay out of trouble and make the team.

Our first response is the most inclusive: we hope they'll learn.
What we really mean, upon reflection, is that we hope they'll
acquire the habit of learning, because the specifics are likely to
become obsolete. Even when information doesn't become obsolete, its quantity is overwhelming. But the other simple things we
hope for and specify so easily, that they'll learn about their culture,
and how to get along with each other, and follow and lead, all

turn out to function within highly complex social structures that we take for granted.

What can a microcomputer in a school do about those goals? Not a lot, it would seem, given the limited vision prevailing in education just now. After all, the Gould Laboratory's computers are much more powerful than micros and are, moreover, connected with each other, the beginning of an elaborate network that will soon include many different knowledge sources, from libraries to laboratories, from dormitories to offices. Their software has been a labor of love, not to mention blood, sweat, and tears, tailored to the purposes of undergraduates in a liberal arts college who are taking computer programming for the first time. Since the ultimate goal at Brown is to provide every faculty member, student, administrator, and staff member on campus with a powerful personal workstation that will connect with all other workstations, just as all telephones now connect with one another, the budget is estimated on Brown's part alone to be between $50 million and $70 million, not counting grants and equipment donations from manufacturers. This is considerably different from the occasional Commodore P.E.T. that stands alone in primary school classrooms here and there.

And yet a single microcomputer in a classroom, even if it hasn't got the power and ambitions of Brown's admirable plan, could still make a difference. Unfortunately, the story of computing in the schools is largely a story of what could be, rather than what is. What could and eventually will be done are topics of great interest (and in some ways more immediate than we might at first think), but instead, consider what could be done right now, if we pushed just a little.

Toward the goal of getting the habit of learning, the microcomputer *right now* can do rapid diagnoses of specific sources of student errors. That capability can be used in many ways: it tells the teacher where each student is in the learning process; it can help in grouping children for activities that will be beneficial to them all; it can occasionally reveal specific weaknesses that might otherwise be assumed to be negligence.

Computer-based diagnosis can support tutoring and coaching. Alan Lesgold of the Learning Research and Development Center of the University of Pittsburgh observes the sad reality of education, that many teachers are operating perilously close to the limits of their own understanding. Consequently, diagnosis, which requires sophistication well beyond the skills being taught, is hard for them, and a computer assist would be a breakthrough. The lack of well-trained teachers is not exaggerated: in some areas, primary- and secondary-school teachers have had difficulty passing the very tests their own students are expected to pass. This is a real, immediate, and pressing problem that could be mitigated by software already in use experimentally.

A second way the computer can foster the habit of learning is to keep a student's attention focused, since the computer can respond so quickly. It is again sad reality, however, that early computer-aided instruction was witless, making decisions only on the basis of the time a student spent on a certain frame or forcing students to spend a predetermined amount of time on it, thus undermining the very strengths the computer brings to the learning process. This need not be so.

The computer can do the impossible—quite literally. When a teacher does a physical demonstration, that demonstration must follow the physical laws. But, as Lesgold says, students often hold views of the world that are incorrect. They would be astonished to confront the specific differences between their own and scientifically accepted views. The computer can illustrate both. "On the computer screen, the sun can orbit the earth, the laws of motion can be repealed, the gambler's fallacy can temporarily hold true." Here are important opportunities, multiple viewpoints.

Games can make certain kinds of low-level learning (especially in languages and arithmetic) more fun, and they can provide an environment to discover things. An Atari researcher, springing across a platform he was lecturing from, in imitation of a lion cub pouncing on a butterfly, once said: "Games are a simulation of life. They've proven to be adaptive for the species. Whereas schools haven't—yet."

In science and mathematics, whose teaching is, by everybody's estimate, dismal in the United States, researchers have evidence that a very large number of students *can* learn more than they typically do at present. Research has further shown that students are actually learning even less than was originally believed: many who pass elementary mathematics and physics courses nevertheless entertain Aristotelian views of physics and have no idea how to apply the mathematical formulas they have memorized. The

computer can change science and mathematics training by analyzing errors carefully; by creating an *experiential,* as distinct from
a theoretical, understanding and foundation for the student to
build upon; by providing an active rather than a passive role for
the student; by transcending a given teacher's knowledge and
personal values; and finally, by changing the word-heavy atmosphere of the classroom toward visual and dynamic alternatives.

Perhaps unexpectedly, the computer can contribute to ordinary literacy. Some of the great problems in teaching reading
right now are that those who choose teaching are no longer the
brightest and best; the quality of children's textbooks is dreadful
(but no surprise to me, who came across the problem in 1946)
and reading relies far too heavily on workbooks and exercise sheets
that are useless for children who don't already understand the
reading and busywork for those who do. But the computer, acting
as an intelligent tutoring system (which will require everything we
know about human learning and about artificial intelligence), could
embody a reading expert's knowledge of texts, a model of the
learner's current state of knowledge, and teaching strategies. Even
if such systems are too costly for schoolchildren to use, at least
teachers could learn how to teach reading from them.

Although computers in schools appear to teach students the
basics of an age they are entering (a point that puts parents in
favor of school computers), *which* aspects of current computer
usage will be relevant in the long term, or even five years hence,
is unclear. As my discussion of computer literacy implies, there is
no consensus about what the basics are. "To a large extent, our
whole society lacks the ability to keep up with the computer revolution," Lesgold remarks. "Finding the right mix of skills to teach
our children is a task to which the best available talent should be
applied."

No doubt. But meanwhile? Does the software that can't do all
we'd wish teach anything? I think so. At a minimum, it teaches
process, a dynamic way of dealing with intellectual abstractions over
time, unbounded by the circumstances of any given set of facts
but adaptable to new facts, new data, change. Well-structured
problems that would require children to use a variety of computing tools at appropriate places would teach perhaps the most
valuable skill of all, which is problem-solving. Beyond that, students acquire the confidence to deal with *complexity,* for even the

simplest programs can transform a certain degree of messy, muddy detail into more clearly structured intellectual representations. And if Brown University's Andries van Dam, professor of computer science, has his way, and scholars' workstations (or students' computers) are connected to each other usefully, then their lucky users will also learn the power of collaborative intellectual effort, which is *community* in the best sense.

When Marc Tucker was director of the Carnegie Corporation's Project on Information Technology and Education, he made some acute observations. If students had the opportunity of using word processing and data-base management software in *every* course, at *all* grades, they would greatly enhance their writing, their ability to express themselves in art and music, their facility with data, and their conceptual grasp of the physical sciences, mathematics, economics, history, and even house construction and plumbing.

But of course that won't happen, he said. Computing in most schools is a separate course (a sort of "theory of the pencil," with a little penmanship thrown in) taught in splendid isolation from a curriculum that, in any event, is in drastic need of reform if we are to prepare citizens for a world and workplace that are knowledge-intensive. "Computers are not a quick fix," he concluded. "They will ultimately prove immensely useful, but only when our schools have been reconceived, restaffed, and reorganized."

Computing as an essential part of education might have seemed revolutionary when Arthur Luehrmann proposed it in 1972, but it was to become a widespread, though vaguely understood, topic of discussion a decade or so later. Most people believed that adding computing to the curriculum meant adding another course called programming and wondered whether eight-year-olds really had a pressing need to know their way around BASIC. That the computer might be a medium to change the way we think across many disciplines, and not an end in itself, was hard to grasp if you'd never actually used one. Moreover, such discussion came at about the same time American schools happened to be in one of their poorest periods, both for funds and national confidence. Federal support had fallen drastically and local school districts were, in some cases, on the verge of, and over into, bankruptcy.

Consequently, the problem of getting computers into the schools set off a sharp debate among legislators and educators. On the one hand, California Congressman Fortney H. (Pete) Stark argued

that the best way was a one-time tax credit to computer manufacturers who donated equipment to the schools, but his oppo-
nents retorted that that would be a waste if the software wasn't
improved. "Yes, this legislation will cost the taxpayers money,"
Stark said. "Yes, it will cause a distortion in the tax code for one
year by adding a 'loophole.' But the ultimate impact of H.R. 701
is worth it. It is a bridge to the future for our children."

There's another fact of computing life that confuses the issue.
Even if the Japanese do not bring their fifth-generation intelligent
computers to market by 1990 (or even some interim form of them,
the likeliest possibility) the soberest of computer scientists in both
industry and the universities forecast that today's supercomputers,
such as the Cray-1, will be desktop items by 1990 and cost thousands, not millions. These estimates are made on the basis of
steady progress in device and software technology: the time and
cost for large IBM computers to complete a fixed amount of data
processing has gone from $14.54 and 375 seconds in 1955 to 7
cents and 1 second in 1983. (Or, to put it Madison Avenue style,
if the automobile industry had done what the computer industry
had done in the last thirty years, a Rolls-Royce would cost $2.50,
get 2 million miles per gallon, and fit on the head of a pin.)

I can easily imagine a prudent school board deciding to wait
and see. After all, five years is a very short time. If the costs are
coming down, and the level of computing ability among teachers
is so low, all the more reason to postpone a decision.

But that timidity has its own costs. China's Cultural Revolution
lasted about ten years, but its effects reverberated up and down
through several generations; perhaps that country will never fully
recover from its paroxysms of anti-intellectualism in the late 1960s
and early 1970s, a particularly bad time in history to have an
ideological tantrum. The rate of change in computing is rapid
and steady, and its cumulative effect compounds inexorably. Five
years isn't what it used to be.

I'm inclined to go along with Stark (though I would make a
few changes in the legislation by adding, at a minimum, input and
output devices) simply because his solution is the easiest and cheapest
and can be implemented almost at once. Some objections to computing in the schools are well-taken, the most difficult to answer
being Tucker's, that the problem is with the schools and not the
technology. All that said, the cost of acting now, and certainly

imperfectly, must be weighed against the cost of lost opportunity. They are almost imponderables.

Andries van Dam, the prime mover behind Brown's ambitious computing plan, has often been asked why other colleges and universities shouldn't just wait and see what Brown does, and then do likewise, at much less cost to themselves. Resorting to one of his favorite metaphors, he admits that pioneers do indeed get arrows in their backs—and up their backsides, he adds saltily. "But come on! This is one of the great intellectual challenges of the century. Are we going to wait until the manufacturers give us what *they* want to give us? Or are we going to take hold of this technology and shape it for our needs as we see them?"

Van Dam began his computing career in graphics, and so he is an ardent advocate of a combination of text and picture, each appropriate to its task. By animating the concepts in computer programming, for example, he has seen the time it takes for students to understand those concepts cut at least in half, a claim I can easily believe when I see those abstract notions made concrete in front of me. Such opportunities exist in every discipline and field. "I don't want to see the end of classrooms," he snorts impatiently, "I want choices, that's all. I want the classroom to be better."

And while he's at it: "I want to see network access, printing, archiving, bulletin boards, calendars, data bases, interactive help programs, and collaborations with colleagues, all supported by our system at Brown. I want to see the computer move from its function as a secretary, which it is now as a word processor, to functioning as a research assistant, to functioning finally as a partner in scholarly work. Will there be problems? Yes, of course. But we're the ones who should be in control; we're the ones who should be shaping this technology to our needs. Carnegie-Mellon and M.I.T. have similar programs under way, and we could have waited for them to do it, but frankly, we were afraid they might not do it right. They're technically oriented institutions; we're a liberal arts institution. There's so much to be done; there's plenty of work to go around."

Van Dam is relying on what he calls the Children's Crusade model. That is, students are so much more open to these new ideas than their parents and teachers that they will lead—or shame—their parents and instructors into the computer revolution.

Marc Tucker says education lacks neither ideas nor resources. It lacks leadership. But John Anderson of the University of Illinois wonders about the resources: "It gives one an odd feeling to contemplate the enormity of the investment in research, equipment, software, and maintenance that would be required for a large-scale introduction of computer technology into the schools when everywhere around the nation there are districts unable, or unwilling, even to finance an adequate supply of paper and pencils."

Caught up in the magic of his own metaphors. Schools have always successfully expected pupils to bring their own pencils and paper.

Interlude: Fairy Tales

In the next section I shall explore some of the major intellectual ideas of the science of computing. I call once more on the Brothers Grimm, not only to illustrate the ideas but, more important, to show that these issues have intrigued us for as long as we have been telling tales, which must be from the beginning of ourselves as the human species.

I was not the first. Though I'd forgotten it until a reader of an early draft of this book reminded me, in 1976 Allen Newell also called computing the Land of Faerie. I mention my forgetfulness only to emphasize how magical—in the best sense—people around the computer find it. In any event, when Newell accepted a chaired professorship at Carnegie-Mellon University in 1976, he held everyone in the audience—I was there—spellbound with what he eventually called "Fairytales." He began:

> Once upon a time when it was still of some use to wish
> for what one wanted, . . .
>   . . . there lived a King and Queen who had a daughter
>   who was lovely to behold, but who never laughed.
> Or perhaps:

234

> ... there lived an old fisherman by the side of a sea
> that had hardly any fishes in it.

"If you are like me," he confessed, "you are already hooked.
You are ready to abandon all talk of present matters, of computers
and electronic technology and professorships, and settle in to hear
a fairy story. Their attraction reaches almost all of us."

He went on to say why we all love fairy stories—how we enter
into an enchanted world where, after some trials, there is always
a happy ending, and happiness is forever, which means at least
for a little while. And though the experts tell us that fairy tales
are for childhood, Newell disagreed: "Fairy stories are for all of
us. Indeed, this is true especially in our current times. For we are,
all of us, children with respect to the future. We do not know
what is coming. The future is to us as new, and as incomprehen-
sible, as adult life is to children."

Fairy tales, he said, have a close connection to technology.
"The aim of technology, when properly applied, is to build a land
of Faerie." Though he regretted that most writers who write about
technology nearly always emphasize the negative (a point, as we
have seen, made in a slightly different way by John McCarthy)
Newell himself saw it differently: "I see the computer as the enchanted technology. Better, it is the technology of enchantment.
I mean that quite literally, so I had best explain."

And what he meant was that computerization provided intelligence and miniaturization. Algorithms and programs are "frozen action to be thawed when needed." The miniaturization of
these physical systems with the capacity for intelligent behavior
means that they are getting smaller, cheaper, less energy-
demanding: "Everything is changing in the right direction." Here
could be the Land of Faerie: "Computer technology offers the
possibility of incorporating intelligent behavior in all the nooks
and crannies of our world. With it we could build an enchanted
land."

The fallacy of the Sorcerer's Apprentice is that technologies
need to be rigid and unthinking. "But every computer scientist
recognizes in the Sorcerer's Apprentice simply a program with a
bug in it, embedded in a first generation operating system with
no built-in panic button. Even with our computer systems today,
poor things as they are, such blunderbuss looping is no longer a

specter." It was only so when computing was so expensive that we didn't know—nor could we have afforded it if we had known—how to make decisions and actions conditional on real situations. "The import of miniaturization is that ultimately we will be able to have the capability for enough conditionality in a small enough space. And the import of our scientific study of computers is that we will know how to make all the conditionality work for us."

Do technologies extract too high a price? Newell was speaking in the midst of the energy crisis, and that was much on everyone's mind. But he demurred: "Ecologically, computer technology itself is nearly magic. The better it gets the less of our environment it consumes." And when it gets better, it is just the right tool to help us cope intelligently with the use of our other resources.

A few toads have entered the Land of Faerie since Newell spoke. People who live in some parts of Silicon Valley are concerned about their groundwater supply having been contaminated by the chemicals that are used to etch chips, and some other people are deeply disturbed by the Valley's labor strife, what they see as an inequitable distribution of income between the very rich technicians and the very poor workers, often minority women, who are easily replaced by workers in faraway lands where the cost of labor is lower yet. There are still other toads.

The entrance of toads into the Land of Faerie does not give lie to the fact that we are in the process of creating an enchanted place. And Newell too reminds us that heroes of fairy tales have help, magic friends who sustain them and help them overcome the witches and giants that beset them.

We humans have made our own best help in this extension of our own intelligence called the computer. Its domain is utterly and completely human, the domain of symbols. If the science of nature is a human construction (and it is), so much the more is the science of the symbol machine. That's why the last section of the book which explores some parts of the scientific study of computers, has earned the right to be called "The New Humanities."

PART 4

The New Humanities

Chapter 23

Hunter-Gatherers of
the Infinite

Sometimes I think of scientists as the hunter-gatherers of the universe, tracking and trying to capture as much of it as they possibly can (all those secrets promised to me in my youth). It is, by and large, a group effort. They swap techniques generously, and news of good spots for quarry, not only among kinfolk but across disciplines too, all in this together (and not a little pride in one's reputation as hunter, tracker, and gatherer). Science, after all, is of, by, and for the human race. God can be presumed to know the material already.

And of course what scientists capture aren't the secrets of the universe so much as symbolic approximations of them: equations, a trace across a bubble chamber or an astronomer's film, the fleeting image on a microelectrograph. The instruments are devices for getting at phenomena in forms accessible to human understanding, a bit like the original hunter-gatherers learned to skin, peel, and cook what they acquired for better human digestion. As scientists hunt and gather, their approximations—symbolic structures all—strike me as a lovely monument to the human quest to understand, the human faith that the universe *is* understandable and worth pushing the hunt for.

But hunting and gathering in the forests, savannas, or even the galaxies of science—the natural world—is one thing; we are used to it and are getting much better at it. Hunting and gathering among the artifacts we have made ourselves, whether human societies or human dreams, is something else, and only began as systematic science in the late nineteenth century. Science surrounding the apparatus is newer yet.

So we ask what role in this larger human quest to understand does computer science play, based as it is on an artifact—a piece of apparatus—made by human beings?* Are computer scientists less hunter-gatherers than agriculturalists, growing their own? It's a pretty question with no certain answer. To be sure, the symbolic processor called the computer is not found in nature but cultivated, so to speak. But the methods of computer scientists are the same as those of their hunter-gatherer cousins in the other sciences: search and find, guess and be wrong, observe for regularities, shape the phenomena into rules and even laws that may or may not hold as new data are brought to bear.

While computer scientists attempt to set up the equivalent of the periodic table of elements or investigate atomic structures, their matter is information, symbols. And since information is a human specialty, there is not only discovery but construction, which is what gives the science its strong engineering, mathematical, and—surprise—artistic flavors.

So the revelations and constructions such science yields are interesting not only for their own sake but for their promised illumination of the other symbolic activities human beings engage in, whether thinking at the level of the individual or moving symbols around a large, multiprocessored system at the level of an economy. This is the stated and central assumption of artificial intelligence, and a much more covert, tentative assumption among other computer scientists.

For the rest of us, our viewpoints are shifting once more. There's ample evidence that Milton's meeting with the telescope changed his metaphors, that Darwin changed the outlook of an

---

*Computer science, that awkward phrase. I prefer the Continental "informatics," but in an unusual display of Anglo-American obstinacy, computer science has prevailed here, and as I've already complained, *ordinateur* isn't doing well outside France. But all credit to the French for their admirable searches for *les mots justes*.

age. Other examples abound, and computing will be no different. But where are we shifting? I offer a small example.

The computer—the emblematic machine of this symbol-besotted century—is deterministic. In principle, one can predict the outcome of any event and its effects on all other events. But as we have already seen, the global atmosphere is also deterministic: in principle, it too can be predicted down to the last molecule's behavior. In practice, it cannot, and that is important. And new. For regarding the atmosphere as a computer reminds us that a deterministic system of any complexity is beyond our puny powers to predict precisely and often beyond our powers to predict approximately.

If the news when Christopher Columbus set out was that the world had open bounds, the news in our century is more complicated. We have good reason to suspect that there are limits on the world after all, at least as we can know it. Here is one of the great departures by computer science from, say, mathematics. Mathematics has long had the notion of problems that are unsolvable—provably, you cannot square the circle—as well as problems that are. But computer science goes a step further. Having ascertained that a problem is solvable, that given enough computing time and memory, an answer can be found, it raises the next question, of practicality or tractability—in short, of cost. Is there an *efficient* solution to the problem? This is a central topic of theoretical computer science, which I shall have more to say about.

An argument is raised. Nature may be deterministic and therefore predictable; computers too; but if free will has any meaning at all, human behavior is not deterministic, and so whatever can safely be said about the natural world, and even this human artifact called the computer, cannot be said about human symbolic behavior. It is not predictable, even by God.

The answer to that from computing is that the use of such terms as *predestination* and *free will* is something like talking about the sunrise and the sunset—useful as a first approximation but really vast simplifications of processes so complex they stop the breath. As well talk about Mahler's Ninth as some tunes. Now we understand why saying that the computer does precisely as it is instructed is in fact almost meaningless, since we can't tell what that is.

For now, it's more pertinent to sidestep the argument and

listen to the message from all of twentieth-century science, biology as well as physics, that so far as humans are concerned it is more useful to view nature as probabilistic than deterministic. Within certain statistical limits, nature can be predicted after all, at least in the large. The same *probably* holds for human beings and their artifacts, though our grasp of the situation is mighty loose at the moment, whether we approach from scientific, philosophic, or even theological points of view.

I have said that a central premise of our century's intellectual inquiry is that beyond biology (and arguably a product of it) the fundamental condition of human existence is a milieu of symbols. We make and manipulate symbols as naturally, elaborately, and prolifically as we turn out cells. Unlike our cellular activity, our symbolic activity is nearly always a community affair. These symbols are complex and contain information. Some theories underlying the science of computing are beginning to give us new insights into complexity and information and the intimate link between them.

Thus *complexity* is a topic of central interest in computer science. It is complexity in the sense that ordinary people mean it, and in a special sense, the determination of the intrinsic difficulty of mathematically posed problems arising in many disciplines, from economics to scheduling airline personnel and planes, to the orderly sharing of resources among many parties.

By asking what the intrinsic difficulty of a particular problem is, theoreticians are asking what the minimal cost is to solve a problem, cost being, say, the time or space (computer memory) required. As might be expected, there are often time-space trade-offs.

Now why would anybody care? Computing gets cheaper and cheaper, and God made lots of time. First, in many applications, computing quickly, accurately, and cheaply is essential—a landing space shuttle has neither infinite time nor infinite computing power to figure out its landing arrangements. Next, as I have said earlier, computer science has introduced the question of tractability. Yes, in principle a problem might be solvable, but *can* it be solved in any practical way? No matter how cheap and plentiful computing is, some classes of problems are tough—even impossible—nuts to crack. These are the parts of the symbolic universe that can never be fully known.

So computer scientists have come face to face with the un-yielding barrier of the unknowable, the infinity of the symbolic universe, and a humbling experience it is. They can prove to their mathematical satisfaction (and human disappointment) that parts of the symbolic universe are forever closed to them. It is not so much that the physical universe has limits (perhaps yes, perhaps not) but that were we humans to arrive at such limits we could nevertheless *imagine* one more step, even if it proves impossible to take it. Thus the power, and ultimate intractability, of the deep space of the symbolic.

I myself am comfortable in this deterministic but not fully knowable universe, for it reminds me pleasantly of a theme that emerges in nearly every human mythology, from the Mediter-ranean to the Orient. It is the idea of a grand plan, a transcendent purpose in life. The plan or purpose eludes surface understanding by the individual, who imagines he is acting freely, when he is really acting out his fate in a process that is morally and meta-physically necessary or determined. Oedipus must kill his father and marry his mother no matter what precautions the family takes; Tristan and Isolde will love each other whether the magic potion causes it or only reveals it to them. Of course, the ancients might have been wrong about all this, and I admit it's eccentric even to make the connection. But I am reminded nevertheless.

So I return to my point that science, including computer sci-ence, is of, by, and for the human race. We are eager to know what we can about our destiny, the universe we find ourselves in. Still, a "science" of an artifact—as opposed to a set of natural phenomena—makes some people uneasy. Let us put aside worries about nomenclature for the moment and propose that computer science is a body of structured knowledge with predictive laws (not all known nor understood at present) about artificial, or human-made, phenomena and objects.

A taxonomic word or two about computer scientists. As with any science, the practitioners fall roughly into two categories: the theoreticians and the experimentalists.

The experimentalists design the machines, build them, and run programs on them to see how things work. And yes, it must be done. To repeat, in systems of any complexity, we humans have great difficulty in telling how the components will behave together until we try out the ensemble. More interesting, such experiments allow scientists to tease out and infer properties of the ensemble that they hadn't the wit to dream up in the abstract, ahead of time. Again, roughly speaking, the experimentalists in computer science are the empiricists in the crowd.

The theoreticians, on the contrary, abstract the essence of a machine; they think about machines that don't really exist or exist only in some general formalized way, such as a universal machine (as they say with fetching modesty, although they mean it in a technical sense; for instance, that many, perhaps most, phenomena, both natural and artificial, can be digitally simulated, hence the universality of the digital computer). Theoreticians seek the grand and unifying principles, true about any computer, though their models of computing depend on whether they are thinking about sequential machines that process one item at a time or parallel machines that process several, or even many, items simultaneously. (There are still other models of computation.) The lingua franca of theoreticians is mathematical.

To confound our little categories, however, Newell and Simon, to name two examples, who consider themselves empiricists, running experiments and making observations, have produced profound theories that are not mathematical. H. T. Kung, also of Carnegie-Mellon and known as a brilliant theoretician, has had a busy hand in building new kinds of computers based on his theoretical models. The field abounds with such unclassifiables, which suggests that the classifications, like predestination and free will, are simply inadequate.

But for convenience, I stand by my rough categories and report that, in addition to the division between theoreticians and experimentalists, there are a number of subcultures among computer scientists, meaning that the practitioners can be viewed in various other ways: software vs. hardware specialists, procedure-oriented language users vs. nonprocedural languages, and so on.

One such division is between algorithmically inclined computer scientists, by far the largest number who work in the field, and the non-algorithmic people, who are mainly in artificial intelligence. The gap between these two groups is rather like the state of affairs between China and the United States in the nineteenth century; some mutually beneficial trade takes place, but each culture, when it thinks about the other at all, regards itself as so obviously superior that the issue of closer relations is hardly

worth pursuing. (However, whereas nineteenth-century America *They were*
sent a lively group of Christian missionaries to China in the rather *reasonably*
vain hopes of claiming souls for the faith, I detect little movement *successful*
on either side here to raise up the heathen.)

The term *algorithm* comes from the name of a famous Persian
textbook author, Abu Ja'far Mohammed ibn Musa al-Khowarizmi
(c. 825), whose name is translated for us by Donald Knuth as
"Father of Ja'far, Mohammed, son of Moses, native of Khowar-
izm," now the Soviet city of Khiva. An algorithm is a procedure
for solving a problem that guarantees (or claims to guarantee) an
answer. It contains steps of actions to be executed in sequential
order, steps that must be precisely defined and unambiguously
specified. (Knuth adds: "A useful algorithm should require not
only a finite number of steps, but a *very* finite number, a reasonable
number.") Examples of these procedures range from the simplest
of arithmetic functions (to find the area of a rectangle whose sides
are 3 meters and 12 meters, multiply 3 times 12) to the most
complex packages of algorithms to model natural phenomena
such as weather, nuclear diffusion, fluid flow, supersonic flow,
and materials elasticity, all involving numerical computations that
were impossible to perform before the introduction of the computer.

However, an algorithm approach to the solution of a problem
presupposes that the problem can be precisely—that is, mathematically—stated and that there exists a procedure, an algorithm,
that guarantees the solution with finite effort. Moreover, the problem cannot change during the time that attempts are made to
solve it.

Many researchers in artificial intelligence—the nonalgo-
rithmic culture—are skeptical about the value of the algorithmic
approach for the kinds of problems they want to solve because,
as they argue, most human problems cannot be mathematically
stated; that is, the information in the most interesting problems
that humans must solve every day is seldom clearly specified.
Moreover, no unique solution can be found to most problems
requiring humanlike intelligence. And finally, it's in the nature of
real-life problems to change out from under you continuously.
Algorithmic computer science is elegant stuff, they say, but its
applications are severely limited. (But then, to make life tangy for
catalogers, the AI community likes to talk about "heuristic search

algorithms" and has developed several to reduce the number of possibilities to be considered in the solution of problems.)

On the contrary, retort the algorithmically inclined, algorithms are all you can depend on in an uncertain universe. And uncharitable remarks are added: Is the mathematics just too tough for you?

Of course the demarcations aren't quite as sharp as that, but the two subcultures nevertheless coexist in mutual disregard. The practitioners of artificial intelligence may be thought of as the ultimate empiricists in computer science; they are relatively short on formal theory and long on observing and then simulating examples of intelligent behavior as best they can. They concede that someday theory might catch up to practice and probably improve it. Meanwhile they attempt to construct intelligent systems any way they can, and thanks to learning-by-doing, thanks to more powerful technology, more of their structures are beginning to stand, be useful, and even inspire.

A synthesis of work in both camps may eventually occur, and if it does, I place my bet that it will happen somewhere between artificial intelligence and theoretical computer science. I say that because in many ways the two camps are asking the same kinds of questions, and it is a given of science that a sound formal theory helps us understand, extend, and finally make strong intellectual structures out of what are otherwise mysterious and unrelated phenomena. Since I have already written extensively elsewhere about artificial intelligence, let me now examine some parts of the theory of computer science, not only to understand the solutions it proposes to problems of interest to human beings but also to ask if its insights can be extended to suggest new ways for us to understand, capture, and think about the rich, indeed infinite, symbolic universe we humans have invented and move about in.

Chapter 24

Chaos, Chance, and Certainty

It might be a scene from the Brothers Grimm. A group of philosophers—the Grimms would have said wizards—are seated at a large round table having lunch. In the center of the table is a bowl of spaghetti. Each philosopher has a plate in front of him and two forks, one on each side. However, the forks are shared: between two people there is exactly one fork.

"Now the philosophers, each in his own good time, are going through cycles," says Michael Rabin, the Albert Einstein Professor of Mathematics at Hebrew University and the T. J. Watson, Sr., Professor of Computer Science at Harvard, who first described to me the dining philosophers problem, formulated by Edsger Dijkstra. "They are not synchronized. Being philosophers and occupied with their thoughts, they may become hungry and want to eat. But each one needs two forks, because that's the way you eat spaghetti. What's the procedure whereby the hungry philosopher picks up his forks, the so-called protocol?"

A classical solution would be a fixed procedure, in computing, a program:

1. If you are hungry, look to your right until a fork is down (meaning the person to your right has released it).

2. Pick it up and look to your left.

3. Wait for the second fork.

4. When the left fork is down, pick it up.

5. Eat.

6. Release your forks, first the right and then the left.

But suppose all the philosophers get hungry at the same time? Following the classical solution, everybody does step one. Then everybody does step two. But step three is impossible: there they all sit, one fork in hand, forever in famished deadlock. Now we are truly in an enchanted place, men frozen by some magic spell that can only be broken by—by what?

"Humans won't behave that way," Rabin says, with a bit more sanguinity on that topic than I have, "but when we are programming computer processes, each needing two resources that are linked together and shared in a way similar to the philosophers, this actually happens: breakdowns occur on account of deadlocks even though the computer is completely healthy and functioning."

Appoint one of the philosophers king? Rabin can still prove that under unfavorable conditions deadlock will occur. If the problem recalls a fairy tale, it is not merely fancy. It is at the heart of computer network design and resource sharing. Like the philosophers, computer processors operate sequentially, but the group operates concurrently. Thus the dining philosophers stand as a paradigm for groups that must share—resources, information, whatever—or else be deadlocked.

The scene shifts to Grand Central Station. You are part of a group of a hundred people who have decided to meet there sometime between 10 and 11 A.M. But when you straggle to the station, you realize there are several entrances, that those entrances are sufficiently far apart that you can't see one from the other. Moreover, enough people are milling around that if you walk from one entrance to another, others in your group may miss you because of the crowd. Even notes tacked to a bulletin board won't help much, because if you attach a message and then walk to the other entrance, perhaps your friends are doing the same, and you'll pass by each other unknowingly. This is an example of the choice-coordination problem: Is there a procedure that will allow you and your group to coordinate choices without having decided beforehand at which entrance you'd meet?

An army with many units, each headed by a general, is mounting a siege on a city. The generals realize that if they are going to attack, they should all attack at once or else they should all do nothing. They pass a message around, trying to decide on a concerted attack to start, say, at noon the next day. But there are Byzantine generals—traitors—among them who are trying to confuse the others and cause a nonconcerted attack. No one can identify the Byzantine generals and no general has any way of knowing whether a message passed to him is true or false. Is there a procedure that will lead to a concerted decision despite the traitors' attempts to confuse the others?

The Byzantine generals problem has long been otherwise known as the interactive consistency problem. It was renamed with some flair by Leslie Lamport of SRI International, when he and his group faced exactly these circumstances in designing a fuel-efficient plane that operated with many processors, some of which might be giving false information.

In each of these chaotic situations, Michael Rabin has proved that orderly decision making can be brought about—the problem can be solved—by introducing chance. To me, it sounds magical.

In any case, it's a solution with at least some irony from a man who bears Einstein's name in his title. It was Einstein who, dismayed by the probabilistic nature of statistical mechanics, exclaimed that he couldn't believe God played dice with the universe.

Rabin is saying that, on the contrary, to introduce randomization, or chance, is the only way the universe, or any other large, complex system that must share resources, can function without deadlock.

We return to the hungry philosophers, each of whom now has a coin with an L for Left on one side and an R for right on the other. When a hunger pang interrupts a philosopher's thoughts, he tosses his coin. If the coin comes up L, he looks to his left and keeps waiting until the fork there is down. When that happens, he picks it up and looks to the other, the right side. If the fork on his right isn't down on the table, then he'll release first fork he is holding. And now he will not automatically look to his left or to his right, but rather toss the coin again and look to whichever side the coin has selected.

The system is symmetrical, in that each philosopher behaves according to the program, but their actual actions are unpredictable, depending as they do on the results of the tosses of their own private coins. Rabin and his associate Daniel Lehmann have proved with statistical certainty that there will be no deadlock, even under the most severe, adverse conditions, including a wicked witch who is *trying* to deadlock the philosophers.

For the puzzled people milling about at Grand Central Station, Rabin has been able to provide another randomized solution, simple and independent of the number of participants. For the Byzantine generals, Rabin has produced still another randomized procedure, which he calls fighting fire with fire: "The Byzantine generals may be trying to foil agreement, so our countermeasure involves confounding them with surprise random moves so as to foil *their* plan."

The imposition of order upon a large number of actors or participants in an ensemble by introducing randomness goes, as Rabin admits, against the intuition. "By deliberately using chance, tossing a coin, we derive not uncertainty but a very, very large measure of certainty that cannot be achieved otherwise. Chance produces not only certainty but simplification. It's one of those intellectual surprises that's completely novel." And, he adds, the issues were meaningless before the advent of the computer: you could hardly pose, let alone answer, such questions.

The imposition of order on a very large number of participants in a system through the use of randomization or chance has immediate computational applications. "Instead of one big monolithic computer, which does more or less one thing at a time, we will soon have a distributed system of many processors on which many computational processes will be running concurrently. However, these computational processes will not be complete strangers to each other because if they were there would be no reason for having them all incorporated into one system. From time to time they want to interact, to exchange information, to access certain shared resources. This raises complex problems of synchronization and coordination, of the actions of these many actors."

But there are wider issues still. "Here in the computer is equipment that can process, store, and transport information at enormous rates, proverbially with the speed of light, and behave in a rather flexible way under given programs that we write for it,"

Rabin says. "We immediately arrive at the question posed right at the start of the computing era in the early fifties: Can we program these machines to behave in an intelligent way to solve problems at a level of our own problem-solving ability? Artificial intelligence is one of the major challenges that the computer age poses."

Rabin has been thinking about that particular question for a while, although he came at it indirectly. At the start of his career, when he was exploring the mathematical notion of information theory proposed by Claude Shannon, he began to suspect that Shannon's approach was insufficient to measure the quantity of real interest in computation, the quantity now called complexity, or inherent difficulty.

"To give a well-known analogy from mechanics, if you want to lift a book, say, from the floor level of your room to the ceiling, there are many ways by which you can do it. You can have a small machine or a small electric motor that lifts up the book; you can do it by hand; two people can get hold of that book and together lift it up; they can do it completely vertically or diagonally. So there are many processes and modes.

"However, in mechanics there is the notion of the *work* required for lifting that book from floor level to the ceiling; this a quantity inherent to that task. In the same way I wanted to define the inherent difficulty, or amount of work, involved in a computational task. So I wrote a paper introducing what was later on called complexity, an axiomatic definition of this inherent amount of work required for the solution of the problem, or the execution of a computational task."

Rabin was able to prove that there were certain computational problems that are inherently difficult, including some of the tasks that were being attempted in artificial intelligence. In 1974 in a talk at an international congress, Rabin showed that some of the programs that people were trying to implement in full generality would eventually break against the stone wall of complexity.

Were there possible ways around this? Could it be that some of these problems were so complex and practically intractable because we insisted on solving with complete certainty? Rabin reflected that human problem solving is not completely reliable, that we make occasional mistakes. Could it be that by giving up the idea of always being right, the solution procedure could be simplified, that in fact a solution to some of these problems could be reached in a practical amount of time? (This is, in fact, similar to an operating principle of AI, but Rabin's aim was to prove it in a mathematically rigorous way.) He showed that by giving up some certainty, in exchange, the complexity of the problem would be reduced, sometimes considerably.

A year later he had devised a test for primality of large numbers (a large number has several hundred digits, and is therefore on the order of a million million million repeated twenty or thirty times). Until then, testing whether a very large number is prime— has no divisors—was not impossible but would have taken hundreds, perhaps millions, of years on a computer. But Rabin's test worked. It had some well-defined computational procedures, and during the process a coin was tossed, figuratively speaking, which decided whether the procedure would do one thing or another. At the end of the test a number could, with very high certainty, be declared prime or composite. The test might produce an erroneous answer, but the possibility of that was two to the minus one hundred, which is smaller than one over a million, million, million. From the practical point of view, this unimaginably small uncertainty that had been introduced bought an enormous reduction in computing time, turning an impossible problem into a possible, even cheap, one. The test was very fast and could be implemented on a small, relatively slow computer. (Two other scientists, Robert Soloway of the University of California, Berkeley, and Völker Strassen, of the University of Zurich, arrived at the same idea independently, but never implemented their test.)

Since then, scientists have published literally hundreds of papers that employ the idea of randomization. By introducing randomization, and accepting minuscule chances of error, hitherto provably impossible computations can be performed. The applications are myriad, including procedures not only for orderly decision making under conditions of false, incomplete, or overwhelming amounts of information but also for dealing with the problems of the dining philosophers, the group at the railroad station, and the Byzantine generals. Rabin's randomness procedures have also found applications in computer security and integrity of information.

I cannot resist going further: the potency of randomness, I suspect, has even wider applications than in computing. Some scientists are already beginning to ask whether nature doesn't make the otherwise unworkable work by supplying a bit of randomness from time to time—jumping genes, for example. I wonder if randomness is an unrecognized but essential part of human decision making and if a time won't come when we shall deliberately and consciously incorporate a sort of coin tossing into all kinds of symbolic activities, not to liven them up but to smooth them out.

Surprising it may be. But to me, this imposition of order upon chaos by the introduction of chance fits securely in the great poetic tradition of paradox, the contradictions in terms—bittersweet, cruel comfort, death-in-life—that saturate the world's great theologies, philosophies, and art—and always suggest a deeper truth.

Chapter 25

The National Football League, the Traveling Salesman, and Complexity

Apropos of the topics I think about these days, I am struck by one theme that recurs in almost every story collected by the Brothers Grimm, the stuff of suspense and plot itself. The innocent—maiden, princeling, orphan—is presented by fate with an impossible task, and unless that task is accomplished in a given time, by sunset, by daybreak, then life will be forfeit. The tasks are wondrous: spinning straw into gold, discovering how the twelve princesses dance their shoes into holes, emptying a pond with a teaspoon, clambering up a glass mountain. Precision is essential, since fate does not forgive those who lapse. The good and clever eventually accomplish the tasks, the wicked are punished by them, at least in the tales of Grimm, though life itself is not so evenhanded.

One message anybody might draw from this theme is our everlasting fascination with puzzles, our everlasting hope of overcoming the clearly insuperable. Like the heros of folktales, computer science theoreticians have been tackling the computational equivalents of emptying ponds with teaspoons and climbing glass mountains with surprisingly successful results.

"In a number of branches of science, engineering, and commerce," said Richard Karp to me one afternoon, "problems arise

254

that have the character of puzzles. These are problems of scheduling, packing, or arrangement." Karp is one of the foremost specialists in these difficult problems, and we spoke in his office at the University of California in Berkeley, where he is a professor of computer science.

"So, for example, scheduling the games in the National Football League is subject to certain restrictions about the number of home and away games, the number of Sunday games, and so forth. Scheduling jobs that have to go through a job shop has similar kinds of restrictions; so does determining the optimal layout of circuits on a chip, which may have tens of thousands of circuits that have to be interconnected. The best order in which a school bus should visit a set of locations is another example."

In principle, these problems are finite and could be tackled by a finite search through all the possible arrangements. For example, all the arrangements of transistors and the wires on a circuit could, in principle, be enumerated. But in practice such an enumeration is beyond all feasible bounds.

"Let's say the problem involved choosing the best way of placing a given number of objects along a line. We say that the number of such placements of an object is N-factorial. And N-factorial is a mathematical function that takes off very, very steeply, so that by the time you have, say, twenty objects to be arranged on a line, the number of possible arrangements is so enormous that it wouldn't be feasible to list them."

This is easy to see. Ten objects to be arranged on a line means about 3 million possibilities of arrangement (what mathematicians call ten factorial). But double those ten objects to twenty, and we must cope with 2 million million million possibilities (twenty factorial, or 2.4×10^{18}). Double again to forty objects, and our possibilities are raised to the number whose first digit is one, followed by about 46 zeroes. The combinatorial explosion is aptly named.

"So shortcuts have to be found," Karp said, "in order to tackle these problems. Over the years, computer scientists as well as workers in operations research and engineering began to investigate these problems, and they found that for some of them the solution was very easy. Even though, from a certain point of view, the number of possibilities to be combed through was vast, enough characteristics of the solution could be identified so that it was possible to actually cut right through to the solution very quickly without having to make any enumeration. Here's such a situation: suppose you've got a bunch of computers that have to be connected together with wires in such a way that there was to be a path from any computer to any other computer. How can you do this in a way that minimizes the total wire length? There's an endless number of ways of choosing the configuration of the wires, but it turns out that an extremely simple procedure—you could teach it to anyone—will find the optimum without any search. You just keep connecting the closest pair of computers (or cities or bus stops) that haven't been joined yet. And that gives you the optimum solution. I can show you on the board."

And here Karp got up and drew little diagrams that, sure enough, seemed to show that what he was saying was true. He assured me that this simple connecting procedure had been proved mathematically to be the optimum solution to the problem. He stood back from the blackboard. "So there's a case where the number of possibilities is vast, but a simple rule gives you the best one. But in many other cases—in fact, in most cases—people were unable to come up with simple rules. And the suspicion began to dawn on many workers that these problems were, in some sense, intractable."

He returned to his chair and sat down. "Now, in order to prove or disprove such a statement, one needs a clear definition of the boundary between a tractable problem and an intractable one. The working definition, the thesis that people adopted, although by no means perfect, turned out to be this: we'll say that a problem is tractable if you can solve it by an amount of effort that goes only as some power of the size of the problem. So if you have N objects to be arranged, and you can do it by looking at all pairs of them, that would be essentially N^2 computation steps, and if you had to look at all triplets of them, if would be N^3 and so on. So some fixed power like N^3, N^4, N^5 is provisionally considered tractable. But on the other hand, if you had to look at all combinations of them, that would be 2^N power, an exponential function that takes off very much faster. If the execution time of the search has to be that big, we say that the problem is intractable."

This definition is clear but somewhat controversial, Karp explained, because some argue that even having to look at all triplets or all quadruplets is too much work to consider the problem tractable. "But as a rough cut, that's the distinction we make. Now the question of complexity becomes a completely well-posed mathematical problem. Does there or does there not exist an algorithm for a given problem whose running time is bounded by one of these power functions (which, by the way, are called polynomial functions)? The reason it's a well-posed problem is that we have a clear mathematical definition of an algorithm based on the concept of an abstract computing mahine, such as a Turing machine. It turns out furthermore that the concept is robust, that the measures of running time or execution time don't change terribly much if we go from one abstract model of the computer to another. So the problem does not depend on some finicky details of definition but is really meaningful in a broader sense."

He considered the example of the traveling salesman, who has given his name to the whole genre of such problems. "In what order should a salesman visit the cities in his territory so as to keep his total travel time to a minimum? It's a yes-or-no question, is there a polynomial time algorithm for the traveling salesman problem? We still don't know the answer to that question! But the concept of NP-completeness, which is what we've been leading up to here [NP-completeness stands literally for nondeterministic polynomial completeness], provides a kind of organizational framework that gives us strong circumstantial evidence about any problems. And the way it works is: we define a certain large class of problems, which includes all the common combinatorial search problems. And this class is called NP. Roughly speaking, NP is the class of problems where it may be very hard to search for an answer, but once you've found it, you can recognize it."

He returned to the National Football League. "It might be very hard to put together all the pieces of the jigsaw to see whether you could satisfy all the constraints—like a team couldn't play at home three weeks in a row, it had to play a certain number of Monday-night games, and so forth. But if I handed you a schedule, it would be a perfectly routine matter to check all these conditions quickly, that is, in polynomial time, and determine yes, the schedule was okay. So most of these puzzle-like problems that we encounter have this characteristic, that even though the solution may be very, very hard to search for, you can quickly check it when it's handed to you. And that class of problems is called NP. NP is more or less coextensive with all the commonly encountered combinatorial problems." He hesitated in a scholarly way, and

added, "Well, there are some technical fine points that I'll skip
over. That'll be good enough for our purpose."

He resumed his explanation. "Within NP we have P. And P
is the name we give to the problems that can be solved easily, the
problems that can be solved within polynomial time. NP, then,
includes P, the easy problems, as well as everything else. NP problems are the hard ones; P problems are the easy ones. NP-complete
is an adjective to describe the problems that are hardest within
NP."

One problem is considered harder than another, he went on
to explain, if the second problem can be reduced to the first one:
problem A is harder than problem B if anybody who could do A
could also do B.

This is well known to wicked stepmothers and other malcon-
tents. In "The Fisherman and His Wife," when the wife is not
content with living in a humble hut but insists upon a pretty cottage
and then a stone castle, all provided by the magic carp whose life
her fisherman husband has saved, and who itself knows a few
things about solving difficult problems, it could be said she is
testing the carp, reducing the problem to harder and harder problems. But her ambitions grow: the stone castle gradually becomes
even larger and more elaborate, for the wife has decided she wants
to be ruler of the land; and then to be emperor; then pope; and
at last rule the sun and the moon. Here the line is drawn, and
her greed and ambition land her back in her little hut.

In scientific terms, the problem of ruling the sun and the moon
is NP-complete. For the way a problem is proved to be NP-complete, the hardest of all, is to show that every problem in that
universe of problems called NP can be reduced to that problem.
The carp can provide the fisherman's wife with everything in the
world that she wants, except to be God.

Our modern scientific applications are, unfortunately, less romantic: Karp cites traveling salesmen, not ambitious wives.

"So the traveling salesman problem turns out to be NP-complete," Karp said. "And the consequence is, if you could do the
traveling salesman problem, you could do all the others. If there
were a shortcut to the traveling salesman problem, if it could be
done in polynomial time, then all the others could be done in
polynomial time too. As we put it, is NP equal to P? Is the whole
domain of problems of interest equivalent to the class of easy

problems? Is every problem easy? We hardly think so. That would mean that anytime you had a puzzle-like problem where at least you could check the solution, you would expect to be able to find it easily. That seems far too good to be true, but it's an open mathematical possibility at the moment.

"Now the working significance of NP-completeness is that we provisionally assume that our NP-complete problem is intractable. If centuries of effort haven't yielded solutions to any NP-complete problems, we don't expect we're going to do it; we think probably P is different from NP, and so these problems are intrinsically intractable. But we still don't know. And that means we ask for less when we work on them. We try to modify the problem so that it ceases to be intractable. Instead of asking for the best tour for the salesman, we ask for a tour that is within 10 percent of the optimum."

Computer scientists call it "relaxing" a problem when they don't insist on strict optimality but will settle for an approximate solution to a problem. That sometimes makes a problem amenable to solution that otherwise wouldn't be. It's desirable to wire a chip with a minimum length of wire (this shortens the length of time that it takes electronic impulses to flow around a chip) but coming within a few percent of the absolute minimum is an easier problem than striving for absolute optimality.

Yet for all their difficulty, people tackle such problems, Karp observed, and solve them in some sort of way. "What people typically do is devise some kind of heuristic, a rule of thumb, and try it out, and if it performs well enough often enough, then they're satisfied with it. In other words, they give up entirely on guarantees but simply try empirically to observe whether some quick and dirty method performs, is satisfactory, in a pragmatic sense. The heuristics that people use are much more complex than the ones I try to analyze."

Another approach, he added, was to try to theoretically validate the performance of those simple rules of thumb that nevertheless perform adequately. For example, even though the traveling salesman problem is hard, you can solve it if you're given a map and destinations. Or, sitting at a screen and given suitably informative displays of information, you could probably trace out a freehand path to connect the parts of a chip that would work. Researchers in AI also duck the combinatorial explosion by rules of thumb that immediately limit their possible choices to tractable dimensions.

Let me repeat that the AI approach to problem solving is decidely and deliberately non-mathematical. It is also non-algorithmic. In his pre-computing studies of human behavior in decision making, Herbert Simon long ago coined the term "satisficing" to describe what humans do in the real world—they may not find the very best solution to a problem they must solve, but they find one that's good enough, and that's the one they settle for. Most AI researchers aren't rabidly anti-algorithmic; an AI rule of thumb says that if you can solve a problem algorithmically, then solve it algorithmically. But AI researchers believe that most problems humans encounter don't satisfy the conditions of algorithmic solution; again, they cannot be mathematically stated, they are not finite, you can't always recognize when you've solved them, and they often change as you're in the process of solving them. People muddle through with their little heuristics nevertheless, settling for the less than perfect solution.

Artificial intelligence calls that winnowing down of possibilities—those methods that humans use to muddle through problems that are mathematically intractable—heuristic search. Faced with a problem to solve, a symbol system, human or computer, generates potential solutions in the form of symbol structures and compares them with the structure of the solution, the goal. This generate-and-test method is always limited, in practical terms, by scarce computational resources (what in humans we might call lack of information, imagination, time, and so on), so it must somehow be made more effective than merely random. And indeed the space of symbol structures exhibits some degree of order and pattern; that order and pattern can more or less be detected; and the problem solver does so by extracting information from the search space and thus generates only structures that show promise of being solutions. The more semantic information the system has access to, the better it performs in this search. But a heuristic search doesn't guarantee the best solution; it doesn't even guarantee any solution at all.

I asked Richard Karp what people had done about such problems before they had computers, and he laughed. He then made a very important point. "I think before we had computers we simply didn't attempt to model problems in the detail that would lead to these complex issues. Most of these very hard puzzle-like problems come because we've raised our aspirations. We try in our modelings to take many more factors and variables into account. We ask for much more, the size of the puzzles we attack is much larger, whether we're talking about economic modeling or weather prediction or laying out circuits. We undertake things on a much larger scale, partly because of the growing complexity of society and partly because of the advantage the computer now gives us to deal with complexity."

But by asking how *difficult* problems might be, theoreticians have also uncovered how easy some other problems are. Certain very important problems can be solved very much faster than had been thought. The fast Fourier transform, a method of computation discovered by theoreticians, collapsed certain kinds of computation from millions of units of time to tens of thousands of units of time and went on to revolutionize entire disciplines, such as crystallography and signal processing. Without the fast Fourier transforms, the startling diagnostic techniques that I have described in the chapter on medicine would have been simply impossible.

In a sense, Karp and his colleagues are in league with the fisherman's wife of the fable, pushing at the boundaries to reach that place where we humans are rulers, emperors, and even popes of the realm of the intellect, but beyond which we cannot go, the unknowable, the incomputable, the nondeterministic polynomial completeness that will elude us forever.

Chapter 26

The Science of
Information

Computer science, to repeat, is a body of structured knowledge
with predictive laws (not all known nor understood at present)
about a class of artificial, or human-made, phenomena and objects
known generically as symbols and sometimes as information. A
group of computer scientists have been trying to tease out some
general laws of information that will help solve certain kinds of
problems that appear in many disciplines, including robotic vision,
distributed computation, resource allocation in a decentralized
economy, seismology, statistics, scientific and engineering computation, medical imaging, signal processing, control theory, and
still others. Typically, each of these disciplines deals only with
problems it considers within its purview, relying on ad hoc techniques for solutions.

And yet scientists in these disciplines have something in common: they must all solve problems with only partial or approximate information. Roughly speaking, information is partial if its
quantity is insufficient to solve a problem exactly, and information
is approximate if it is contaminated by error. (This is different
from, say, routing the traveling salesman or scheduling the National Football League, where all information is complete and
exact.)

262

"For most systems and problems, the available information is partial and approximate," says Joseph Traub, who is the Edwin Howard Armstrong Professor of Computer Science and Professor of Mathematics at Columbia. Together with Henryk Woźniakowski of Columbia and the University of Warsaw, he has founded a field known as information-based complexity. Its goal is to create a general theory about problems with partial or approximate information and to apply the results to solving specific problems in varied disciplines.

"For example, in weather prediction, thousands of weather stations make measurements at various altitudes. In addition, planes, ships, and satellites also make measurements. As with all measurements, these will inevitably be contaminated with errors. Furthermore, since there are only a certain number of measurements that can be taken, the information is partial." Partial information contaminated with errors is a fact of real life, but it puts severe limits on, for example, long-term predictions.

In the interests of full disclosure, Traub and I are married to each other, and so I have seen his interests in information and complexity evolve over many years, becoming more refined and deeper as time goes by.

Information-based complexity aims at a general theory for dealing optimally with uncertainty. It takes what is called the information-centered approach, as distinct from the algorithm centered approach. This does not mean that workers here do not use algorithms. On the contrary, their theory provides a provably optimal algorithm for a given problem. Working at the information level, a higher order of abstraction that transcends the details of each particular field, offers extremely powerful tools that are not available at the algorithm level.

Not everybody believes that the goals of information-based complexity can be achieved. Because scientists can already solve some problems with partial or approximate information without the benefit of any general laws, some of them don't believe such laws exist, or if they do, they question whether Traub and his group are on the right track of discovery.

And yet the argument against ad hoc solutions to problems is not that they shouldn't be used—everybody is interested in solving problems, and sooner rather than later. Instead, the arguments against ad hoc solutions are that they remain at a low and relatively impotent intellectual level: it is difficult to be sure that they are the best solution (cheapest, fastest, most accurate), and they are seldom extendable to other domains.

Whether Traub and his group are on the right track will only be answered in time. But he is optimistic.

"Since for most problems," Traub says, concurring with researchers in artificial intelligence, "information is partial and approximate, we can't hope for an exact answer; we must live with uncertainty. There are examples everywhere: in the physical and biological sciences, engineering, control, prediction, decision theory, tomography, economics, designing experiments, seismology, sociology, medicine. Typically, the larger the system, the less likely you are to have exact information, especially if the system is changing with time. You settle for knowing that a certain outcome is probable, but you can't be sure."

Those fields look very different from each other—economists don't have much to say to seismologists, nor biologists to decision theorists. But Traub and his colleagues are asking whether, at this information level of abstraction, laws exist governing how well problems that apply to all such fields can be solved. They believe there are such laws and are trying to discover them.

Why? "One of the central theses of science is that the correct level of generality, that is, of abstraction from the particular, leads to simplicity. Unimportant details are ignored. Progress is made by showing that diverse phenomena can be uniformly explained. A sound general theory exhibits structure that is invisible to someone looking only at a particular problem. It also suggests entirely new questions and approaches. Newtonian mechanics provides an archetypal example. Before Newton, any 'reasonable' person believed that the heavens and earth were different domains and that apples and planets were very different objects, obeying very different laws. For some characteristics this is true; you can verify that by biting into an apple and biting into a planet. But if the correct variables, which are force, mass, and acceleration, are considered, then there *are* laws that apply equally well to apples and planets as well as to carriages, waterwheels, and buildings."

The discovery of general laws about science has proved in the long run to be an efficient way to achieve practical results. Chemistry stopped being alchemy when general, predictive laws began to emerge about the elements, and medicine became more than hand holding as biologists discovered the nature of microbes and their relation to disease. Laws about information would lead to effective solutions of problems routinely inundated by staggering amounts of information that must be scanned with the hope of choosing the best information. In addition, the laws would lead to economical solutions when information is scarce and very costly.

What do the first emerging laws of information look like? Traub and his colleagues have looked at problems as different from each other as planets and apples and yet identified as common to them all some basic properties and a fundamental quantity, which they call the radius of information.

Just as complexity measures the inherent *difficulty* of a problem, the radius of information measures the intrinsic *uncertainty* in the solution of a problem based on the available information. It is stated in their information principle: "There exists a quantity called the radius of information which measures the intrinsic uncertainty of solving a problem if specified information is known."

The radius of information is a powerful mathematical notion, and applied to problems with partial and approximate information, it not only says how well a problem can be solved but also leads to the best algorithm and the best information. The "best information" is an abstract notion that is explained most easily by example: in seismology, readings by sensors located at the best places provide the "best information."

"Because of the emphasis on information, we call this the information-centered approach," says Traub, comparing it with the algorithm-centered approach, which at present is in widespread use. There, an algorithm is created and analyzed, then another algorithm is proposed and analyzed, and so on. "It's all pretty ad hoc; you don't have a benchmark of the best possible algorithm. In contrast, using the information-centered approach, you merely state how well a problem should be solved, and indicate the type of information available. The theory then tells you the best information, the best algorithm, and the complexity."

But it bears repeating that such problems must be mathematically stated, which at present rules out certain kinds of applications. However, just because something is considered, say, an artificial intelligence problem, doesn't mean it cannot be mathematically stated; indeed Traub's colleagues are applying the information-centered approach to the classical AI problem of robotic vision—how can a robot make its way visually around the world?

Traub and his colleagues observe that if information is partial or approximate, a problem cannot be solved exactly. "Some computer scientists are unfamiliar with such problems because they have worked primarily with complete and exact information. Therefore they can solve their problems exactly, and the only issue is minimal cost, that is, complexity. But statisticians and economists to whom we've explained our ideas don't have any trouble at all. Of course you can't solve problems exactly, they say, let's go on from there. How can you solve them best?"

There are times when even with complete and exact information, scientists *choose* not to solve exactly. Traub cites artificial intelligence techniques in chess as an example: they avoid "brute-force" methods, because of their expense in time and computing power, and rely on heuristic approaches, which usually, but don't always, yield a solution. "In other words, we live with the uncertainty of heuristics to decrease complexity."

Suppose that the information-centered approach provides the best algorithm and the minimal cost of solving a problem. Does it offer anything else?

"Another thing it can do is tell you whether a problem can be decomposed for a solution on a parallel computer or, more generally, on a distributed network. Let me illustrate: Let's play twenty questions. You tell me you're thinking of an integer between 1 and 16. I ask questions concerning that integer to which you respond yes or no. If you're thinking of, say, 15, the sequence of questions and answers might go as follows:

"Is the number between 1 and 8? No.

"Is the number between 9 and 12? No.

"Is the number between 13 and 14? No.

"Is the number 15? Yes.

"I obtained your number with four questions, and it's well known that one of sixteen possibilities can always be identified with four yes-or-no questions.

"Now, I waited for your answer to each question, then adapted my next question to your answer. That's known as *adaptive* information. But what if I asked all my questions simultaneously? Then I wouldn't have a chance to adapt my questions to your answers: that's an example of *nonadaptive* information. In the example I gave you, four adaptive questions are sufficient; fewer than four aren't enough. But the surprising thing is that four *nonadaptive* question are also enough if you ask the right questions. Thus for this problem, and for many problems, nonadaptive information is just as powerful as adaptive information."

The importance of that lies in the future of computing, in distributed computing, for example, where computation on machines with many processors, capable of simultaneous operation, will be increasingly important. Adaptive information is a sequential process: you must know the answer to one question before you ask the next. Nonadaptive information can proceed in parallel, since questions are answered independently of each other. If nonadaptive methods are as powerful as adaptive methods, then they are ideally suited to distributed computation. But the twenty-questions example is a toy problem. Does this insight also hold for real problems?

Traub replies, "Almost everybody believes that *usually* adaption helps. However, almost everybody is mistaken. Although there are problems where adaption helps, information-based complexity lets us show that there are many important problems—problems that we can identify by mathematical means—for which adaption is no help at all. That's a pleasant surprise for people who want to take advantage of the speed and power of parallel computing for their problems." And decomposition is only one example of the power of the information-centered approach to problem solving, Traub says. He and his colleagues are working on other parts of this emerging science of information.

"Coping with complexity is a central issue for us individually and collectively, whether we're talking about managing a large organization or putting a man on the moon. We hope these studies will eventually provide us with a general scientific framework for coping with complexity in the everyday sense of the word."

Richard Karp had made the same point and added that our aspirations for coping with complexity rise as we master the difficulties.

And so I tease computer science theoreticians about their use of the term *the universal machine,* but they can lay good claim. The computer exhibits, and is beginning to help elucidate, a whole new set of phenomena that cross over disciplines and topics in very unexpected ways. Central to understanding those disparate disciplines and topics are concepts of complexity, information, process, and adaption. Surely more such helpful concepts will come as this young science matures. And while my sympathies lie ever with the scientists struggling to make artificial intelligence a full reality, by hook or by crook, one important lesson from the history of science is that the discovery of general laws is more powerful, in the end, for increasing knowledge than are dozens of special cases that work well enough.

Meanwhile, most of us would be grateful indeed for a better understanding of complexity and information, topics that seem to baffle and frustrate us at every turn. Even people who accept the computer as a helpful artifact look warily at the quantity—never mind the quality—of the solutions it produces. Surely this is no great improvement over matters as they were. Some claim it's worse.

Perhaps. But I suspect we stand in relation to complexity and information as our forebears a century ago stood in relation to disease: lacking a comprehensive theory, we see it as countless special cases and have no idea how to handle it except to apply the computational equivalent of hot compresses, ice packs, and taking the sea air, as all those languid Victorian invalids once did. These are palliatives—not bad, but not very effective in the long run. The theoreticians of computer science hope to rescue us from all this even as biologists rescued us from fevers, infections, and convulsions. It won't be all at once, and it will take a while for theoretical concepts to be translated into practical solutions. But it doesn't seem reckless to believe that it will happen.

Chapter 27

The Structures of
Information

The first written catalogs humans made of the natural world were—
of all things—alphabetical. How we thought about the natural
world before we had the alphabet mystifies me. I suppose there
was no systematic way. As texts were translated into different
European languages from Greek and Latin, the alphabetical
order of plants and animals varied, of course, depending upon
the language being used. It was all confusing, provincial, and
inflexible.

Then Linnaeus finally devised his System of Nature, two Latin
names for each specimen, denoting genus and species. His scheme
was not only a great and useful revision of data that were already
known: perhaps more important, it permitted the orderly addition
of new data, a process denied by previous schemes.

All this is to say that the arrangement of data is as much an
artifact as anything. The structures of information and knowledge
are cultural, and they guide or imprison us in various ways. Europeans arrived in Africa to tell people who had lived there since
the dawn of humankind that they lived on a *continent,* a notion
that had no equivalent in the indigenous languages. Thus Africans
began thinking of themselves in that European-imposed term

at the same time they thought of themselves as Maasai or Wolof.

So it is that a computer program operates not on shapeless masses of information or data but on elements whose relationships are carefully structured, depending on the purposes we have for them. There are different kinds of structures, with static and dynamic properties; different structures require different representations in the machine (and elsewhere in life).

Even in the simplest structure, a linear list (a laundry list, a shopping list), it is important—at least if you plan to do anything with it—to know its order: which element is first? Last? How many elements are there? When the structure becomes more complicated, say, a two-dimensional array (having both horizontal and vertical structures, such as a timetable) or a tree, which might represent hierarchical or branching relationships (a genealogical chart) or a network, a complex multi-linked structure with many interconnections (the telephone system), the complexity of the structure makes it impossible to handle the elements perfectly.

Lists are put to different purposes, and their arrangements can be made to suit such purposes. Computing was not the first discipline to understand the importance of these structures—accountants, for example, use LIFO and FIFO—and as Donald Knuth observes, the very multiplicity of these names attests to the importance of the ideas in many abstract disciplines. How these list elements should be stored, linked, and arrayed is a subject of much intense study.

Trees, which are considered the most important nonlinear structures arising in computer algorithms, follow the shape of nature's own trees, which is to say, a root with branches. Like lists, abstract tree structures are a familiar pre-computing notion. Those most of us are familiar with are, in fact, upside-down trees, with the "root" at the top and the branches beneath, for example, organization charts, with the chief executive officer at the top and the officers beneath branching away. Genealogical trees, however, vary, depending on who has captured our interest, a subject's ancestors or his descendants.

But for all the apparent simplicity of a tree structure, it is a very powerful way of representing large amounts of information. Mathematicians study tree structures (and have done so since before the computer), discovering mathematical properties about them that can be put to use in applications as varied as chemistry or engineering. Psychologists are interested in tree structures because they can represent many aspects of human memory and reasoning, allowing the computer to remember associatively (and forget) in human fashion and also to reason: a tree is a good representation of the and/or concept, the if/then concept, and still others.

A tree can stand for a hierarchy, which is by far the most significant structure of information. Hierarchies did not originate with computing either, but the computer, both as example and as simulator, has allowed—compelled—the examination of hierarchies in a broader and more accurate way than pre-computing tools permitted. But, intuitively, we knew the intellectual and emotional power of the hierarchy long ago. Much of the impact of Tolstoy's *War and Peace,* for instance, comes from its shifts among the levels of a hierarchy, from individuals caught up in the war— Pierre, Natasha, Prince Andrey—to the great movements of troops under the respective commands of Napoleon and the emperor of Russia. Political governance relies on hierarchies and so does musical organization: the list might contain the breadth and depth of human endeavor.

Rules can be formulated about the behavior of elements within a given level of a hierarchy (what computer scientists call a subsystem), the influences of one level upon others above and below it, and the connections between distant parts of the hierarchy. Theorems about the dynamic properties of hierarchies were published in 1961 by Herbert Simon and Albert Ando, which subsequently appear anew as various scientists, ignorant of the Simon-Ando work, discover for themselves the potency of hierarchical dynamics in their own fields.

As I have spoken of information structures here, they seem malleable and almost chancy, depending on who designs them and for what purpose and depending too on what nature compels (much that is incomplete and contaminated). Yet in the previous chapters, I have spoken of the science of information and the search for scientific laws and invariants about information. Which is so? The answer is both, because symbol systems (which is what information is) are artifacts, adaptive, goal-seeking, and at the same time subject to natural laws. All this has been made explicit by computer science, which is itself a science of the artificial. One more important insight from computing, first revealed in artificial intelligence research, is that structures of information are impotent without processes embedded in them. In the realm of symbols, they can no more be pulled apart than style and sense in a poem.

Whether they were investigating simple lists or arrangements of the cosmos, computer scientists soon learned that conventional, intuitive reasoning about processes fails us as we enter realms of any complexity. We see this everywhere in real life. Programs are written but do not produce what we expected; laws, enacted with high-minded intention by our legislators, turn out to have unexpectedly unpleasant results; medicines, developed for curing a disease, afflict some patients worse than the disease they wish to cure. These are unanticipated effects, and we blame ourselves for not seeing far enough ahead.

It has been a modest hope of computer scientists to find formal, mathematical proofs of the correctness of their otherwise impenetrable programs, but the number of areas where such formal proofs were useful has been small. Formal proofs have been notably absent in artificial intelligence, where solutions cannot be proved correct because problems cannot be posed mathematically. The proof is whether the program seems to be doing what it is supposed to do.

The Japanese fifth generation of computers, whose aim is to bring artificial intelligence on a large scale to everyone, is also trying to approach that problem. Kazuhiro Fuchi's address, at the 1981 Tokyo conference, announcing the ten-year fifth-generation project, dwelled on the fact that, traditionally, computer technology had driven software instead of the other way around and that now it was time for software to assume supremacy and at the same time open itself to verification—was it doing what it was supposed to? Both these goals could be met only if software had an underlying formal logic that permitted investigations and proofs.

A few years later, Fuchi would muse on the evolution of the first four generations of computers and suggest that their underlying paradigm, the Turing machine, was really only a special case of logical machine, quite different and somehow less natural than predicate logic. (Predicate logic is the logic we all learned in school: Socrates is a man; all men are mortal; therefore, Socrates is mortal. It is the simple causal logic we use to get through the day: if I don't take my umbrella and it rains, then I will get wet.) Fuchi half agreed, he said, with people who hold that the evolution of the computer has been a gigantic historical detour away from more natural, perhaps more humanlike, predicate logic. He speculated that since memory elements were so expensive—and I would add unreliable—in 1940, it was therefore necessary to use as simple a hardware configuration and as few vacuum tubes as possible. Complexity of function was achieved by clever software. Now that the cost of computing components and cycles is diminishing drastically, Fuchi suggested that the time was approaching to return to predicate logic.

In the last ten years programming languages have been developed that are based on predicate logic, and such a language is at the heart of the Japanese fifth generation. This has caused some controversy, especially among American artificial intelligence workers who distrust what they consider overly rigid formalisms. And yet, as Fuchi points out, those same researchers are building expert systems that are based on rules, and rule-based knowledge "means a return to predicate logic." (Some leading American AI researchers, such as Allen Newell and John McCarthy, think the distrust of their colleagues for formal logic is unwarranted. As early as 1958 McCarthy proposed that all human knowledge be given a formal, homogeneous representation, the first-order predicate calculus. However, whether the language the Japanese have chosen and are developing further is the best means to achieve these desirable ends is unclear.)

Ordinary human language is also a species of predicate logic, Fuchi went on. "This may be only natural because logic itself came from a desire to formulate part of the mechanism of natural language," and he added that the impulse toward logic programming had come, as it happened, from researchers in natural language.

What a provocative idea this is. Can it be that logic is as natural a human process as language and intimately bound to it? How will that come to affect the structures of information in the future?

Significantly, it may be the Japanese who structure knowledge for all the world in their large knowledge-information processing systems (or KIPS, as they are known) some ten or fifteen years hence, just as Europeans did for—or imposed upon—the rest of the world during the centuries of the European hegemony. Europeans gave us a linear, logical, cause-and-effect knowledge, with an acute sense of time moving forward (as opposed to cycling around), of rationality as an instrument of inquiry (and inquiry as a splendid thing to pursue). It was a powerful way of apprehending the world, in every sense of that term, and lent Europeans a hauteur about themselves in relation to the rest of humanity that they were able to maintain unselfconsciously and, in many ways, even justify for several centuries.

I'm not sure anybody could predict what will happen to the worldwide structures of knowledge when the new computer amplifies our rational processes to such a degree. That it might very well be the Japanese who provide the structures adds another imponderable to the future shape of knowledge. Alan Kay has pointed out that Japanese culture is the "blackboard" model of knowledge representation and processing writ large: that is, the consensual nature of Japanese decision making provides a good analogy to the consensus of many sources of expert knowledge in a computerized expert system, each providing, concurrently and cooperatively, its opinion about something to be decided, as I have described earlier (and which, indeed, grew out of a consensual milieu). The blackboard model has proved to be a potent intellectual structure in applications as varied as Harold Cohen's art-making program, AARON, and systems to interpret continuous human speech.

The comparison between Japanese culture and the blackboard model may be apt. It may further be that the Japanese ethos of cooperation, that culture's explicit fascination with symbols, and its comfort with complexity, all fit the Japanese to be uniquely ready to lead the world intellectually into the next century.*

Then again, it may be that such comparisons are specious. All that can be said for sure is that, come the new machines, come

---

*Certainly their educational system does: the Japanese understand its importance in their very bones. Merry White, on the faculty of the Harvard School of Education, writes: "If Americans realized how powerful the relationship is between Japanese school achievement and social and economic successes we might see the same kind of protectionist language aimed at the Japanese educational system that we see directed at their automobile industry. ('The Japanese must stop producing such able and committed students because *it isn't fair.*')"

the further pervasiveness of the computer, things in our minds will be different.

But already, thanks to illumination by the computer, an intellectual structure called dynamic process has replaced the notion of static property. Intelligence used to be thought of as a property—you were born with it or not; you had a high IQ or not. Now it is more usefully described as a process: intelligence seems to consist of choosing an internal representation for a problem, using strategies for manipulating that representation, and executing elementary information processing steps.

To consider intelligence as a process instead of a property is not an inconsequential change in terminology. The splendid thing about processes is that they can be changed—even better, improved. We need only begin to understand them. In cognitive psychology, the computer, as both laboratory instrument and model for discovery, is helping us to do just that. (As it happens, the Japanese have long held the view that intelligence is the equivalent of effort: ability depends not on some inherent human property but on diligence.)

In the future, we shall deal differently with complexity. In the preceding chapters I have talked about some pioneering work and speculated about where it might lead us. In more concrete terms I picture our descendants wondering how we had the courage to get out of bed in the morning in the face of so much uncertainty.

Intellectual achievement is a collective effort, more or less, but that's acknowledged more forthrightly in some places than in others. In science, for example, the intellectual network is sensitive and intimate (and, as a consequence, charged with high emotion); it is just as sensitive and intimate (and charged with high emotion) in the arts, but less easily seen, less easily admitted.

The same might be said of the two hemispheres, West and East. The Western ethos celebrates individuality and unique accomplishments, while the East (perhaps because of centuries of rice cultivation, which demands intense cooperative farming) has long celebrated the group. While some significant things have *wow!* been accomplished by individuals in computing, the machine seems best suited for community effort. It not only eases cooperation, as, for example, Donald Straus's work in computer-aided conciliation shows. In addition, the machine's own structures of information, arrived at experimentally and empirically, suggest how such efforts among humans and their machines can work even better.

Process, complexity, community—these are some of the great themes of computing, and they are coming to pervade our intellectual milieu. The other great themes are rationality, symbols, and, by extension, the artificial. These I take up again now.

Chapter 28

The Personal Computer

My father was a part-time optimist. He became both an American and a salesman at the age of thirty-three, and optimism came with the territories. Self-help books, promoting hope and cheer as vital to successful sales, floated into our house. They remained largely unread; their jackets faded (the author's photo always on the front, not the back, a man with rimless glasses, winning smile), moved here and there for dusting. They must have been thin stuff after the Shaw and Dickens he'd grown up on. When my grandmother came to visit us in the New World, my father asked her only to bring along his beloved copy of *Barnaby Rudge,* a gloomy book, distended with violence.

He was sales manager of the northwest territory, whatever that was: he went to look it up in the New York Public Library after he said yes to the job. He later heard that he had been interviewed only as a joke. The picture on his application—homburg, black overcoat, British mustache—was so comical that the company president expected to amuse himself for fifteen minutes by meeting this exotic in person. Instead, the exotic made such an impression that even without sales experience (though he might have lied about that) he was hired.

My father had a great capacity to laugh at such things; one of his most appealing virtues was that he turned humiliations into sidesplitting epics, playing all the parts—skeptical boss, innocent immigrant—with no more than a lift of the brows, a roll of the eyes, few words of dialogue. The star was really the narrator, the one who stepped back for the larger view. That these were humiliations didn't occur to us as we sat around the dinner table being entertained in traditional Irish storytelling style. Tell us again, we'd say, about the time your rich aunt sent the weird clothes from Pretoria and you had to wear them to school (and he made us see him in the pith helmet, a spectacle in a Liverpool primary school, slugging it out with his tormentors); tell us again about the time you came back from the aunts in London so well-mannered you didn't get anything to eat from the rest of the family. The job interview was part of the same. Now I can see he felt the humiliations—agonizingly—but for the family, they were transmuted into laughter. But the phrase also implies the opposite: he could see the tragic side too, and that was always with him.

So he went off to the northwest territory, in this case, the states of Washington, Oregon, Idaho, Montana, Wyoming, Colorado, Utah, Nevada, and northern California, and sold his firm's products, which were mainly hair dyes and shampoos. I try to imagine what it was like to sell hair dyes in Butte, Montana, or Laramie, Wyoming, in 1948 where the frontier was still a reality, not a memory. My father's homburg was now a fedora, but he had the same overcoat and mustache, a British accent, and called on a hundred dusty little beauty parlors (as they were then known) and chatted up a thousand beauty operators (as they were also then known); he rode Greyhound buses between the cow towns and checked into the salesmen's hotels. In his sample case he carried nothing less than dreams of the Beautiful and the Good.

Artifice, in its smallest, but not negligible, forms is hair dye and permanent waves, perfumes and rouge. For a while in my early twenties I dyed my naturally brown hair blond, and loved the internal transformation the external permitted: from mousy to brassy, in every sense. It gave me courage in a time of need. Artifice in a larger sense makes the transmutation from pain to laughter. (Or action. Justin Kaplan lists some men who have changed their names and organically changed their lives: Lenin, Trotsky, Stalin, Malcolm X.) How could I disdain the artificial when I saw its value to the living of a real life?

And as I grew up on storytelling, his, the Brothers Grimm (and more and more, which is why it wasn't really accidental I chose literature in college), I also began to see in the artificial something like truth. Trying, I think, to refine my tastes, my professors at first closed more books for me than they opened, making literature a caste system, the best barely tolerable and the rest untouchable. But the power of art overcomes even that. After a few years, I returned to stories, to write as well as read them. (I've even gone back to Eliot, ill-served by his 1950s interpreters.)

In an oblique way, the mind-body problem is connected with this. If dyeing your hair can give you courage, if transmuting your pain to laughter can ease your way through the world, where is this much-discussed boundary between mind and body to be found? Though I made all the conventional noises about dualism in college philosophy courses, I couldn't honestly regard it as a problem, because for me it didn't exist, never had and never would. I've proposed that the mind-body problem is one only a man could have invented, women dwelling in their bodies as they do, but perhaps my own history has more to do with it than my gender.

So I am glad enough, but not really surprised, to see that artificial intelligence research, among its many other contributions, has come up with a scientific hypothesis to dispose of the mind-body problem. This, of course, is the physical symbol system hypothesis: a symbol system can only arise within a physical system and no other place.

Outside my study window the Hudson River and the sky are examples of relatively pure "nature," though even they are compromised by effluents and *craft*. But Riverside Park was treeless at the turn of the century and hand-planned and -planted to be what it is now; across the river are warehouses, factories, trucks, a ferryboat converted to a restaurant. I ponder the fact that each of these arose in the minds of human beings before they were fashioned into artifacts, and in a funny way that thrills me far beyond any intrinsic value those warehouses and other structures have. Perhaps I'm a natural city dweller on that account. But I'm also moved to tears as my plane lifts off out of Mombasa and I stare down on the shambas, the farming villages, fashioned by other humans for other purposes. It's not their beauty that moves me but their very existence.

So what is this stuff, these warehouses and street cafés and gritty subways and garbage trucks, these grass-roofed huts and

carefully cultivated corn rows, and museums and music and my
Oriental rugs and the morning mail, French, good manners, and
friendship, all the things that make me glad to be part of the
human race? I mean what *essentially*? (For I'm not without judgment: the subways are a scandal; the garbage trucks disturb my
sleep; the morning mail brings foolish letters with welcome ones.)
No, I want to rise above the particular, in its good and its bad
instantiations, to the general. These things are artifacts, every last
one of them.

And what is an artifact? Artificial intelligence research suggests
an illuminating definition. Herbert Simon writes: "An artifact can
be thought of as a meeting point—an 'interface' in today's terms—
between an 'inner' environment and an 'outer' environment, the
surroundings in which it operates. If the inner environment is
appropriate to the outer environment, or vice versa, the artifact
will serve its intended purpose."

A meeting place, an interface, an idea or set of them, made
manifest. Artifacts begin in human minds but must burst out to
exist in the external environment. Their success in that outer
environment depends on how well they achieve their goals, a
process that is guided by rationality. Rationality doesn't mean that
tepid caricature of reasoning so boringly deplored by the romantics among us. Rather, rationality means the seldom smooth movement toward goals, achieving subgoals, searching the large space
of possibilities, finding sometimes, but not always. It encompasses
emotion, sometimes passion, as an intrinsic part of the process.

And lo, it now seems that passion itself can be quantified.
Neurophysiologists have discovered that each emotion has its own
distinct signature, involving the facial muscles, brain areas, and
autonomic activity. Thus anger, sadness, disgust, and surprise can
be consistently distinguished. The distinguishing—the measuring,
to give it its correct name—is so complicated and massive that it
must be done by computer.

I am personally glad to see reason, or rationality, brought to
bear on feelings in this new way. The cognitive and computer
sciences I've been drawn to over these decades have until now
had little to say about human emotions, and none of it very interesting. But already this particular effort to quantify is showing
us a few things, suspected but not known for certain, in the relationships between feelings and, say, health. Thus the most pre-

liminary evidence suggests that some negative emotions are bad for your health, but not others; sadness, hopelessness, and loneliness seem to suppress the immune function, whereas anger may help the immune system fight such diseases as cancer. The research is also helping to illuminate the differences between human male and female passions; between Germans, Spaniards, and Japanese, and so on.

The hope in this effort of bringing reason to bear on passion is that it will explain, help us understand, and perhaps eventually control our passions, curb our excesses, correct our deficiencies, accommodate those different from us. It strikes me as a modest and virtuous hope.

Yet the irony is heavy. Reason, as any reader knows, is these days in bad repute. For some of us, pure reason is an ideal, inevitably compromised by boundaries and limits but otherwise desirable and worth approaching; for others of us, reason cripples honest passion and is thus the cause of all our problems. The latter is a back-to-basics view: reason has led us up some inhuman paths. I see that once more I've described the catechisms, if not the practices, of the two cultures.

Let me confess an inclination for reason over passion, and I run risks. Better to confess incest, murder, opium eating, adultery, a weakness for demon rum, treason (to name a few of the great confessional themes of literature). Social workers will come to my case, rehabilitators will be found for me, moral squalor will be forgiven as no more than life-style. Let me only phrase it well, and I am heroic.

But of course. Just so. It's the phrasing, the rational reshaping of those passions toward pellucidity that matters, their reordering (by words, music, images, even equations) into design, harmony, tension, balance, precision. Into artifacts. Medea is the pathetic mom who kills self and kids in the daily headlines until Euripides or Robinson Jeffers or Shozo Sato, in his shattering *Kabuki Medea*, seizes her and shapes her passions into art. The phrasing—the choosing and shaping of symbols—is, like it or not, the task of reason.

Thus it is that reason and passion are not antithetical but complementary, and one without the other is, at the very least, banal. One without the other can be fatal.

Reason is a process, not a state. A true path in reason is as nonsensical as a true path in religion. It is not faulty reason that leads us to two different places; it is the bounded nature of the process itself, moving through a large and complicated environment. The process begins with premises, me with mine, you with yours, that are different, and thus we arrive at different places. But that is not to say all premises are equally valuable, all reasoning equally robust. There is such a thing as quality. Reason of quality is, for example, unaccommodating to fanaticism. It exposes the parochial brutally.

Then perhaps people are angry with reason because it hasn't done all we hoped. We gave ourselves over to reason, to science, to the Western tradition of rationality and are now on the brink of world annihilation. Well, yes; we did expect too much. The fault is not with reason itself but with the impossibilities we demand of it. Reason is a precious but fragile process for apprehending and acting in the world. It is not at all accidental that the Christian notion of original sin is bound up in the search for knowledge: those canny oldsters knew all about the limits of reason. And that is how I sometimes read original sin, that reason is bounded by our evolutionary legacy, and the sin is in forgetting, pretending infallibility.

In humans (and provably in other intelligent agents) rational behavior in real life is always bounded, limited, not only by the complexity of the real world but also by the nonrational and even irrational elements beyond. It is also bounded by the human ability to know, not just because our brains are limited but because information, itself an artifact, is always incomplete, faulty, even false. The computer will improve the quality of our information, and therefore of our reasoning, but limits will always be present. Moreover, even if we work toward goals, sometimes those goals are so ill-defined that they reveal themselves to us only after patient search (which is how Le Corbusier defined creation).

A computational view of the world, which is what I have been describing, turns out to be congenial with the inner point of view I have been carrying around (in rather formless shape, to be sure) since I can remember. Perhaps this accounts in part for why I came to feel so at home among computer scientists when I had no scientific or mathematical training and must still struggle with some of the technicalities of computing. And yet here I am, Old Hand if not native, ducking through the alleys, bargaining at the market, and murmuring the language, albeit with a decided accent. To make that choice has been the story of a life, the yearning to connect not just the two cultures, art and science, but also the interior and exterior, passion and reason, which came together for me at first intuitively and finally explicitly, not in computing but in writing about computing.

It's a strange place to be. Not respectable. Although, come to think of it, writing was an outsider's game for me from the start. Moved, at a tender age, from one of the Old Country's modern primary schools to an old-fashioned inner-city Liverpool one, they discover that the lax modern school hasn't yet taught me to write my own name. The master ponders this astonishing lapse. And then, ostensibly for my edification, but mainly for my public shame, he writes my name in blue chalk on the blackboard. "This is for Pamela McCorduck," he says solemnly to the class, "who doesn't know how to write her own name." I learn instantly. But the name stays on the board for days all the same, corpse on a gibbet to deter intellectual sins.

So here I am still, disreputable, outsider to both cultures, scribbling about them both. Heaven knows I appall the border guards, who keep insisting on the difference between science and art (do they moonlight on the mind-body border?). The usual doctrine is that science is the abstract, the general, unconcerned with particulars; whereas art, on the contrary, is the singular, there for immediate human encounter. From this there follows much pernicious nonsense about art being human, science not, and so on.

This book has meant to point out that such doctrine is false to both science and art—why one-man shows, why describe art in terms of periods or movements, why read collected works, if there isn't something valuable beyond the immediate encounter with a particular artifact? And even if it were once true about science (but it never was, only a convenient burlesque), with the arrival of the sciences of the artificial, everything needs redefinition.

I hear that even to venture into the land of science without all papers in order is to patronize and vulgarize it. Could be. (And what a charming excuse to make no efforts. Who'd want to risk being either vulgar or patronizing?) But since I'm no longer the young woman who was too shy even to take tea with Sir Charles and Lady Pamela, these days I state my terms calmly, fashion my own artifacts. Here is where my search has led. So far.

Arriving here, at first I told myself my pleasure was in the people I met who did computing (in artificial intelligence, and then in theory, and then in engineering). They were so intelligent it was just exhilarating to hang around them. That was true, but not the whole truth. I next told myself that I liked their world view: their optimisim and their zest, their own self-confidence. That was also true, but again, not the whole truth.

Then it must be the machine itself that engages me. Yes, but at a certain distance. The quotidian technology is seldom as interesting to me as the machine's entrance into one symbolic realm after another, disturbing and transforming. The computer is a kind of theater for me, one part magic show, one part tragedy; it's a gallery, a listening room, a text. Yet its difference from all those is something that matters mightily to me: I am no mere spectator, but drawn in—to myself and others: what will this medium called the computer reflect back about minds and their symbols?—and sent out to press against my hypercube, to see, for example, a strand of DNA, its image synthesized by the computer. Its beauty leaves me in tears. How wonderful that life is beautiful, I say to the scientist Robert Langridge, who's shown me this, and he laughs: what else could it be?

The personal computer, the universal machine, enchants me. Simultaneously it reflects, models, and amplifies the human mind, acts as metaphor, is itself artifact. In a new way, it reveals the inner structure of the most human of properties, our urge to symbolize. If the dynamo broke Henry Adams by raising questions he couldn't answer about power and force, the computer does just the opposite: supplies answers and restores composure. Human thought and deed are magnified, but not disproportionately. At the same time, the computer does not imply that power is constant and growing: it speaks sharply of limits, mocks self-important illusions of control.

Here is the meeting place of the natural and the artificial, the ideal and the material, blurring boundaries with serene disregard. Here is not the bridge between the two cultures so much as the transcendence of them. In other words, here's more than science, it's the new humanities too, since I define the humanities as the best and the most important artifacts we are fashioning, whether structures to grasp the natural world or those to express and shape our own deepest longings. The computer, symbol processor as it is, is the essence of human truth, specific to the species.

I'm at home. It's an illuminated place, cheery on the whole, where opposites can coexist peacefully, and limits are a fact, not an occasion for despair. From here I have an orderly, harmonious, rich, continuously surprising view of the world I live in, which is also the world I'm in the process of creating every day. (A bit batty, of course, like the Widow Winchester, carpentering and transforming her house every day of her life; but she hoped for immortality, while I'm only after understanding. But still, a bit of crust conscripting the universal machine to tend to my idiosyncrasies.)

The universal machine is present, called upon far and near, by the ordinary and the grand, the harmless and the lethal, wherever we choose, all the while describing, calculating, illuminating, amplifying, and finally changing things. Up against the hardest questions, we are humbled by their complexity, grudgingly reconciled to some eternal mystery. But come here, there are grounds for part-time optimism. Which is to say, hope.

Notes

2. Two Centuries

Braudel, Fernand. *Civilization and Capitalism, 15th–18th Century: Structures of Everyday Life*. Vol. 1. New York: Harper & Row, 1981.

———. *Civilization and Capitalism 15th–18th Century: The Wheels of Commerce*. Vol. 2. New York: Harper & Row, 1982.

Coughlin, Ellen K. "Literacy: 'Excitement' of New Field Attracts Scholars of Literature." *Chronicle of Higher Education*, 9 Jan. 1985.

Eisenstein, Elizabeth L. *The Printing Press as an Agent of Change*. 2 vols. New York: Cambridge University Press, 1979.

Lassaigne, Jacques, and Guilio Carlo Argan. *The Fifteenth Century from van Eyck to Botticelli*. New York: Skira, n.d.

McNeill, William H. *The Pursuit of Power*. Chicago: University of Chicago Press, 1982.

———. *The Rise of the West*. Chicago: University of Chicago Press, 1963.

Meskill, John. *An Introduction to Chinese Civilization*. New York: Columbia University Press, 1973.

Rice, Eugene F., Jr. *The Foundations of Early Modern Europe, 1460–1559*. New York: W. W. Norton, 1970.

Stock, Brian. *The Implications of Literacy.* Princeton, N.J.: Princeton University Press, 1983.

3. Technologies of the Intellect

Anderson, Marie, ed. *Transborder Data Flows: What Is the Appropriate Strategy for the United States?* The Wilson Center Report, Washington, D.C., 5 Oct. 1982.

Eisenstein, Elizabeth L. *The Printing Press as an Agent of Change.* 2 vols. New York: Cambridge University Press, 1979.

Feigenbaum, Edward, and Pamela McCorduck. *The Fifth Generation.* Reading, Mass.: Addison-Wesley, 1983.

Friedman, Thomas L. "Computer Digests the Talmud to Help Rabbis." *New York Times,* 23 Nov. 1984, Section A, p. 1.

Havelock, Eric A. *The Literate Revolution in Greece and Its Cultural Consequences.* Princeton, N.J.: Princeton University Press, 1982.

Simon, Herbert A. *The Sciences of the Artificial.* 2nd ed. Cambridge, Mass.: M.I.T. Press, 1981.

4. Books

Battin, Patricia A. "The Electronic Library—A Vision for the Future." Columbia University Fourth Annual Lectures in Computer Science, New York, 2 Apr. 1984. Also, *EDUCOM Bulletin,* 19, no. 2 (Summer 1984), pp. 12–17.

Friedman, Thomas L. "Computer Digest the Talmud to Help Rabbis." *New York Times,* 23 Nov. 1984, Section A, p. 1.

Gass, William. "Of Speed Readers and Lip-Movers." *New York Times Book Review.* 1 Apr. 1984.

5. Texts

Barthes, Roland. *The Pleasure of the Text.* Tr. Richard Miller, New York: Hill & Wang, 1975.

Frase, L. T. "The UNIX Writer's Workbench Software: Philosophy." *Bell System Technical Journal,* 62, no. 6 (July–Aug. 1983), pp. 1883–1890.

Gerola, Humberto, and Ralph E. Gomory. "Computers in Science and Technology: Early Indications." *Science,* 225, no. 6 (July 1984), pp. 11–17.

Gingrich, P. S. "The UNIX Writer's Workbench Software: Results of a Field Study." *Bell System Technical Journal,* 62, no. 6 (July–Aug. 1983), pp. 1909–1921.

Heidorn, G. E., K. Jensen, L. A. Miller, R. J. Byrd, and M. S. Chodorow. "The EPISTLE Text-Critiquing System." *IBM Systems Journal,* 21, no. 3 (1982), pp. 305–326.

Macdonald, N. H. "The UNIX Writer's Workbench Software: Rationale and Design." *Bell System Technical Jouranl,* 62, no. 6 (July–Aug. 1983), pp. 1891–1908.

Spence, Jonathan. *The Gate of Heavenly Peace.* New York: Viking Press, 1981.

6. The Transmutations of Texts

Catano, James V. "Poetry and Computers: Experimenting with the Communal Text." *Computers and the Humanities,* 13 (1979), pp. 269–275.

DeFanti, Thomas A. "The Mass Impact of Videogame Technology." In *Advances in Computers.* Vol. 23. Ed. Marshall C. Yovits. New York: Academic Press, 1984.

Feigenbaum, Edward A., and Pamela McCorduck. *The Fifth Generation.* Reading, Mass.: Addison-Wesley, 1983.

Hawes, Ralph E. "Logos: The Intelligent Translation System." An invited address to the ASLIB Technical Translation Group and the Translator's Guild, 10 Nov. 1983.

Nelson, Ted. *Literary Machines.* 3rd ed. Swarthmore, Pa.: Published by the author.

Strandberg, Josiah R. W., Carol L. Chomsky, Robert Scholes, and Andries van Dam. "An Experiment in Computer-Based Education Using Hypertext." Final report to the National Endowment for the Humanities, 3 June 1976.

Turner, Judith Axler. "An Electronic 'Soap Opera' and 'Hyper Media' Backed by $3-Million CPB Grant." *Chronicle of Higher Education,* 29 Aug. 1984.

7. The Computer

McCorduck, Pamela. *Machines Who Think.* San Francisco: Freeman, 1979.

Newell, Allen, and Herbert A. Simon. "Computer Science as Empirical Inquiry: Symbols and Search." *Communications of the ACM.* Mar. 1976.

8. Other Computers, Other Views

Adams, Henry. *The Education of Henry Adams.* Introd. D. W. Brogan. 1918; reprint ed., Boston: Houghton Mifflin, 1961.

Campbell, Jeremy. *Grammatical Man: Information, Entropy, Language and Life.* New York: Simon & Schuster, 1982.

Simon, Herbert A. "Cohabiting the Planet with Computers." In *Cohabiting with Computers.* Ed. J. F. Traub. Los Altos, Calif.: William Kaufmann, 1985.

Venturi, Robert. *Complexity and Contradiction in Architecture.* 2nd ed. New York: Museum of Modern Art, 1977.

9. *The Empire of Reason: Artificial Intelligence*

Commager, Henry Steele. *The Empire of Reason*. New York: Oxford University Press, 1982.

McCorduck, Pamela. *Machines Who Think*. San Francisco: Freeman, 1979.

Simon, Herbert A. *The Sciences of the Artificial*. 2nd ed. Cambridge, Mass.: MIT Press, 1981.

10. *The Protean Machine*

Abercrombie, Stanley. "Waltzing to the CRT." *Interior Design*, Mar. 1984.

Bell, Gordon. Untitled manuscript.

Mowshowitz, Abbe. *The Conquest of Will*. Reading, Mass.: Addison-Wesley, 1974.

Turkle, Sherry. *The Second Self: Computers and the Human Spirit*. New York: Simon & Schuster, 1984.

Brennan, Jean Ford. *The IBM Watson Laboratory at Columbia University: A History*, Armonk, New York: IBM, 1971.

12. *AARON*

Cohen, Harold. "What Is an Image?" In *Proceedings of the Sixth International Joint Conference on Artificial Intelligence*, Tokyo, 20–23 Aug. 1979.

Danto, Arthur C. *The Transfiguration of the Commonplace*. Cambridge, Mass.: Harvard University Press, 1981.

Steinberg, Leo. *Other Criteria*. New York: Oxford University Press, 1972.

Interlude: The Twilight of Heroics

Campbell, Joseph. *The Hero with a Thousand Faces*. Princeton, N.J.: Princeton University Press, 1973.

Chaiken, Jan M., and Marcia R. Chaiken. "Crime: Coping with Justice." *Wilson Quarterly*, 7, no. 2 (Spring 1983), pp. 102–115.

13. *The Medical Microcosm*

Alderson, Philip C. "Emission Tomography (SPECT and PET): Clinical Applications of an Evolving Technology." Informal paper, Columbia-Presbyterian Medical Center, New York, 1984.

Bischoff, Miriam, Edward H. Shortliffe, A. Carlisle Scott, Robert W. Carlson, and Charlotte D. Jacobs. "Integration of a Computer-Based Consultant into the Clinical Setting." In *Proceedings of the Seventh Annual Symposium on Computer Application in Medical Care*, Institute of Electrical and Electronics Engineers

Computer Society, Washington, D.C., 23–26 Oct. 1983, pp. 149–152. Also Stanford Heuristic Programming Project, Memo HPP-83-14, Stanford University, Palo Alto, Calif.

Davis, Karen. "Health Implications of Aging in America." In *Proceedings of the Seventh Annual Symposium on Computer Applications in Medical Care*, pp. 625–631.

Kaplan, Bonnie. "The Computer as Rorschach: Implications for Management and User Acceptance." In *Proceedings of the Seventh Annual Symposium on Computer Applications in Medical Care*, pp. 664–667.

Kunz, John, Edward H. Shortliffe, Bruce G. Buchanan, and Edward A. Feigenbaum. "Computer Assisted Decision Making in Medicine." Stanford Heuristic Programming Project, Report No. HPP-83-23, Apr. 1983, Stanford University, Palo Alto, Calif.

Naditch, Murray P. "PLATO STAYWELL: A Behavioral Medicine Microcomputer Program of Health Behavior Change." In *Proceedings of the Seventh Annual Symposium on Computer Applications in Medical Care*, pp. 363–365.

O'Connell, Joan. "Cutting the Guesswork Out of Surgery." *Business Week*, no. 2889 (8 Apr. 1985), p. 80.

Reggia, James A. "The Case for Artificial Intelligence in Medicine." In *Proceedings of the Seventh Annual Symposium on Computer Applications in Medical Care*, pp. 4–7.

14. Flatland: The Micro Universe

Abbott, Edwin A. "Flatland: A Romance of Many Dimensions." In *The World of Mathematics*. Ed. J. R. Newman. Vol. 4. New York: Simon & Schuster, 1956.

Van Gelder, Lindsy. "Women in Computing." *PC, the Independent Guide to IBM Personal Computers*, 2, no. 1 (June 1983), pp. 148–153.

15. War

Cong. Rec., 140, no. 8 (1 Feb. 1984).

De Voto, Bernard, ed. *The Journals of Lewis and Clark*. Boston: Houghton Mifflin, 1953.

Dyson, Freeman. *Weapons and Hope*. New York: Harper & Row, 1984.

Hawke, David Freeman. *Those Tremendous Mountains*. New York: Norton, 1980.

Ornstein, Severo, Brian C. Smith, and Lucy Suchman. "Strategic Computing: An Assessment." Computer Professionals for Social Responsibility, Palo Alto, Calif., 21 June 1984.

16. The Computer and Conciliation

"Computer-Assisted Negotiations: A Case History from the Law of the Sea Negotiations and Speculation Regarding Future Uses." (Donald B. Straus, moderator; panel members: T. T. B. Koh, J. D. Nyhart, Elliot L. Richardson, and James K. Sebenius.) *Computer Culture: The Scientific, Intellectual and Social Impact of the Computer.* Ed. Heinz Pagels. New York: Annals of the New York Academy of Sciences, 426 (1984).

"Process Assessment of the Conference on Multiple Objective Decision Procedures for Power Plant Site Selection." Research Institute of the American Arbitration Association, 20 June 1980.

Straus, Donald B., and Peter B. Clark. "Computer-Assisted Negotiations: Bigger Problems Need Better Tools." *Environmental Professional,* 2 (1980), pp. 75–87.

17. *Computing in Senegal*

Kurian, George Thomas. "Senegal." *Encyclopedia of the Third World.* Vol. 3. New York: Facts on File, 1982.

UNESCO Statistical Yearbook, 1983. Paris: United Nations Educational, Scientific and Cultural Organization, 1983.

18. *A Wider View of Third-World Computing*

Bogod, Julian. *The Role of Computing in Developing Countries.* The British Computer Society Lecture Series, No. 2. London: British Computer Society, 1979.

Leff, Nathaniel H. Rev. of *Technological Trends and Challenges in Electronics,* by Staffan Jacobsson and Jon Sigurdson. *Science,* 223, no. 27 (Jan. 1984), pp. 386–387.

19. *Computing in the Soviet Union*

Davis, N. C., and S. E. Goodman. "The Soviet Block's Unified System of Computers." *Computing Surveys,* June 1978.

Goldman, Marshall I. "Chernenko's Inheritance: A Low-Tech Economy at Home . . ." *New York Times,* 19 Feb. 1984.

Goodman, S. E. "Advanced Technology: How Will the USSR Adjust?" In *The Soviet Union in the 1980s.* Washington, D.C.: Smithsonian Institution Press, 1984.

———. "Computing and the Development of the Soviet Economy." In *Soviet Economy in a Time of Change: A Compendium of Papers Submitted to the Joint Economic Committee, Congress of the United States,* vol. 1. Washington, D.C.: U.S. Government Printing Office, 1979.

Graham, Loren. "The Computer Revolution Is Bypassing the Soviet Union." *Washington Post National Weekly Edition,* 2 Apr. 1984.

Kennan, George. "Reflections (Soviet-American Relations)." *New Yorker,* 24 Sept. 1984.

Schmemann, Serge. "Trying to Reconcile Secrecy and Computer Use in Russia." *New York Times,* 28 Dec. 1984.

Shulman, Marshall. Interview.

Tagliabue, John. "Hungary Encourages Interest in Computers." *New York Times,* 6 Jan. 1985.

20. Work

Beauvoir, Simone de. *The Coming of Age.* New York: Warner, 1973.

Boffey, Philip M. "Automation Seen by Experts as a Job-Saver for Industries." *New York Times,* 28 May 1983.

Cairns, John. *Cancer: Science and Society.* San Francisco: Freeman, 1978.

"Consumers Pay for Auto Quota." *San Francisco Chronicle,* 27 June 1984.

Gilchrist, Bruce, and Arlaana Shenkin. "The Impact of Computers on Employment." Columbia University Computing Center, Nov. 1979.

Goulianos, Joan, ed. *By a Woman Writt.* Baltimore, Md.: Penguin, 1974.

High Technology in the Work Place: Japan and the United States. A Seminar Report. New York: The Japan Society Public Affairs Series 20, 23 Apr. 1982.

Miller, William F. "Perspectives on a High Tech Society." In *Cohabiting with Computers.* Ed. J. F. Traub. Los Altos, Calif.: Kaufmann, 1985.

Nilsson, Nils. Private communication.

Reddy, Raj. "Robots, Unemployment, and New Jobs." Speech at the inauguration of the World Center for Human Resources, Paris, France, 15 Mar. 1982.

Webb, R. K. *Modern England from the 18th Century to the Present.* New York: Dodd, Mead, 1968.

21. Aiming at Computer Literacy

Leuhrmann, Arthur W. "Should the Computer Teach the Student, or Vice Versa?" Proceedings of the Spring Joint Computer Conference, 1972.

"Preliminary Report of the Task Force on the Future of Computing at Carnegie-Mellon University" (Feb. 1982). Quoted in *Current Issues in Higher Education,* No. 2 (1983–84), pp. 3–24.

22. Computing in the Schools

Computers in Education: Realizing the Potential. Report of a Research Conference, U.S. Department of Education, Office of Educational Research and Improvement, Pittsburgh, Pa., Nov. 1982.

Dallaire, Gene, Fortney H. (Pete) Stark, and Hal Berghel. "Should Congress

Provide Special Tax Incentives for Firms Donating Computers to Schools?" *Communications of the Association for Computing Machinery,* Mar. 1984.

Tucker, Marc S. "The Schools We Need—But Never Had." Unpublished manuscript.

———. "The 'Star Wars' Universities: Carnegie-Mellon, Brown, and M.I.T." *Current Issues in Higher Education,* No. 2 (1983d–84).

Interlude: Fairy Tales

Newell, Allen. "Fairytales." Carnegie-Mellon University Computer Science Department Research Review, 1977.

23. Hunter-Gatherers of the Infinite

Knuth, Donald E. *The Art of Computer Programming.* Vol. 1: *Fundamental Algorithms.* 2nd ed. Reading, Mass.: Addison-Wesley, 1973.

24. Chaos, Chance, and Certainty

Kolata, Gina. "Order Out of Chaos in Computers." *Science,* 2 (Mar. 1984).

26. The Science of Information

Traub, J. F. "Information, Complexity, and the Sciences." University Lecture, Columbia University, 6 Feb. 1985.

———, and H. Woźniakowski. "Information and Computation." In *Advances in Computers.* Vol. 23. Ed. Marshall C. Yovits. New York: Academic Press, 1984.

27. The Structures of Information

Boorstin, Daniel J. *The Discoverers.* New York: Random House, 1983.

Courtois, P. J. "M 83: On Time and Space Decomposition of Complex Structures." Philips Research Laboratory, Brussels, Belgium, June 1984; also the Landsdowne Lecture, University of Victoria, Victoria, British Columbia, Canada, Apr. 1984.

Fuchi, Kazuhiro. "Significance of Fifth Generation Computer Systems Research and Development." *ICOT Journal,* No. 3 (1984).

Knuth, Donald E. *The Art of Computer Programming.* Vol. 1. 2nd ed. Reading, Mass.: Addison-Wesley, 1972.

McCorduck, Pamela. *Machines Who Think.* San Francisco: Freeman, 1979.

Simon, Herbert A. *The Sciences of the Artificial.* 2nd ed. Cambridge, Mass.: M.I.T. Press, 1981.

Simon, H. A., and A. Ando. "Aggregation of Variables in Dynamic Systems." *Econometrica*, 29 (Apr. 1961), pp. 111–38.

White, Merry I. "Japanese Education: How Do They Do It?" *Japan Society Newsletter*, Sept. 1984; reprinted from *Public Interest*, No. 76 (Summer 1984).

28. The Personal Computer

Goleman, Daniel. "Human Emotion Under New Scrutiny." *New York Times*, 23 May 1984.

Simon, Herbert A. *The Sciences of the Artificial.* 2nd ed. Cambridge, Mass.: M.I.T. Press, 1981.

Index

AARON, 123–132, 274
Abbott, Edwin A., 150–151
Academy of Sciences, 198
Accounting, 270
ACE (Automated Cable Expertise), 103
Acid-based paper, 43
Adams, Henry, 78, 132, 284
Advanced Research Projects Agency (ARPA), 157, 159, 160, 163
"Aesthetic objects," 128
Agat, 199
Age of Symbols, 2–3, 78
Agincourt, battle of, 19
Agriculture, computers used in, 192
Aleksandrov, Anatoly P., 199
Alexander VI, Pope, 23, 28
ALGOL, 111
Algorithms, 235, 244–246, 257
Alphabets, 30, 33–34, 39, 269
Altdorfer, Albrecht, 121–122
American Arbitration Association, 169
Anatomical information, 143
Anderson, John, 233
Ando, Albert, 271
Annenberg/Corporation for Public Broadcasting Project, 67
Anti-satellite weapons, 109
APL (A Programming Language), 111
Apple II, 199
Apple IIe, 183, 184, 185, 221
Apple Computers, 68, 114, 190
Apple Fellows, 68
Apple Lisa, 216
Apple Macintosh, 67, 113, 216, 224
Aquaculture, 192
Architecture, 109–110
Arid area agriculture, 192
Aristotle, 40
ARPA (Advanced Research Projects Agency), 157, 159, 160, 163

Arrays, two-dimensional, 270
Art:
    abstraction in, 77–78
    computer, 1, 115–132, 150, 232, 274
    personality and, 129–132
    representation in, 127, 128–129, 132
    science vs. 15, 283
    technology and, 117, 127–132
Artificial intelligence (AI):
    computability, 90
    criticism of, 94, 95, 96, 99–100, 102–103
    as developed in Japan, 103–104, 157, 161–162, 163, 231, 272, 273–274
    as development of reason, 94–104
    expert systems for, 37, 38, 103, 125–126, 142–146, 192, 273
    historical precedents for, 97
    human intelligence transcended by, 88–90, 91, 275
    impact of, 50, 211
    intelligent behavior vs., 77, 79, 80, 82
    invention of, 83–93, 98–99, 102
    as non-algorithmic, 244–246, 260, 265–266
    problem-solving ability of, 251–253, 259–260, 264
    reason and, 94–104
    research in, 11, 163, 264, 271–272, 279, 280
    as result of "Yankee ingenuity," 97–98
    structures of information analyzed by, 271–272, 273
    translations by, 61–70
Assassinations, political, 163, 164–165
Association of American Publishers, 55
Atari, 68, 114, 228
Atmospheric systems, as computers, 84–86, 87, 91
Atonal music, 217
Authors Guild, 55
Automated Cable Expertise (ACE), 103
Automation, 56, 201, 209–211, 214

297

Automobile industry, 212, 231
Ayensu, Edward, 189

Bach, Johann Sebastian, 130
Ballistics calculations, 156
Banking, electronic, 72, 210
Bar Ilan University, 40, 51
Barnaby Rudge (Dickens), 277
Barthes, Roland, 52, 77
BASIC (Beginner's All-purpose Symbolic In-
    struction Code), 111, 188, 216, 223, 230
Battin, Patricia, 47–48
Battle management systems, 157, 160
Bauhaus, 119
Beauvoir, Simone de, 208
Bedouins, 191
Bell, Gordon, 111
Bell Laboratories, 55–56, 116, 117
Berkeley, University of California at, 7–
    10
"Big MOMA" (Schwartz), 119–120
Billing, computerized, 139
Binary numbers theory, 219, 222
Biological systems, as computers, 91
"Blackboard" model, 111, 125–126, 274
Black Death, 19, 20–21
Blinn, James, 116
Bogod, Julian, 194–195
Books:
    purchase of, 43–45
    as replaced by computers, 42–51
    (*See also* Printing)
"Boom box phenomenon," 182, 187, 190
Boorstin, Daniel, 97
"Boxe Internationale" style, 109
Bradford, William, 95
Bradley, William, 167
Braille, 69
Branching relationships, 270–271
Braun, Wernher von, 8–9
Brennan, Jean Ford, 113*n*
Brezhnev, Leonid, 163
British empiricism, 10
Brookings Institution, 212
Brooklyn Bridge (Lozowick), 120
Brown University, 65–67
    computer literacy project at, 225–227, 230,
        232
Bureau of Indian Affairs, 98
Byzantine generals problem, 249, 252

Calculus, first-order predicate, 273
California, economy of, 210–211
Calisher, Hortense, 160–161
Camps, computer, 220–224
Cancer research, 37, 143, 281
Carnegie-Mellon University, 53, 111, 189, 218–
    219, 223, 232
CAT (computed axial tomographic) scanners,
    141, 142, 145
Catano, James V., 65, 66
Catholic Church, effect of printing on, 20, 23–
    24, 28–29
Cell theory, 78, 80, 242
Censorship, 23, 38

Centre Mondial Informatique et Resource Hu-
    maine, 184–185, 189, 194
Chance, in mathematical solutions, 249–253
Chaplin, Charlie, 16, 119, 153
Chekhov, Anton, 196, 204
Chemistry, 264
    computers used in, 142–143
Chemotherapy, 37, 143
Chernenko, Konstantin, 202
Chess, computer, 266
Chicago Manual of Style, The, 56
Children:
    chronically ill, 140
    computers used by, 110, 114, 183–188
    education of, 229
    literature for, 42–43, 98, 155
    in work force, 205–206
"Children's Crusade" model, 232
China, 20, 36, 231
    computer languages used by, 111
Chou dynasty, 97
Christina's World (Wyeth), 119
"Closed forms," 125
Cloud seeding, 85
COBOL, 111
Code-breaking, 156
Cognition:
    literacy and, 24–27
    non-intuitive, 175, 250
"Cohabiting the Planet with Computers"
    (Simon), 83
Cohen, Harold, 117, 122, 274
    computer art by, 123–132
Colette, 54
Collages, computer, 119
Columbia-Presbyterian Medical Center, 141
Columbia University, 47, 83, 109, 113*n*, 263
Columbus, Christopher, 29, 98, 241
Combinatorial explosion, 255, 260
Commager, Henry Steele, 94, 96, 99
Commerce Department, U.S., 174
Commodore P. E. T., 227
Communication:
    asynchronous, 53
    computers as medium for, 52–53, 107, 113–
        114
    digital, 198
Communist ideology, 197, 199, 209
Complexity:
    as concept, 229–230, 241, 282
    of functions, 273
    information-based, 263, 266, 267–268
    as inherent difficulty, 251–252, 265
    solutions to, 254–261, 263
Composite numbers, 252
Computational space, 88–89
Computed axial tomographic (CAT) scanners,
    141, 142, 145
Computer-aided design and manufacture, 141,
    201–202
Computer-aided instruction, 66
Computer Professionals for Social Responsibility
    (CPSR), 159–160, 163
Computer revolution, 16, 49, 91–92, 229
Computers, computations by, 257–261

Computers (*cont.*):
advertisements for, 149–154
as aid to human intellect, 16, 28, 38–40, 41,
    86, 100–101, 112–114, 133–135, 148,
    236, 243, 284
as artifacts, 50, 92, 134, 268, 279–280, 283,
    284
as artifice, 99–101, 114, 135, 278–279, 284
atmospheric systems as, 84–86, 87, 91
as automated reasoning machines, 36
automobile vs. piano analogies for, 217–218
biological systems as, 91
books replaced by, 42–51
as calculators, 22, 34
camps for, 220–224
as civilized and human tool, 15–16
as communications medium, 52–53, 107,
    113–114
compatible, 200, 216–218
cooperation fostered by, 40, 64–65, 92, 230,
    274–275
criticism of, 105–110, 113
design of, 105–106, 110–111, 159–160, 216–
    217
determinism of, 85, 241–242, 243, 261
displays for, 225–226
as dynamic medium, 113–114
ecological impact of, 236
economics of, 37–38, 142, 143, 215, 218, 231,
    236, 242
economic systems as, 86, 87, 91
fear of, 49–51, 223
fifth generation, 36–37, 64, 157, 231, 272,
    273–274
graphics by, 1, 115–122, 150, 232
hardware for, 147–155, 194, 198, 201, 203,
    216
human relations impaired by, 106–110
impact of, 16, 49, 91–92, 229, 236
incompatible systems of, 144
industry for, 198, 200–202, 230–231, 232,
    236
interactive nature of, 217–218, 225
interface with, 217–218, 280
as "Land of Faerie," 234–236, 254
languages for, 67–68, 79, 111–112, 188, 200,
    273
legal aspect of, 145
legislation for, 230–232
"librarian" vs. "oracle" images of, 68–69
linked resources in, 248
literacy in, 1, 2, 51, 181–188, 194, 195, 199,
    215–227, 229, 230, 232
magazines for, 147–155
mainframe, 198, 200
maintenance of, 190
manuals for, 71–72, 219, 224
manufacturers of, 230–231, 232, 236
memories of, 125, 126, 200, 222, 242, 273
micro-, 46, 153–154, 202, 223, 227
military use of, 62, 103, 156–167
mini-, 202
miniaturization of, 35, 235, 236
models generated by, 170–180
musical training and, 154

nature of work changed by, 54, 55, 205–214
networks for, 45, 53, 84, 94, 134, 139, 144,
    161, 202, 217, 270
obsession with, 108–109, 110
in offices, 112
parallel, 80, 84, 266–267
as pedagogical tools, 56–60, 65–67, 185, 187–
    188, 193, 220–221, 224, 225–233
personal, 45, 46, 54, 65, 113–114, 140, 147–
    155, 190, 199, 203, 215, 225–226, 277–
    285
as physical symbol systems, 75–82, 84, 85, 279
political systems as, 86–87, 91
potential capacity of, 88–90, 91, 105–114,
    178, 218
printing press compared to, 21, 22, 24, 28,
    29, 37, 45, 48, 157
processes analyzed by, 121–122, 248, 272
as processors of symbols, 2–3, 16, 22, 34, 49,
    75–82, 86, 90, 92–93, 100–101, 132, 236,
    240, 284
productivity increased by, 54, 55
programs for, 55–56, 105–106, 114, 125–
    126, 131, 152, 154, 189, 226, 235, 250,
    270, 272
as reasoning machines, 94–104
reliability of, 159–160
security systems for, 252
self-perpetuating, 193
self-referential, 82, 84
sequential, 244
serial, 199
as singularity, 35
software for, 28, 147–155, 184, 185, 187, 194,
    198, 201, 216, 227, 229, 230, 231, 272, 273
solar system as, 84, 85, 87, 91
teachers of, 185, 187–188
third-generation, 35–36
as universal machines, 3, 122, 139, 244, 267,
    285
women as users of, 110, 153–154
workstations for, 227, 230
(*See also individual computers*)
Computer science
development of, 90–91, 100–101, 104, 106,
    110, 214, 217, 231, 236
experimentalists vs. theoreticians in, 243–246
as hunting and gathering of artifacts, 239–
    246
information-centered vs. algorithm-centered
    approach to, 263–264, 265
as science of information, 262–268, 271
theoretical problems of, 247–261, 262–264,
    267–268
Constantinople, fall of (1453), 20
Constitution, U.S., 104, 212
Control Data Corporation, 140, 221
Conway, Melvin, 110–111
Corporations, multinational, 195
Council on Library Resources, 55
CPSR (Computer Professionals for Social Re-
    sponsibility), 159–160, 163
Cray-1, 231
Creationists, 105
Cruise missiles, 164

Crystallography, 261
Culture:
 literary vs. scientific, 7–17, 29, 281, 283, 284
 oral, 26, 219
 print vs. scribal, 22–23, 27, 29
 values of, 36
Cursors, 1
Cystic fibrosis, 140

Daffe, Balla Moussa, 184
Dance, The (Matisse), 121
Danto, Arthur C., 128–129, 130, 131, 132
Dartmouth College, 215
Darwin, Charles, 240
Data, digital, 116, 120–121, 198, 244
Data bases, 45, 106, 230
"David and Goliath deployment," 164, 165
Decision-making:
 in computer-aided negotiations, 168–180, 275
 false conditions for, 252–253
 as process, 172–173, 247–250, 274
 support systems for, 139
Defense Department, U.S., 103
 computer projects of, 157–165
Demoiselles d'Avignon, Les (Picasso), 119, 120–121
Denning, Peter and Dorothy, 59
"Deteriorating image" canvases, 116n
Diabetes, 140
Diagnostic imaging techniques, 143
Dickens, Charles, 277
Digital Equipment Corporation (DEC), 111
Dijkstra, Edsger, 247
"Dining philosophers" problem, 247–248, 249–250, 252
Diouff, Jacques, 184
Diseases:
 chronic, 140
 diagnosis of, 141–146
 neurological, 141
 prevention of, 206–207
Doctor-patient relationship, 143–144, 145
"Doctor's Dilemma, The" (McCarthy), 11–15
Documentation, 55–56
Duchamp, Marcel, 117–118
Dynabook, 67–68
Dynamic process, 275
Dynamo, Virgin vs., 78, 132, 284
Dyson, Freeman, 164, 165

École Normale Supérieure, 182, 183, 184, 185, 187
Economic systems, as computers, 86, 87, 91
Economies of scale, 193
Editing, 55, 56, 63–64, 66, 152
Education:
 computers used in, 56–60, 65–67, 185, 187–188, 193, 220–221, 224, 225–233
 "gap" in, 194–195
 (See also Teachers)
Einstein, Albert, 249
Eisenstein, Elizabeth L., 22, 23, 25, 27, 29
Elderly, health care for, 144–145
Electronic Numerical Integrator and Computer (ENIAC), 156n–157n
Eliot, T. S., 7, 8, 86, 113, 279
Em, David, 116, 122

"Empire of Reason," 94–104
Encyclopaedia Britannica, 68
ENIAC (Electronic Numerical Integrator and Computer), 156n–157n
"Entitality," 129
Entrepreneurship, 37–38
Environmental energy negotiations, 169, 170–172, 178
EPISTLE, 604
Equipoise, 133–135
Erasmus, Desiderius, 134
Euripides, 91, 281
Europe:
 computer research in, 38, 40
 as nation-states, 28–29, 34, 36
European Economic Community, 63
EUROTRA, 63
Evolution, human, 88–89, 282
Expert systems:
 development, 37, 38, 103, 125–126, 192, 273
 in medicine, 142–146
Expletives, 59

Factory system, 207–208, 209
Fall, Sega Seck, 183
False Mirror, The (Magritte), 119
Family unit, 207–209
Farming, cooperative, 275
Fast Fourier transform, 261
Feedback, 170
Feigenbaum, Edward, 98
Fish and Wildlife Service, U.S., 170–172
"Fisherman and his Wife," 258, 261
Fishman, Katharine Davis, 154
Flatland, 150–151, 155, 163
Food and Drug Administration, U.S., 145–146
Forster, E. M., 49–50
FORTRAN, 111
"Fortress family," 107
Founding Fathers, 95–96, 98–99, 102, 104
Fowler, Henry, 56
Franco-Senegalese School, 185
Franklin, Benjamin, 95
Frase, Lawrence, 56
Free will, 241–242, 244
FRESS, 66
Freud, Sigmund, 3, 77
Fuchi, Kazuhiro, 272, 273
Fuel-efficient airplanes, 249
Fugue-writing machines, 130

Galen, 40
Gallagher, William, 220–224
Games, as learning experience, 228
Gas chromatographs, 79
Gass, William, 48–49
Genealogical charts, 270
Generality, correct level of, 264
"Generate-and-test" methods, 260
GIGO (garbage in can only lead to garbage out), 222
Goodman, Seymour E., 197, 198, 199, 200, 201, 202, 203
Gorbachev, Mikhail, 202
Gorée Island, 1
Gothic architecture, 26

Gould Laboratory, 225–227
Graham, Loren, 194, 202
Grand boubou, le, 183
Grand Central Station problem, 248–249, 250, 252
Graphics, computer, 1, 115–122, 150, 232
Great Depression (1873–1896), 205
Great Exposition of 1900 (Paris), 78
Greek culture, 33–34, 97, 207
Grimm, Jakob and Wilhelm, 42–43, 98, 155, 234, 247, 254, 278
Grinnell Glacier, 3
Gutenberg, Johann, 21

Hackers, 108–109, 110, 112
Harmon, Leon, 115n–116n, 116
Harris, Mark, 58
Havelock, Eric, 33
Hawthorne, Nathaniel, 99–100, 101, 104
Helsinki Agreement (1975), 167
Heroes, 133–135
Heuristic search algorithms, 245–246, 259–260, 266
Hierarchical relationships, 270–271
Hippocratic oath, 134
Historical consciousness, 26
Holistic view, 214
Home advisors, 140
Hommage à Duchamp (Schwartz), 117–118
Hospitals, computers used in, 139–146
Hundred Years' War, 19
Hungary, 21, 203
  computer research in, 203–204
Hydrogen bombs, 164
Hypermedia, 67

IBM, computer research by, 60, 111, 118, 120, 194, 231
IBM 360 computers, 198, 200
IBM 370 computers, 198, 200, 201
IBM 610 Autopoint Computer, 113n
IBM PC, 16, 147–155, 188, 190
IBM Watson Laboratory at Columbia University: A History, The (Brennan), 113n
Immune system, 281
Implosion method, 156
Incidents at Sea Agreement (1972), 167
Income distribution, 210
Individuality, collective effort vs., 274–275
Infanticide, 209
Informatics, 240n
Information:
  adaptive vs. non-adaptive, 266–267
  approximate, 262–268
  best, 265
  decentralization of, 196–197
  digitized, 116, 120–121, 198, 244
  distribution of, 267
  "gap" in, 194–195
  general laws of, 264–265, 268
  integrity of, 252
  partial, 262–268
  processing of, 31, 38–39, 81, 121–122, 157, 185, 218, 229, 248, 272, 275
  quantity of, 226–227
  radius of, 265

science of, 262–268, 271
semantic, 260
structures of, 269–276
  as symbol systems, 271–272
theory of, 251
Innocent VIII, Pope, 20
Inquisition, 20, 40
Insulin pumps, 145
Integrated circuits, 35–36
  layout of, 255, 259, 261
Integration, of public schools, 101
Interactive movie games, 114
Interface, 217–218, 280
Interior Design, 109
International Institute for Advanced Systems Analysis (IIASA), 177–178
I/O devices, 200
IRMA, 153

Japan:
  artificial intelligence as developed in, 103–104, 157, 161–162, 163, 231, 272, 273–274
  computer research in, 2, 36–37, 38, 112, 198
  culture of, 2, 274–276
Japanese Ministry of International Trade and Industry, 157
Jeffers, Robinson, 281
Jefferson, Thomas, 104, 158, 163
Jet Propulsion Laboratory, 116
Jewish law, 40, 51
Jewish question, 8
Johns, Jasper, 119
Johnson, Pamela Hansford, 10, 283
Jordaens, Jacob, 130
Josephson junctions, 75
Judson, Horace Freeland, 9

Kabuki Medea (Sato), 281
Kâne, Boubacai, 2, 183–184
Kaplan, Bonnie, 146
Kaplan, Justin, 278
Kaprow, Alan, 128
Karp, Richard, 267
  as computer theoretician, 254–261
Kay, Alan, 67–68, 113–114, 274
Kemeny, John, 215–216
Kennan, George, 197
Khowarizmi, Abu Ja'far Mohammed ibn Musa al-, 245
KIPS (knowledge-information processing systems), 273–274
Knowledge:
  democratization of, 39
  dynamic vs. static, 146
  equipoise and, 133–135
  intensity of, 230
  as power, 38–39
Knowledge-information processing systems (KIPS), 273–274
Knowledge-value theory, 213
Knowledge workers, 22
Knowlton, Kenneth, 116
Knuth, Donald, 245, 270
Koh, Tommy, 173–174, 175, 176
Kuhn, Thomas, 178

Kung, H. T., 244
Kurtz, Thomas, 216

Laboratories, computerized, 139–140, 143, 193
Labor-management negotiations, 169, 175, 179
Labor-value theory, 213
Lachaise, Gaston, 119
Lamport, Leslie, 249
Landscape architecture, 219, 220
Langridge, Robert, 284
Languages:
  in animals, 78–79, 80
  computer, 67–68, 79, 111–112, 188, 200, 273
  conceptualization in, 25–26, 27, 31, 34, 39
  invention of, 16
  as linear, 25
  literacy and, 25–26, 157
  translation of, 61–70
  written, 30, 33–34, 39, 69–70, 269
  See also individual computer languages)
"Launch-on-warning," 159
Law of the Sea negotiatons, 173–176
Lay intelligentsia, 22, 27
Learning:
  by example, 192
  experiential, 193, 229
  habit of, 226–227
  (See also Education)
Le Corbusier, 109–110, 282
Leff, Nathaniel, 195
Legal profession, computers used in, 2, 135
Lentz, John, 113n
Leontief, Wassily, 210
Lesgold, Alan, 227–228, 229
Leukemia, 140
Lewis and Clark, 158
Libraries:
  computers in, 44, 47–48
  electronic, 193
  in medical schools, 145, 146
Library of Congress, 55
Lincoln, Abraham, 115n–116n
Linear lists, 270
Linguistics, 220–221
Linnaeus, Carolus, 269
LISP, 79
Literacy:
  cognition and, 24–27
  in computers, 1, 2, 51, 181–188, 194, 195,
    199, 215–227, 229, 230, 232
  languages and, 25–26, 157
  memory and, 26, 28
  printing and, 24–27, 30–32
  (See also Reading)
"Literary Exercises in Pessimism and Paranoia"
  (McCarthy), 12–13
Literate Revolution in Greece and Its Cultural Conse-
  quences, The (Havelock), 33
Literature:
  children's, 42–43, 98, 155
  science vs., 7–17, 29, 281, 283, 284
  as technology, 25
"Little Tramp, The," 16, 153
Logic, predicate, 272–273
LOGO, 114, 184, 185, 186, 189

Logos Corporation, 62–64, 184
Longbows, 19
Louisiana Purchase, 158
Lozowick, Louis, 120
Lucas, George, 123
Luehrmann, Arthur, 215–217, 218, 224, 230
Luray Caverns, 124

McCarthy, John, 11, 79, 98, 193, 235, 273
McCarthyism, 8
Macdonald, Nina, 56, 57
Machine or assembly code, 200
Machine Stops, The (Forster), 49–50
Machines Who Think (McCorduck), 97
Madison, James, 104
Magritte, René, 119
Mahler, Gustav, 241
Mail, electronic, 52–53
Malpractice, medical, 146
Marxist theory, 209
Mass spectrographic data, 143
Materialism, spiritualism vs., 92
Mathematical problems:
  ad hoc solutions to, 263–264
  choice-coordination, 247–253
  combinatorial search, 254–261
  connecting procedure for, 255–256
  heuristic solutions to, 245–246, 259–260, 266
  ill-conditioned vs. well-conditioned, 32, 35, 41
  interactive consistency, 249
  "NP" vs. "P," 258–259
  optimality of solutions for, 259–260
  puzzle-like, 254, 257–258, 259, 261
  "relaxing" of, 259
  scheduling, 254–261
  solution of, 229, 241, 245–246, 250–253, 256,
    259–260, 263–264
  uncertainty in, 249–253
Mathematics:
  algorithms in, 235, 244–246, 257
  proofs of, 32, 241, 272
  teaching of, 228–229
  tree structures analyzed by, 270–271
Matisse, Henri, 121
Medea (Euripides), 91, 281
Medical Devices Act (1976), 145
Medicare, 140
Medicine:
  computers used in, 103, 139–146, 191–192,
    261
  cost-effectiveness of techniques in, 143–144,
    145
  family practice, 142
  government regulation of, 145–146
  technology of, 134–135, 206–207, 264–265
Memory:
  computer, 125, 126, 200, 222, 242, 273
  hierarchical nature of, 271
  list structures of, 31–32, 79
  literacy and, 26, 28
  long-term, 31–32
  printing as artificial, 31–32, 34
  as process, 80
Metaphors, 25
"Meta-things," 125–126

MetPath, 139–140
Microprocessors, 3, 140
Microsynergy, 152
Milton, John, 240
Mind-body problem, 279, 283
Mining, deep-sea, 173–176
Minsky, Marvin, 98
Miró, Joan, 119
MIRVs, 164, 179
M.I.T., 67, 108n, 111, 232
M.I.T. Deep Sea Mining Model, 173–176
M.I.T. Press, 44
Modigliani, Amedeo, 119, 121
Monet, Claude, 122
Mongols, 20–21
Monroe, Marilyn, 119
Moore, Henry, 119
Morris, William, 207
Mortality rate, 207
Moslems, 181, 186, 191
Mowshowitz, Abbe, 107
Museum of Modern Art (MOMA), 1, 116
  computer graphics poster for, 118–122
"Mutually assured destruction," 159
MYCIN, 142–143

National defense, computers used for, 157–165
National Defense Education Act, 162
National Football League, game schedules of, 255, 257–258, 262
National Institutes of Health, 103, 158
National Library of Medicine, 55
National Science Foundation, 61, 159
N-dimensional hypercube, 88–89, 93, 284
Negotiations, computer-aided, 168–180, 275
  international, 173–178
  multilateral, 176–177
Nelson, Ted, 65
Neocortex, 92–93
Neurophysiology, 280
Newell, Allen, 244, 273
  computers as viewed by, 76–77, 78, 79, 80, 85, 234–236
New Man concept, 88, 91
Newtonian mechanics, 264
New York Academy of Sciences, 175
New York Times, 121
N-factorial, 255–257
Nilsson, Nils, 211
1984 (Orwell), 196
NMR (nuclear magnetic resonance) scanners, 141, 145
Nominalizations, 59
Noms d'ordinateur, 107
NP-completeness, 257–259, 261
Nuclear family, 107
Nuclear magnetic resonance (NMR) scanners, 141, 145
Nuclear Risk Reduction Centers, 165–167
Nuclear weapons, 156–167
  arms race in, 164–167
  disarmament of, 161, 164–165, 166–167, 179
  global destruction from, 163–164, 165
  non-nuclear vs., 164
  proliferation of, 166
  smart, 161
Nyhart, Daniel, 173, 176

Oedipus (character), 243
ONCOCIN, 143, 144
One Chase Plaza, 109, 110
Order-of-magnitude effect, 31, 32, 70, 122, 141
Original sin, 282
Orwell, George, 196
Ouagou-Niayes School #1, 185, 186–187

Pacemakers, 140, 145
Pac-Man, 34
Painting, electronic, 122
Papert, Seymour, 106, 114
Paradox, 253
Parricide, 208–209
Pascal, 111, 188
PC: The Independent Guide to IBM Personal Computers, 147–155
Perkins, Maxwell, 55
Perlis, Alan, 88–90, 111–112
Phoenician script, 33
Physics, theoretical, 89–90
Picasso, Pablo, 119, 120–122
Pictographs, 69
Pilots' assistants, 157, 160
PLATO, 140, 220–221
Plutonium bomb, 156
Poetry, teaching of, 65–67
Political systems, as computers, 86–87, 91
Polynomial functions, 257–259
Porsche, 152
Positive-sum results, 175
Power plants, 170–172
Predestination, 241–242, 244
Preemptive nuclear strikes, 159
Preindustrial work, 205–209
Pre-Raphaelites, 207
Primality of large numbers, 252
Printing:
  as artificial memory, 31–32, 34
  collective activity fostered by, 23, 26–27
  computer compared to, 21, 22, 24, 28, 29, 37, 45, 48, 157
  economics of, 26, 27–28, 209
  impact of, 21–29, 39, 40–41
  literacy and, 24–27, 30–32
  science influenced by, 24, 27
  (See also Reading)
Printing Press as an Agent of Change, The (Eisenstein), 22
Probability, 241–242, 249
"Pro-cybernetic euphoria," 199
Programs, structured, 105–106
Project on Information and Technology, 46
Protocol, 247–248
Prynne, Hester (character), 99–100, 101, 104
Psychology:
  cognitive, 79–80, 275
  information-processing, 31
  visual, 115n–116n
Psychology Today, 107
Publishing, 44–45, 46, 55
Puzzles, 254, 257–258

Rabin, Michael, 247, 248, 249, 250–251, 252
Ralph, Miss, 42, 43
Randomization, 249–253
Rationalists, 22
Reading:
  as perception, 69–70
  as processing of symbols, 48–49
  teaching of, 229
  (*See also* Literacy)
Reagan administration, 174
Reason:
  in computers, 94–104
  passion vs., 7, 15, 35, 104, 134, 165, 280–283
Reclining Nude (Modigliani), 119, 121
Reddy, Raj, 189, 190, 191–194, 195, 213
Reductionists, 22
Rembrandt van Rijn, 121
Research Libraries Group, 47
Revolutions, political, 88
Rice cultivation, 275
Richardson, Elliot, 173, 174, 175, 176
Robotics Institute, 189
Robots, 94, 123, 157, 209
  vision of, 265–266
Robust concepts, 257
Rolls-Royce, 231
Roosevelt, Eleanor, 168
Ross, Harold, 55
Roux, M., 185
Rubens, Peter Paul, 130
Russell, Bertrand, 3, 77
Ryad, 200–201

Sabenius, James, 173, 174
Sahel area, 182
Sartre, Jean-Paul, 54
Satellite links, 193
"Satisficing," 260
Sato, Shozo, 281
Saussure, Ferdinand de, 77
Scarlet Letter, The (Hawthorne), 99–100, 101, 104
Schlemmer, Oskar, 119
Scholarly Information Center, 47
Scholarship, computers and, 46–48
Scholes, Robert, 66–67
Schwartz, Lillian, 116–122, 126
Science:
  art and literature vs., 7–17, 29, 281, 283, 284
  as artifact, 15
  empirical, 10, 90–91
  ethics of, 9, 11–15
  general laws of, 264–265, 271
  as influenced by printing, 24, 27
  long-range research in, 158–159
  military use of, 158–159
  objective, 110
  pure, 158
  teaching of, 228–229
  (*See also* Computer science)
Science fiction, 94, 153
Scott, Bernard, 64
Sears Roebuck catalogs, 147
Second Self, The (Turkle), 106, 108, 110
Semiology, 77

Semitic script, 33
Senegal, computer literacy program in, 1, 2, 181–188, 194, 195, 199
Senghor, Léopold Sédar, 181, 195
Sentence types, 59
Shaiken, Harley, 209, 211
Shakespeare, William, 7, 19
Shannon, Claude, 251
Shaw, J. C., 79
Shulman, Marshall, 197–198, 203
Siege guns, mobile, 19
Signal processing, 261
Silicon Valley, 236
Silkscreens, 117
Simon, Herbert A., 98, 244, 260, 271, 280
  computers as viewed by, 31, 76–77, 78, 79, 80, 83–93
Single photon emission computed tomography (SPECT), 141
Skidmore, Owings, and Merrill, 109
Smalltalk, 67, 68
Smith, Henry Nash, 58
"Snail-mail," 53
Snow, C. P., 9, 10, 13, 283
Social sciences, 9–10
Sodium levels, cellular, 141
Solar system, as computer, 84, 85, 87, 91
Soloway, Robert, 252
"Solution from Morality, Common Sense and Technology" (McCarthy), 13–15
Sonar signals, 103
Sorcerer's Apprentice, fallacy of, 235–236
Soviet Union, computer research in, 2, 177–178, 196–204
Space programs, 8–9, 89, 116, 193, 211
SPECT (single photon emission computed tomography), 141
Spenser, Edmund, 94
Spreadsheet programs, 152, 189, 223
Sputnik, 8–9
SRI International, 210
Stalin, Joseph, 199
"Stand-alone" devices, 54
"Standing-for-ness," 127
Standing Woman (Lachaise), 119
Stanford University, 107, 142
Stanford University Medical Center, 143, 144
Staples, Charles, 64
Stark, Fortney H., 230–231
Star Wars (film), 123, 222
"Star Wars" defense initiative, 109, 160, 179
Static property, 275
Statistical mechanics, 249
Staywell, 140
Steel industry, 212
Steinberg, Leo, 127–128
Stella, Frank, 77–78
Stock, Brian, 26
Strassen, Völker, 252
Strategic arms control agreements, 166–167
Strategic Computing Project, 157, 159, 160, 163
Strategic Defense Initiative, 109, 160, 179
Straus, Donald B., 275
  computer-aided negotiations as viewed by, 169, 170, 171, 174–180
Streetcar Named Desire, A (Williams), 8

Strunk, William, Jr., 56
Subsystems, 271
Supreme Court, U.S., 101
Surgeon's work stations, 141
Sylla, Fatimata, 183, 186, 195
Symbols:
    Age of, 2–3, 78
    computers as physical systems of, 75–82, 84, 85, 279
    computers as processors of, 2–3, 16, 22, 34, 49, 75–82, 86, 90, 92–93, 100–101, 132, 236, 240, 284
    as important to human intelligence, 2–3, 77–82, 86–87, 90, 92–93, 132, 214, 236, 240, 241, 242, 246, 284
    information as systems of, 271–272
    reading as processing of, 48–49
    solutions generated by, 260
System of Nature (Linnaeus), 269

Target with Four Faces (Johns), 119
Tax credits, 230–231
Teachers:
    of computers, 185, 187–188
    training of, 228–229
Technology:
    art and, 117, 127–132
    change as result of, 11, 16, 50, 190–191, 203
    in developing countries, 1, 2, 181–195, 199, 211
    dissemination of, 34, 209, 211
    fairy tales and, 235–236
    "fixes" by, 15, 161, 193
    "gap" in, 195
    of intellect, 28, 30–41
    literature as, 95
    medical, 134–135, 206–207, 264–265
    moral problems solved by, 11–15, 133–135
    new jobs created by, 209–212
    opposition to, 207–208
    quality vs. quantity in, 31, 32, 34, 35, 55, 70, 122, 141
    as "shade of gray" advantage, 32–33, 36, 37, 39, 40, 41
    in workplace, 205–214
    (See also Science)
Technology Bill of Rights, 211–212, 213
Telecommunications, 103, 203
Terrorism, nuclear, 165–166
Texts:
    editing of, 55, 56, 63–64, 66, 152
    electronic, 50–51, 52–55, 60
    hyper-, 65–67
    literary, 52–60
    perception of, 69–70
Thomas, Eliza Agnes, 205–206, 207, 208, 209
Tolstoy, Leo, 271
Tractability, 242–243, 256, 259, 260
Translations, automatic, 61–70
Traub, Joseph, 263–267
Traveling salesman problems, 257, 258–259, 262
Tree structures, 270–271
Triage, 183
Tristan and Isolde, 243

Tucker, Marc, 46, 230, 231, 233
Turing Award, 76
Turing machine, 257, 272
Turkle, Sherry, 106, 108, 110
Turnkey plants, 202
Two Cultures debate, 7–17, 29, 281, 283, 284

Ultrasound imaging, 141
UNESCO, 194
United Nations, 168, 173, 194
Unterweger, Peter, 214

Van Dam, Andries, 66, 230, 232–233
Van Dyck, Anthony, 130
Van Gelder, Lindsy, 154
VAX, 124
Venturi, Robert, 84
Videocassette recorders, 72
Video games, 34, 68, 76, 114, 154, 222
Video terminals, 154
Vietnam war, 11, 162
Visifile, 152
VLSIs (very large scale integrated circuits), 75
Volkswriter, 152
Von Neumann, John, 86, 105

Wang, 63
Warhol, Andy, 116n, 119
Warsaw pact countries, 200
Watson Scientific Computing Laboratory, 113n
Weather prediction, 263
Wells, H. G., 50
"What-if" scenarios, 170
White, E. B., 56
White, Merry, 274
Whitehead, Alfred North, 3, 77
Williams, Tennessee, 8
Winpisinger, William W., 211–212, 213
Wirth, Niklaus, 111
Wolof language, 184, 188
Women, as users of computers, 110, 153–154
Women's Computer Literacy Project, 224
Woolf, Virginia, 9
Word processors, 68, 154, 189, 217, 223
    advantages of, 47, 54, 63, 230, 232
World Bank, 173
Woźniakowski, Henryk, 263
Wright, Deborah, 220, 224
Writer's Workbench, 56–60
Writing styles, as corrected by computers, 56–60
Wyeth, Andrew, 119

Xerox Corporation, 68, 216
Xerox Palo Alto Research Center, 67
X-ray machines, 142

Yamani, Sheikh Ahmed Zaki, 191
Yeats, William Butler, 32
Yershov, Andrei P., 199
Yoshida, June, 168

Zero-sum results, 87, 169–170, 175

About the Author

Pamela McCorduck published two novels before she wrote the highly acclaimed *Machines Who Think*, a history of artificial intelligence, and coauthored *The Fifth Generation*, about the world-wide future of artificial intelligence. Her books have been translated into most of the major European and Asian languages. Ms. McCorduck is a Lecturer in English and Comparative Literature at Columbia University and divides her time between New York City and Berkeley, California.